Thomas Hardy

by
Norman Page
Professor of English
University of Alberta

Routledge & Kegan Paul
London, Boston and Henley

First published in 1977
by Routledge & Kegan Paul Ltd
39 Store Street,
London WC1E 7DD,
Broadway House,
Newtown Road,
Henley-on-Thames,
Oxon RG9 1EN and
9 Park Street,
Boston, Mass. 02108, USA
Reprinted in 1979
Reprinted and first published
as a paperback in 1980
Set in Monotype Bembo
and printed in Great Britain by
Caledonian Graphics Ltd
Cumbernauld, Scotland

British Library Cataloguing in Publication Data

Page, Norman
Thomas Hardy.
1. Hardy, Thomas – Criticism and interpretation
823'.8   PR4754

ISBN 0 7100 8614 8 (c)
ISBN 0 7100 8615 6 (p)

To Milly

Contents

Preface

Books on Hardy are legion. The first of them, Lionel Johnson's still readable study, appeared in 1894, more than thirty years before its subject's death; and since then Hardy criticism has established itself as a growth industry. In our own time, every year produces an impressive – or, from another point of view, daunting – quota of books and articles, editions and casebooks, monographs, notes and queries and dissertations. My justification for venturing to add to their number is, I believe, twofold. First, most studies of Hardy concern themselves with only a portion of his total *œuvre*: among recent major critics, for example, Ian Gregor and Michael Millgate have limited their field of reference to the fiction, whilst others have been mainly interested in Hardy the poet. The sheer bulk of Hardy's work in prose and verse makes such decisions understandable; but his unusual position as a major poet who was also a major novelist (to put the emphasis where he would have put it, and where it is increasingly being put by contemporary critics) seems to demand a more comprehensive treatment, even if inclusiveness has to be purchased at the price of a measure of superficiality. In this book, therefore, I have tried to give some account not only of Hardy's major novels and of his poems, but also of his minor novels and short stories, his autobiography, his essays, letters, notebooks, and other miscellaneous writings – to offer, in fact, to the reader or student who may be unfamiliar with the full range of his achievement a map of the whole area, the by-ways as well as the major landmarks. Without insisting that all the literary productions, public and private, of his long lifetime constitute a seamless garment, or that they are all of equal interest and value (which is certainly not the case), I would maintain that they are all stamped with his highly idiosyncratic personality, and that an understanding of each area can help to illuminate the others. Hardy himself would not, I think, have disagreed with this claim; in an unpublished fragment found among his papers after his death, and quoted elsewhere in this volume, he urged that his writings, of which 'the last line' was his own death, be judged as a whole – be regarded, as it were, as constituting a single enormous volume written over a period of more than six decades.

Second, and arising naturally from what has just been said, in writing this study I have been able to make use of material, much of it still unpublished or in process of publication, which contributes to an understanding of Hardy but which has not usually been taken into account by previous critics. It seems likely that the late 1970s will prove to be a very important period in Hardy scholarship, and that materials which have hitherto been accessible only to a small number of students will soon become widely available, partly thanks to the emergence of Hardy's works from British copyright in 1978. Within the next few years, we can expect to see editions of Hardy's letters, notebooks and diaries, as well as important new editions of his novels and poems. (Details of some of these projects are given in the Bibliographical Notes at the end of this volume.) I have myself examined a large proportion of the material in question, as well as most of Hardy's surviving literary manuscripts, on which a great deal of further research needs to be done; and my discussion of his work utilizes some of the observations and conclusions derived from this study.

The Bibliographical Notes serve both to acknowledge some of the main published sources to which I am indebted, and to furnish the reader with a minimal guide to further works of Hardy scholarship and criticism. I have also given some account of important collections of Hardy material, published and unpublished, and of significant work in progress.

My discussion of Hardy's short stories has already appeared, in a slightly different form, in *Studies in Short Fiction* (vol. II, Winter 1974), and is here used by kind permission of the editor. A small portion of Chapter 2 has already been published in *Etudes Anglaises* (vol. 25 (1972), pp. 486–92, Paris, Librairie Didier), and is reprinted by kind permission of the editor of that journal. Some other passages in Chapters 2 and 6 are taken from a series of lectures titled 'Thomas Hardy: Fact and Problems', which I delivered at the University of Alberta in February 1975; my thanks are due to the Department of English, whose invitation to deliver the annual Broadus Lectures stimulated me to think and write about certain aspects of Hardy. The Canada Council have generously assisted my researches by making grants which enabled me to spend a good deal of time in England in 1973 and 1975. The Curator and staff of the Dorset County Museum,

Dorchester, showed unfailing patience and helpfulness on my numerous visits to the Thomas Hardy Memorial Collection housed there. Finally, I should like to record my gratitude to the many individual scholars with whom I have had the opportunity of discussing Hardy, and especially to those who have given me information concerning their own work in progress.

Acknowledgments

Quotations from *The Complete Poems of Thomas Hardy*, ed. James Gibson, are made with the permission of the Trustees of the Hardy Estate, Macmillan, London and Basingstoke, and St Martin's Press Inc., Macmillan & Co. Ltd. Quotations from unpublished material appear by kind permission of the Trustees of the estate of the late Miss E. A. Dugdale.

I

Life and Career

HARDY, Thomas, author; O.M. 1910; Hon. LL.D. Aberdeen; Litt.D. Cambridge and D.Litt. Oxford; LL.D. St. Andrews and Bristol; Hon. Fellow Magdalene College, Cambridge, and Queen's College, Oxford; J.P. Dorset; *b*. Dorsetshire, 2 June 1840; *s*. of late Thomas and Jemima Hardy; *m*. 1st, 1874, Emma Lavinia (*d*. 1912), *d*. of J. A. Gifford, and *niece* of Archdn. Gifford; 2nd, 1914, Florence Emily, J.P. for Dorchester, *d*. of Edward Dugdale, and author of numerous books for children, magazine articles, and reviews. *Educ*: Dorchester; King's College, London. Pupil of John Hicks, ecclesiastical architect, 1856–61; read Latin and Greek with a fellow-pupil, 1857–60; sketched and measured many old country churches now pulled down or altered; removed to London and worked at Gothic architecture under Sir A. Blomfield, A.R.A., 1862–67; prizeman of Royal Institute of British Architects, 1863; the Architectural Assoc., 1863; wrote verses, 1865–68; gave up verse for prose, 1868–70; but resumed it later. Holds Gold Medal of Royal Society of Literature; Member of the Council of Justice to Animals; is against blood-sport, dog-chaining, and the caging of birds. [A long list of his publications follows.] *Address*: Max Gate, Dorchester, Dorset. *Club*: Athenaeum.

To the basic biographical information provided by this entry, composed by Hardy for *Who's Who*, needs to be added the fact that he died on 11 January 1928, in his eighty-eighth year. But the entry offers something more than facts: as with so many of Hardy's writings, its unexpected emphases and unobtrusive evasions seem to betray, for the most part unconsciously, the peculiar cast of his mind and personality. The quiet hint of modest origins and an education largely self-conducted, almost drowned by the muster-roll of honorary degrees; the trivial half-deception of 'King's College, London' (he had attended an evening class in French there for 'a term or two', apparently in 1865-6); the slightly absurd parading of his first wife's kinship with an archdeacon; the space devoted to his architectural career, the dryness of 'gave up verse for prose . . . but resumed it later', and the sudden passion of the reference to cruelty to animals – all these suggest that the long and productive journey from early-Victorian Dorset to the Athenaeum, two honorary fellowships, and the Order of Merit had not been pursued without the creation or exacerbation of certain tensions or compulsions. Which is perhaps no more than to say that, like any major artist, Hardy is a man difficult to understand and foolish to attempt to seize in a neat phrase or two, and that his work both provides an insight into his complex and remarkable individuality and itself demands some understanding of that individuality in order to be fully understood.

Hardy's work is strongly localized – firmly rooted in an intimately known region and, especially in the case of the fiction, a specific epoch in the history of English rural society. To have been born in a certain place at a certain moment in history was his first and indispensable qualification as a writer: indeed, born ten years later, or in the next county, or in a different social group, he might never have become a writer at all, and would certainly have been a very different one. In Hardy's verse and prose, however, time and place are repeatedly transcended, and the vast and the minute, the timeless and the transitory, continually juxtaposed. He was fascinated by the intrusion of the particular upon the universal, and by the quirkiness of the individual lot in relation to the endlessly repeated cycle of human existence; but he could also view the situation the other way round, and whereas most writers deal in years and generations, Hardy is fond of placing human destiny against a background of millennia. He found especially appealing the way in which even a single human existence is capable of spanning a whole epoch of history, and thus in a sense overcoming the normal temporal limitations of the lonely personality. He treasured his acquaintance with Mrs Anne Procter, the famous literary hostess, whose memories went back to the age of Wordsworth and Keats, and who survived to become the subject of a ribald rumour that Henry James had made her a proposal of marriage. And, when he was nearly eighty, he wrote in his diary: 'It bridges over the years to think that Gray might have seen Wordsworth in his cradle, and Wordsworth might have seen me in mine.' (Gray was born in 1716, more than 200 years before these words were written.) Hardy's own lifetime was remarkable for this 'bridging' quality, covering as it did an unprecedented era of change in the public sphere, in scientific and technological development, and in intellectual and moral life, as well as embracing a career of some sixty years as a continuously active writer. Hardy was born when Victoria had been on the throne for only three years, and survived to welcome her great-grandson (as the Prince of Wales) into his home. He began his schooling in the year in which the *Communist Manifesto* was published, and he lived to see the Russian Revolution; he was already a young man when Darwin's *Origin of Species* appeared, and in his old age he took an interest in the theories of Einstein; he belonged to the generation which was overwhelmed by the poetry of Swinburne, he heard Dickens read, and met Tennyson and Browning; but he lived to ponder the poetic techniques of T. S. Eliot and D. H. Lawrence, and to discuss his work with Virginia Woolf. In studying Hardy and his writings, therefore, we study the two or three generations in which modern England, and modern literature, came into being.

It is scarcely thinkable that these revolutions in life, thought and feeling should not have left their mark on an author's work, especially one who served the art of fiction for a quarter of a century. But if Hardy's work is not fully intelligible without reference to external circumstances and processes, it also draws much of its characteristic strength from deeply felt private experiences and preoccupations. It is important, consequently, to see it in relation to his personal life as well as to its wider context. Such an aim, however, is more easily conceived than fulfilled: Hardy was an intensely, almost morbidly, reserved man who clung tenaciously to an inviolable privacy even when he was world-famous and persistently lionized. This is not to say that he was a recluse or a misanthrope, for one of the many paradoxes of his character is that his deep reticence did not prevent him from going into society and enjoying the friendship or acquaintance of many men and women, including some of the leading figures of his day. If half of him had a hermit's nature, the other half was a rather conventional late-Victorian gentleman, 'a good clubman' (as the *Dictionary of National Biography* was later to record), 'a gracious host' (as one of his friends, Frederic Harrison, attests), a practical man of affairs, managing his investments shrewdly, a respected member of the local bench, a governor of the grammar school and a writer of letters to the newspapers. But it remains true that to understand his inner nature, and the sources from which his best poetry and fiction originated, is peculiarly difficult. It is not, as in the case of some writers, that evidence of various kinds is lacking; it is, if anything, over-abundant and frequently contradictory. And the difficulty is increased by the deviousness (not to put it more strongly) Hardy often displayed in his comments on his own life and work, most notably in that extraordinary monument, his autobiography. Outside his books, his long life was relatively uneventful: with only a few exceptions (and perhaps some others which still puzzle or elude his biographers), the real landmarks of his eighty-seven years are the shelf-full of volumes of prose and verse, and much of the outward drama of his existence relates to the vicissitudes of their composition, publication and reception. But his inner life, so much less easily known, was rich and intense; it involved an unusual sensibility which finds expression in almost every line he wrote, and has commended his novels, stories and poems to millions of readers all over the world; and for this reason, while the present chapter can concern itself mainly with the outward circumstances of Hardy's life as man and author, it is in the more detailed discussion of his work in later chapters that we may hope to come a little closer to the essential Thomas Hardy.

Early Years

Hardy was born on 2 June 1840, in the hamlet of Higher Bockhampton, a few miles from the town of Dorchester – within walking distance, that is, of a small but busy community which formed the commercial and social centre of an agricultural region, yet at the same time in a secluded corner set well back from the main road. The railway, which had already transformed both landscape and life-style in most other parts of England, had not yet come to Dorset, though it was to do so within a few years. Although the interior of the Hardy cottage has changed since his childhood, and although some neighbouring dwellings have disappeared, the setting is still peaceful, with woodland beginning a few paces from its door. Yet it would be wrong for the modern admirer imaginatively to recreate the environment of Hardy's childhood in wholly idyllic terms. The living conditions of the rural poor within a short distance of his birthplace are graphically brought home by the *Eight Letters to His Royal Highness Prince Albert* published in 1855 by the Rev. Henry Moule, Vicar of Fordington St George, just outside Dorchester, and father of a man who was to become an important influence on Hardy's personal and intellectual development. Moule's letters describe the cholera outbreak of 1854 and the local conditions which encouraged the spread of the disease. In his parish some 1,100 persons lived in a space covering five acres. The typical cottage consisted of a single room, which might be as little as eight feet square, opening on to the street, with a similar room above it. Four feet away, on the opposite side of a lane, was another row of dwellings. Most lacked a privy: sewage was commonly disposed of in the mill pond, which also provided water for washing and sometimes even 'for culinary purposes'. Hardy's neat and comfortable home was at least as far removed from such dwellings as it was from the manor-houses of the local aristocracy; but, as he grew up, he must have been aware of the extremes of a society in which he occupied a place somewhere near the middle.

He was later to claim kinship (not always quite plausibly) with various Hardys notable in Dorset history over several centuries; certainly both his parents came from long-established Dorset families. His father had risen to be a builder and an employer of labour – a matter of some importance in the nice discrimination of social levels to which Hardy was always to be highly sensitive. Like his own father before him, Thomas Hardy senior was also a gifted amateur musician, his activities centring on (without being confined to) the parish church. Hardy later noted in the margin of one of his books that his father spoke dialect to his workmen, but that standard English was spoken in the home. Such a childhood acquainted the physically fragile and withdrawn boy with the sights and sounds of rural life and the beliefs and superstitions of country folk; it accustomed his ear to local speech, while at the same time implanting an awareness of different social levels. His first 'love affair', at the age of about ten, and in a strictly Shelleyan sense, was with a lady more than four times his age and considerably above his station: Mrs Julia Augusta Martin was the lady of the manor, and his affection for her seems to have been reciprocated. He was a very early reader: among his books were Dryden's *Virgil*, Johnson's *Rasselas*, and a popular illustrated history of the Napoleonic wars which was to give birth to a lifelong enthusiasm for the period. He also read Shakespeare, Scott and Bunyan, as well as such popular novelists as Dumas and G. P. R. James. The catalogue of his mild precocity also includes early talent as a violinist, and he was to remain deeply sensitive to music throughout his life. His family were orthodox church-going members of the Church of England, and (as he relates in the *Life*) a favourite game of the young Hardy was to wrap a tablecloth around himself and to preach a sermon in imitation of the local vicar; it was predicted that he would become a parson. Later Hardy, whom one of his critics was to refer to as 'the village atheist', taught for a time in the parish Sunday school. His deep familiarity with the language of the Bible, as well as the liturgy and hymnody of the Anglican church, remained with him, and finds expression in hundreds of passages of prose and verse.

His formal education was limited to some eight years of schooling, first at the village school, then, from the age of nine, in Dorchester. He began Latin, as an 'extra', at twelve. At sixteen he entered into pupillage with Hicks of Dorchester, architect and church-restorer; and architecture was to be the major concern of his working life for the next sixteen years, his career as an architect (not without its own modest distinction) overlapping that as novelist. This training, combined with what must have been a naturally acute visual sense, is manifested at many levels in his writings. It was a period of energetic 'restoration' – often a euphemism for extensive rebuilding in accordance with modern tastes – of medieval churches; and Hardy's architectural career was to be responsible for the important early years in London and the 1870 visits to Cornwall, so fateful in his emotional life. At the same time that he was acquiring his training in Hicks's office, however, he pursued a self-ordained course of private study in non-architectural subjects, especially languages and literature. Before this time he had added to his schoolboy Latin a beginning in French and German; now he began the study of Greek, both the classical authors and the New Testament, reading hard for two or three hours before breakfast and the daily walk into Dorchester. Among the books he read at this period was the controversial *Essays and Reviews* (1860), which questioned the bases of religious orthodoxy. Sixty years later, Hardy recalled that he lived at this time 'a life twisted of three strands': his work as an architectural student, the daybreak studies which must have been undertaken as some measure of compensation for the lack of a university education, and his continuing participation in the rustic community, which included playing the fiddle at local weddings and other festivities.

One of his closest friends was Horace Moule, Cambridge graduate, sound Greek scholar, and son of the vicar of Fordington. Moule's role seems to have been that of mentor to the younger man; Robert Gittings has recently argued convincingly that his suicide in 1873 left an ineradicable impression on Hardy, whose 'emergence as a fully tragic artist' can be dated from that event. Hardy, who had the instincts and tastes of a scholar but who was under the necessity of earning his living and qualifying in the profession to which he was committed, evidently turned to Moule for intellectual guidance and personal encouragement. He was bitterly disappointed when the latter advised him to abandon Greek, as of doubtful value to architectural success; one suspects that

6

what he really longed for was a little urging to make his way to a university, whatever the price, though in later years he claimed that he might have gone to Cambridge had he wished. His escape from architecture, however, was to be by another route, and to take much longer. Moreover, he probably succeeded in acquiring a wider store of knowledge through his own efforts than would have been conferred by any university in that period. His intellectual self-help was to place at his disposal a reasonably sound acquaintance with classical and modern languages and literatures, history, theology, philosophy, science and art history. His writings constantly bear witness (at times, obtrusively so) to the range and, sometimes, the depth of his knowledge: *Two on a Tower*, for instance, demonstrates his keen interest in astronomy, most of his novels are scattered with references to the history of painting, and his preparations for *The Dynasts* involved extensive historical researches.

In 1862 he moved to London and found work in the office of a well-known architect, Arthur Blomfield. It was six months before he threw away the return half of the railway ticket he had bought for the journey from Dorchester; as it turned out, he was to spend more than five years in the metropolis. During 1863 we find Moule writing to him on the acquisition of a literary style and the use of prose models. Clearly Hardy has sought his advice and is already combining his architectural duties at this date with literary aspirations. He was not neglectful of these duties, however, and the omens for prosperity as an architect were favourable. In 1863 he was awarded the essay prize of the Royal Institute of British Architects. But he was also by this time beginning to use the pen as well as the pencil. After abandoning a short-lived notion of becoming an art critic for the press, he set his literary sights higher, and by the middle of the decade was writing poems and submitting them to magazines, with a signal lack of success. A few, however, survived to achieve publication more than thirty years later, and the earliest of the *Collected Poems* belong to 1865–6. Later he toyed with the idea of writing blank-verse dramas, and in his efforts to learn something of the theatre from the inside he even appeared briefly in a walking-on part in a Covent Garden pantomime. In the event his first published work, apart from a few trifles in a Dorchester newspaper, was a humorous sketch, 'How I Built Myself a House', which appeared in *Chambers's Journal* in 1865. In London he went to theatres and dances, operas and oratorios, attended French classes in the evening at King's College (later listed in *Who's Who* as one of his places of education), heard Dickens read at the Hanover Square Rooms, and was present at Palmerston's funeral in Westminster Abbey, characteristically noting in a letter to his sister that the former Prime Minister was a link between their own age and that of Pitt and Burke. He also read at the British Museum, and at one period walked every day 'for many months' from Blomfield's office in Adelphi Terrace to the National Gallery, where he would spend twenty minutes after lunch on a self-conducted course on the history of painting, 'confining his attention to a single master on each visit'. He had moved away from Dorset in more than a merely physical sense, and his intellectual and emotional development had left the village church far behind, though he was never to forsake it entirely. His diary for these years shows that he was much impressed by Newman's *Apologia Pro Vita Sua*, but found himself unable to accept the premises on which Newman's eloquent religious arguments were founded.

In the summer of 1867 ill health drove him back to Dorchester, and he resumed his earlier mode of existence, walking from his parents' cottage to Hicks's office. It seems to have been at this time that, after a further brief flirtation with poetry, he decided to abandon verse in favour of prose, as a more promising avenue to seeing his work in print, and wrote (in the latter half of 1867) his first novel: *The Poor Man and the Lady. By the Poor Man.* It is clear that his decision to turn to the novel sprang from necessity rather than choice: he felt no consuming interest in prose fiction, and his favourite reading was in the poets, not the novelists; but he must have realized that it offered the only possibility of making literature his profession. The careers of Dickens, George Eliot, Trollope (all still writing at this time) and others had proved that fortune as well as fame could be the reward of the successful novelist.

This first novel has disappeared. We have, however, a fair notion of its nature from a long letter written to Hardy by Alexander Macmillan, the publisher, to whom he had sent it in July 1868. We also have Hardy's own description of it, half a century later in his autobiography, as 'a sweeping dramatic satire of the squirearchy and nobility, London society, the vulgarity of the middle class, modern Christianity, church-restoration, and political and domestic morals in general . . . the tendency of the writing being socialistic, not to say revolutionary . . .'. It was evidently a sardonic treatment of the theme of class-distinction, and an exposure of the hollowness of 'good' society – working off, no doubt, diverse and keenly felt personal frustrations; and it was apparently loosely constructed, with an absence of 'plot' but some well-written scenes. (At least one of them, praised by Macmillan's reader,

John Morley, seems to have been salvaged for *Under the Greenwood Tree*.) Undaunted by Macmillan's rejection, Hardy sent his manuscript to another publisher, Chapman and Hall, where it was read by the novelist and poet George Meredith. Hardy set down (again, fifty years after the event) his recollections of an interview with Meredith: the gist of the latter's advice was that, while the book was publishable, it invited hostility from 'the conventional reviewers', and would do his future as an author no good. Meredith suggested that the young novelist should either drastically rewrite the book, or, better still, begin another novel with a more strongly constructed plot. Hardy opted for the second alternative, and took Meredith at something more than his word – the result being *Desperate Remedies*, his earliest surviving novel.

For the next few years, Hardy continued to follow his architectural career and to devote his leisure time to further efforts at fiction. This phase of part-time authorship coincided with his courtship of Emma Lavinia Gifford, whom he had met in Cornwall, while engaged on church-restoration business, in the spring of 1870. Their relationship over the next forty years was to be the source of much joy at first, of a longer period of pain and bitterness, and eventually, after her death, of some of his finest poems.

In the novels written during this period, one has a sense of Hardy groping for a type of fiction that was both congenial to his temperament and experience and likely to find acceptance in the literary market-place. *Desperate Remedies* is a conscientious exercise in the 'sensation novel', which in the previous decade had proved enormously successful and lucrative in the hands of such best-sellers as Wilkie Collins and M. E. Braddon. *Under the Greenwood Tree* represents a complete change of direction: it is a village love-story, written at Bockhampton in the early stages of Hardy's courtship, and it rejects the sensation novel as a model in favour of the school of realistic fiction popularized by George Eliot. In it, for the first time, Hardy exploited his deep knowledge of rustic life and speech, no doubt seen and heard the more clearly after his long absence. He may well have been prompted to this change of direction by the fact that two of the most influential critical organs of the day, the *Athenaeum* and the *Spectator*, had praised the presentation of rustic life in *Desperate Remedies*. *Under the Greenwood Tree* was written shortly after the appearance of these reviews. Already one notes a pattern emerging in Hardy's early ventures into fiction: he characteristically effects a compromise between the kind of novel he is, by nature and gifts, best qualified to write, and the kind that his study of the market suggests as likely to be saleable. *Desperate Remedies* had been published as a 'three-decker' at half a guinea a volume – the traditional and expensive fictional format of the period. His second novel appeared in two volumes. Both were published by William Tinsley, the first in 1871 at the author's expense, the second in the following year on slightly more favourable terms.

During the next twenty-three years, all Hardy's remaining novels were to appear as serials before being issued in volume form. Earlier in the century, serialization, most commonly in monthly 'parts' (paper-covered instalments of a novel sold over a period often as long as nineteen months), had enabled Dickens and others to reach an unprecedentedly wide audience with their fiction. By the time Hardy began to write, the separate issue of parts had lost ground to the rival mode of serialization in magazines: from the point of view of the public, there were obvious attractions in obtaining between the covers of a single, relatively cheap publication not only a regular dose of fiction but a variety of other material. Thus *A Pair of Blue Eyes* appeared in *Tinsley's Magazine*, and subsequently in a New York newspaper, as well as being published by Tinsley in three volumes.

Hardy as a Professional Novelist

The *Spectator* had attacked *Desperate Remedies*, to Hardy's deep distress, on moral grounds; but the next two novels received favourable notices, though the sales of neither could be regarded as brilliant. It was his fourth published novel, *Far from the Madding Crowd*, which established him as a novelist with a growing reputation on both sides of the Atlantic. Like its predecessors, it was published anonymously, and there was speculation – perhaps puzzling to the modern reader, but flattering to Hardy – that the author might be George Eliot. (The possibility was mooted by the *Spectator* after the appearance of the first number.) The novel was written with the encouragement of Leslie Stephen, editor of the prestigious *Cornhill*, which had already serialized not only George Eliot but Thackeray, Trollope, Mrs Gaskell, and other established authors. Stephen had been much impressed by *Under the Greenwood Tree*, and wrote to Hardy on 30 November 1872 to invite him to contribute a serial to his magazine. Hardy at that time had *A Pair of Blue Eyes* on hand, but by September of the following year he was able to send him a portion of his new novel. Even though the book was still largely unwritten, Stephen promptly accepted it, and serialization began in January 1874, publication of the earlier portions proceeding simultaneously with the composition of the remainder. To Hardy's delighted surprise, he found his story occupying pride of place at the beginning of the magazine. Stephen was staking a good deal, perhaps, on this judgment of a little-known author, but he was justified by events; for the novel was widely reviewed, brought Hardy his largest audience to date, and in volume form was more successful than any of his previous books. The editorial path was not entirely smooth, however. *Far from the Madding Crowd* raised a problem that was to recur many times in a more or less acute form during Hardy's career as a writer of fiction, for the seduction of Fanny Robin by Sergeant Troy led to protests from 'three respectable ladies and subscribers', and hence to a warning from editor to author that that element in the story needed to be handled with special tact. Stephen's dilemma as editor of a family magazine is conveyed by a sentence in one of his letters written to Hardy at this time: 'Excuse this wretched shred of concession to popular stupidity; but I am a slave.'

The success of this novel may have enabled Hardy to feel justified in embarking on marriage, for it was in September 1874, while it was still appearing each month, that he married Emma Lavinia Gifford. She was, as she later liked to remind him, a lady, and the niece of an archdeacon; so that the title of his first, unpublished novel had proved prophetic. None of his family was present at the wedding. One of Emma's diaries has survived to give us a vivid account of the wedding tour, which took them to Rouen and Paris; Hardy's autobiography scarcely mentions it, however. It was his first trip abroad, and cannily combined business with pleasure by enabling him to collect material for his next novel, *The Hand of Ethelberta*. This too appeared in the *Cornhill*, and seems to have been a deliberate, and somewhat perverse, attempt on Hardy's part to avoid being typecast as a chronicler of rustic life. He comments wryly in his autobiography that its appearance produced 'general disappointment at the lack of sheep and shepherds'. Not surprisingly, it was less successful than its predecessor, and for his next novel, *The Return of the Native*, Hardy wisely returned to the rural scene. (It seems that he had been 'anxious to get back to verse' at this time, and had even suggested to Stephen a series of 'tragic poems' for the *Cornhill*; but the proposal met with no encouragement, and he continued with fiction.) After the early part of the new novel had been written, it was offered to Stephen, who declined to commit himself until he had seen the complete work – an act of editorial prudence, or timidity, dictated by doubts as to the outcome of the potentially explosive sexual situation in which Hardy had placed his principal characters. It duly appeared in 1878 in another monthly, *Belgravia*, and was widely discussed, though reviewers combined praise and criticism in roughly equal proportions. Some detected in it a Shakespearean quality; one compared its heroine, Eustacia Vye, to Emma Bovary, though Hardy later denied that he had read Flaubert's novel at that time. Much of the discussion focused on the rendering of peasant life and the realism or otherwise of the dialogue: Hardy, it seems, was already becoming generally identified as a regional novelist.

The Return of the Native was followed by three minor novels. (The distinction between major and minor fiction in relation to Hardy will be discussed in a later chapter.) *The Trumpet-Major* (1880) is a short historical novel, and the first of Hardy's books to exemplify his deep and lifelong interest in the Napoleonic period. The notebook in which he collected research material for this novel still survives. *A Laodicean* (1881) illustrates the hazards to which authors and publishers of serialized fiction exposed themselves. Dickens and Mrs Gaskell had died during the run of uncompleted novels; Hardy did not die, but he fell seriously ill with internal haemorrhages when the first number was about to appear, and avoided surgery only by keeping to his bed for several months. It was in these painful circumstances that he dictated most of the novel to his wife. It was also during this period that he noted in his diary the idea, with which he may already have been toying for several years, of an ambitious historical and philosophical drama – the idea which, many years later, was to develop into *The Dynasts* (see Chapter 6). The third, *Two on a Tower* (1882), was written for an American magazine, the *Atlantic Monthly* – evidence of Hardy's growing transatlantic reputation. In the course of planning it he visited Greenwich observatory and engaged in reading and correspondence to collect material illustrative of his hero's passion for astronomy.

More than one reviewer of *Two on a Tower* took Hardy to task for a trifling slip – the bestowal of an incorrect form of address upon a titled widow who married a bishop. The error was corrected in later editions, and Hardy's sensitivity to the incident is a reminder that the village boy who was now moving with apparent ease in the literary and social circles of the metropolis was still at heart a little unsure of his qualifications for such a role. His diaries and notebooks show that at this period of his life he assiduously went into society in quest of material that might be useful to a busy and prolific professional novelist (he had produced four novels in five years). We can imagine that, at least initially, such activities must have been somewhat less than congenial to one of his reserved disposition, and one who was still conscious of his modest provincial origins. Nevertheless, he dutifully attended dinners and 'at homes', joined country-house parties, turned up at exhibitions and private views, and generally studied the upper reaches of British society at close range. Ironically enough, it was only in his lesser fiction that he was to make extensive use of the material thus accumulated: his major novels owe almost nothing to his conscientious frequenting of dinner-tables and drawing-rooms and his careful compilation of observations and epigrams in his notebooks, but draw on deeper and earlier levels of experience in a world geographically and socially remote from the London homes of the wealthy and the celebrated. Still, the list of those who were among his acquaintance during these years is impressive, and gives the lie to any notion that may prevail of Hardy as a peasant or a recluse. It includes publishers and editors such as Leslie Stephen, Alexander Macmillan and George Smith; eminent authors such as Tennyson, Browning and Matthew Arnold; notable Americans such as William Dean Howells, John Russell Lowell and Henry James; Henry Irving the actor; Frith, Alma-Tadema and Burne-Jones the painters; Thomas Henry Huxley the scientist; and many others. The popular image of Hardy, like that of Henry James, relies heavily on his later years, but it is important to remember that he did not have a permanent home in Dorset between the time he left his parents' house and his mid-forties. During the time that all the novels so far discussed were written, he and his wife lived in a series of rented rooms and houses in London and Dorset, moving frequently and making numerous tours in England and abroad. And even after he built himself a country home, he was for many years in the habit of migrating annually to London for the 'season'.

When at last he decided on building a house to his own designs, he considered various sites and finally settled on a spot on the outskirts of Dorchester. (He took a mildly snobbish pride in the fact that the land was purchased from the Duchy of Cornwall.) There was surely something symbolic about this return to within a few miles of his birthplace; and certainly the years immediately following his decision to settle at Max Gate saw the production of four of his finest novels. The first of them, *The Mayor of Casterbridge* (written in 1884-5), is significantly set in Dorchester, for which Casterbridge is the fictional name. Several episodes in the book owe their origin to a careful study which Hardy made, soon after moving to Dorchester, of the back numbers of the local newspaper, the *Dorset County Chronicle*, for the years 1826-30. It is almost as if, having returned to his native soil, he had been anxious to attempt to recover, in minute and circumstantial detail, not only his own past but that of his parents' generation. (The novel opens in the 1820s, and the main action is set in the 1840s.) Max Gate was to remain his home until his death forty-two years later. As his fame grew, he was to receive there a remarkable procession of visitors, from the Prince of Wales downwards, and to become more and more identified in the popular mind with the Wessex he had helped to define in his work.

The Woodlanders appeared in the popular monthly *Macmillan's Magazine*, in 1886–7; some idea of the size of its readership is given by the fact that the ten thousand copies of its first number were sold immediately, and a further printing was called for. (One must also remember, of course, that each copy might be perused by several readers.) To the same period belongs Hardy's first book of short stories, *Wessex Tales* (1888). He was to contribute nearly fifty stories, on widely assorted themes and of uneven quality, to a great variety of periodicals, and to collect the best of them in a series of four volumes.

The publication of Hardy's next novel was to cause him more trouble than any previous one. He was now fifty, and had for many years been a professional author with a considerable international fame; but the treatment to which *Tess of the D'Urbervilles* was subjected before it finally achieved publication in a seriously mangled form might have been a source of bitter humiliation even to a younger and less eminent author. To a man of Hardy's deeply sensitive nature, capable of being wounded by even moderate criticism (he had 'wished that he were dead' when he read the *Spectator*'s review of *Desperate Remedies*), the situation must have been almost intolerable; yet, curiously enough, his handling of it seems, after some initial ingenuousness, to have been almost cynical. Perhaps cynicism was the only alternative to despair or total abandonment of the novel; certainly one is tempted to say that it was not only the heroine who was violated but the book itself. *Tess* was written for Tillotson & Son, a Lancashire firm of strong nonconformist traditions whose 'Newspaper Fiction Bureau' supplied serial novels and short stories to a large number of provincial newspapers. When Hardy sent them the first half of his new novel on 9 September 1889 – the portion containing such scenes as the seduction of Tess and her improvised 'baptism' of her dying child – they became disagreeably aware that it was hardly likely to be suited to the kind of publication, designed for family consumption, in which their fiction was syndicated. Hardy refused to agree to their proposal that the offending scenes should be excised and the whole story reworked, and the agreement between them was thereupon cancelled. What seems never to have been satisfactorily explained is why Hardy did not anticipate the objections that would inevitably be made to crucial elements in his story by a firm of whose traditions and moral standards he must have been aware. He proceeded to offer the novel successively to two editors. *Murray's Magazine* refused it on the grounds of its excessive frankness in dealing with sex and marriage; Mowbray Morris, editor of *Macmillan's Magazine*, who had earlier warned Hardy that he was sailing too near the wind in *The Woodlanders*, also rejected this new novel. Hardy's solution to this impasse was to set about the 'dismemberment' (his own word) of the novel, removing the two episodes referred to above, publishing them with some modifications as separate sketches 'for adult readers', and patching up the remainder somewhat clumsily, many changes being necessitated by these drastic amputations. The serial version eventually published in the *Graphic* thus incorporates numerous additions, omissions and bowdlerizations; it was not until publication in three volumes was achieved at the end of 1891 that the original text was substantially restored.

It was, of course, this publication in volume form which provoked violent reactions from many reviewers. *Tess* was more widely discussed than any previous novel of Hardy's, and, perhaps for this reason, sold far better than any of them – some 19,000 copies had been sold by the end of 1892. Several critics, among them the spokesmen of such influential organs as *The Times* and the *Westminster Review*, hailed it as a great novel and lauded its tragic power and moral seriousness; but others attacked it roundly, the *Quarterly*, for instance, commenting that 'Mr. Hardy has told an extremely disagreeable story in an extremely disagreeable manner', which echoes the slightly earlier verdict of the widely read *Saturday Review* ('Mr Hardy . . . tells an unpleasant story in a very unpleasant way'). As usual, Hardy seems to have been more deeply affected by criticism than by praise. It was after reading the *Quarterly*'s attack that he noted in his diary: 'Well, if this sort of thing continues no more novel-writing for me. A man must be a fool to deliberately stand up to be shot at.' It was while he was embroiled in the difficulties over the publication of *Tess* that he wrote one of his most important statements on the art of the novel, his essay 'Candour in English Fiction' (see Chapter 5 below).

Tess, then, had the double effect of raising against Hardy a storm of hostility, much of it based on moral rather than artistic objections, such as he had never before faced, and at the same time of granting him a larger measure of success in terms of sales than he had hitherto enjoyed. He was now generally recognized, at home and abroad, as one of England's leading novelists. *Jude the Obscure*, his last novel, continued and accentuated the double trend described above. It sold even better than its predecessor, reaching its twentieth thousand within three months; and again it evoked the loud protests of critics, who found it 'coarsely indecent' and 'obscene'. Indeed, it was the object of a remarkable barrage of vituperation which recalls the attacks on Ibsen quoted in Shaw's *Quintessence of Ibsenism*: an American lady reviewer (whose subsequent encounter with Hardy, as described in the *Life*, makes amusing reading) commented that its subject was 'pigs – animal and human', and claimed to have been driven to open the window to let in the fresh air; the *Pall Mall Gazette* found in it 'dirt, drivel, and damnation'; A. J. Butler said in the *National Review* that it depicted the 'night-cart' side of nature; R. Y. Tyrrell in the *Fortnightly Review* found it 'a dismal treatise', 'steeped in sex'; while a New York critic condemned it as 'a moral monstrosity and an outrage upon art'. It is true that the denigrators did not have it all their own way: the more progressive wing of critical opinion hailed it as a fine achievement, the *Saturday Review* making up for its attack on *Tess* by perceptively applauding Hardy's presentation of his working-class hero, the *Daily Telegraph* recognizing it as a 'masterpiece' (though deploring its 'prevailing gloom'), and the *Westminster Review* hailing Hardy as 'the greatest living English writer of fiction'. The establishment, however – as represented, for instance, by a letter from a bishop in the *Yorkshire Post*, and the banning of the book by a circulating library – were more demonstrative; and again Hardy reacted to this reception with a dignity which concealed a deeply wounded and indignant spirit. Nor were the wounds quick to heal or the indignation quick to subside: a quarter of a century later, when many of those involved were dead, he wrote in his autobiography several passages which show that the bitterness still rankled. (Most of them were deleted before publication, but they can be read in the original typescript.)

Once again, though, one has to register a certain surprise at Hardy's ingenuousness – or disingenuousness. He surely ought to have been prepared for trouble; for *Jude*, like *Tess*, had had a rough passage before it ever reached volume form, having been sadly mangled in its progress from manuscript to serial. Hardy wrote the novel in 1893–4, after a longer gestation period than was usual with him, the first notes relating to it dating back (according to his own account) to 1887. It was intended for serialization in *Harper's Monthly*; and at an early stage, in response to the publisher's tactful reminder that it should be 'in every respect suitable for a family magazine', he had replied that it 'would be a tale that could not offend the most fastidious maiden'. That he should ever have made such a guarantee can only be explained by the unforeseen shift of focus from Jude's quest for an education to what the period called 'the marriage question'. Within a few months, no doubt recalling his experiences with *Tess*, he asked that the agreement should be cancelled, since the story was taking unforeseen directions which could scarcely fail to offend. It was not cancelled; but the familiar protests followed when the editor had the earlier parts of the novel in his hands, and once again Hardy set about the distasteful task of bowdlerization. The presentation of his hero's relationships with Arabella and Sue was drastically modified, with (as R. L. Purdy puts it) 'amazing sacrifice of art and credibility'. Hardy was later to make the modest claim that the novel, 'as abridged in the magazine', was 'a not uninteresting one for the general family circle'. The process of restoration was duly performed for its appearance in volume form. By this time he had acquired a considerable measure of skill in damaging the fabric of his original version of a novel in such a way that, once the hazards of serial publication had been successfully negotiated, the damage could be repaired with relative ease; he noted in his diary, however, that 'on account of the labour of altering *Jude the Obscure* to suit the magazine, and then having to alter it back, I have lost energy for revising and improving the original as I meant to do'.

The *Well-Beloved* had been serialized in 1892, and therefore precedes *Jude* in date of composition; it was not issued in volume form, however, until 1897, some revision, including a completely new ending, having taken place in the meantime. A letter to Edmund Gosse written the day after its publication in volume form indicates that Hardy's original intention had been to subject it to a thorough revision; but, as with *Jude*, that intention had been abandoned – evidence, perhaps, of his increasing weariness with fiction. Yet again, his bland claim in the prospectus supplied to his publisher that 'There is not a word or scene in the tale which can offend the most fastidious taste; and it is equally suited for the reading of young people, and for that of persons of maturer years' is not easy to reconcile with the actual theme of the novel, the protagonist's remarkably enduring sexual impressionability. Hardy seems yet again to have been surprised and pained by its reception: in a cancelled passage in his autobiography, he refers to the 'bewildering' effect upon him of the hostile criticism directed at a book which he had intended as a romantic fantasy, but which was attacked for immorality; and in a letter he offered the explanation that it might be the reviewer, and not the author, who was afflicted with 'sex mania'. Its publication brought to a close more than twenty-five years of uninterrupted activity as a novelist: aside from a few short stories, Hardy was to write no more prose fiction in the remaining thirty-one years of his life.

To the question: why did Hardy abandon the novel? a variety of answers is possible. The legend that distress or disgust at the reception of his last novels caused him to take a vow of silence as a novelist is probably no more than a half- or even a quarter-truth. It is possible to exaggerate (as Hardy himself may well have done) the extent of the hostility: as has already been suggested, *Tess* and *Jude* evoked high praise as well as abuse. Another, less romantic, explanation is that the success of these novels, combined with the steady income derived from the continuing sales of his earlier books, made it possible for Hardy to write for himself instead of for editors, publishers and reviewers – and writing for himself had always meant writing verse. Scattered remarks in his letters also suggest that Hardy regarded the possibility of writing more fiction as still open after *Jude*, and as late as 1901–2 he was still noting ideas for short stories in his diary: there was apparently nothing in the nature of a solemn vow or dramatic renunciation. But, whatever the reason, his prediction after the attacks on *Tess* ('. . . no more novel-writing for me') was fulfilled. At the same time, it would be a mistake to interpret his abandoning of prose fiction as stemming from a cynical and opportunistic contempt for the genre. Although in a notorious phrase (on which it would be unwise to lean too heavily) he quite early limited his ambition in his field to being considered 'a good hand at a serial', the manuscripts of his novels and short stories indicate that he took considerable pains over even minor questions of style. Even such a labour of expediency as the extraction from *Tess* of the two sketches published independently bears the evidence of considerable thought and pains: rather than, as might have been supposed, carrying out the mutilation with cynical perfunctoriness, he took the task seriously and performed it conscientiously. Nor did he give up revising his novels as new editions were called for even after he had given up the novel itself. During the years when he was explicitly disparaging his own achievements in fiction, and deploring the widespread tendency to regard him as a novelist rather than a poet – his un-published letters contain many such observations – he showed considerable interest in making such revisions as time and reflection called for.

One further possibility calls for mention: that Hardy did not so much abandon fiction as find that fiction had abandoned him. For developments in the novel during the years from 1870 to 1895 had made Hardy's type of fiction seem somewhat old-fashioned. Hardy had little interest in the theory of the novel or in those writers who, during this generation and the next, transformed the art of fiction; and it may be that he realized that he was becoming less and less equipped to practise the public art of fiction, as opposed to the private art of poetry, and was disinclined, at nearly sixty, to begin learning new tricks.

Hardy the Poet

Hardy had written verse during his years in London (1862–7), but his preoccupation with fiction in the following decades left little time for poetry, though he seems to have written and preserved a few poems from the 1870s and 1880s. As Michael Millgate has pointed out, his turning to poetry in the late 1890s did not represent a complete break with the world of the novels. His first volume of verse was significantly entitled *Wessex Poems* (1898); and much of his poetry reflects the same closely observed rural world, expresses a similar range of moods and emotions, and displays the same taste for irony and the same pre-occupation with the past, as the Wessex Novels. At times the parallels between prose and verse are very close: Hardy wrote a number of poems which employ similar material to passages in the fiction (e.g., 'Midnight on the Great Western', based on a passage in *Jude the Obscure*). Of more than 900 items in the *Collected Poems*, though, most were written during the thirty years after the end of his career as a novelist. To trace the development of his art as a poet is no easy task, for the order of publication was by no means always that of composition. Hardy frequently put aside a draft of a poem, sometimes for years or decades, before returning to it; and his habit seems to have been to incorporate in a given volume both poems recently composed and others dating from a much earlier period. Since he also destroyed his drafts, it is difficult to ascertain to what extent these earlier poems were revised. Of *Late Lyrics and Earlier* (1922), for example (the title of which illustrates the point in question), Hardy commented that 'about half the verses were written quite lately'; the others seem to range over some fifty-five years, though only about one in five can be dated with any precision. Even more strikingly, his last collection, *Winter Words*, published posthumously in 1928, brings together poems of over sixty years. As it happens, however, the question of dating is not of crucial

importance, for Hardy's poetry shows relatively little of the development or the division into phases or periods that we associate with such
a poet as Yeats or Eliot. He was curiously impervious to 'influences',
and although he wrote verse of various kinds – lyrics, ballads, dramatic
monologues, narratives – and although he exhibits an extraordinary
variety of metrical forms and some fascinating experiments with
language, the later work is not significantly different in mood or
style from the earlier.

Concerning the relative value of the fiction and the poetry, Hardy's
own views are quite unambiguous. In a letter to one of his earliest
critics, Harold Child, on 7 May 1915, he insisted that his verse (including *The Dynasts*) represented his 'essential' writings, while the prose
was 'accidental' – in other words, written out of the necessity to earn a
living; and he often insisted that the condensation demanded by the
poetic medium was more congenial to his natural mode of expression
than the diffuseness of prose. In his letters and conversation, he was apt
to disparage the novels, and to discourage those who seemed inclined
to take an interest in them at the expense of the poetry.

It would be natural to suppose that the poetry is more personal than
the fiction, drawing more heavily on actual and perhaps identifiable
experiences, personalities and places. But while there may be some
truth in this supposition, the distinction between them in this respect is
far from clear-cut. Hardy vigorously denied the existence of autobiographical elements in his novels, and indignantly repudiated attempts
to interpret the fortunes of his heroes as versions of private experience.
He was obviously irritated, for instance, by the reading of *Jude the
Obscure* as personal history, and in a letter written in 1923 insisted that
there was 'not a page' of personal experience in that book – a statement
impossible to accept as it stands. On the other hand, he commented
that there was 'more autobiography in a hundred lines of [the] poetry
than in all the novels', and it is true that many of the poems have
names and dates attached in such a way as to suggest that they embody
fragments of actual experience and memory. Hardy is probably guilty
of some degree of evasiveness, and the truth may well be that he drew
more heavily on his personal life, in both prose and verse, than he was
prepared to acknowledge, but that, like most other writers, he never
hesitated to adapt fact to the demands of art. Such evasiveness would be
quite consistent with his attitude towards biographers, critics, journalists, interviewers and anyone else who displayed an unwelcome
curiosity concerning his private life and personality.

Reviewers were in general slow to take Hardy seriously as a poet, and both the melancholy cast of much of his verse and its unorthodox diction and syntax seem to have been obstacles to instant popularity. Even his admirers must have been disconcerted at his turning from the novel to poetry, and it is striking that his first collection of poems was issued in an edition of only 500 copies. The steady rise of his poetical reputation is attested by the progressively larger printings of later collections: 2,000 copies of the first edition of *Time's Laughingstocks*, for instance, in 1909; 3,000 of *Moments of Vision* (1917); and 5,000 of *Human Shows* (1925), with two further impressions within a few weeks of publication. But, as a later chapter will suggest, it is only in our own generation that Hardy's own valuation of his verse in relation to his novels has begun to win wide and authoritative acceptance.

To the same period as the early volumes of verse belongs *The Dynasts*, an 'epic drama' on the Napoleonic wars. In spite of its dramatic form, it was never intended for the theatre, and indeed would be impossible to stage in any adequate sense. Hardy said that it was written for 'mental performance', though somewhat inconsistently he produced an abridgment which was staged by his friend Harley Granville-Barker and which ran for seventy-two performances in 1914–15. Although much of the verse is irredeemably pedestrian, the sheer magnitude of conception on the human and supernatural levels is impressive, and something of Hardy's own excitement at the real-life drama of such events as the retreat from Moscow and the death of Nelson succeeds in coming across. This work, the largest and most ambitious of all Hardy's undertakings, also illustrates his remarkable capacity for allowing a literary idea to mature slowly in his mind before the process of composition began. The notion of writing 'an Iliad of Europe from 1789 to 1815' (one of his earliest references to the general intention which eventually found fulfilment in *The Dynasts*) occupied him intermittently for well over thirty years; starting as a straightforward historical poem or play, it developed over the years into a cosmic drama with an elaborate philosophical framework. Its three parts were published separately, in 1904, 1906 and 1908; one effect of publication in 'parts' was to educate the public in the reading of the work, and reviewers, who were not kindly disposed to the early portion, grew gradually more appreciative as the philosophical and technical interest of the work became more apparent.

Last Years

With one major exception, Hardy's outward existence during the last thirty years of his life was uneventful. Public honours included the Order of Merit in 1910 (he had earlier refused a knighthood), and honorary fellowships of Oxford and Cambridge colleges: the Dorset boy who had felt his lack of a university education ended by dining at high tables as a distinguished member, and the writer who had scandalized respectable opinion in one generation lived to become part of the establishment in the next. As he grew older, he left Max Gate less often, though the stream of visitors seems to have shown little diminution, and he maintained an extensive correspondence with the celebrated and the obscure in all parts of the world, and kept a scrupulous eye on his business interests and on matters of copyrights and royalties. But the death of his wife in 1912 was an emotional landmark. The marriage which had begun so brightly had turned to bitterness and, although they remained under the same roof, to emotional estrangement. Her sudden death, however, revived the emotions of forty years earlier, and combined them with the poignant realization that the experiences and feelings which survived so freshly in memory belonged irrevocably to the past. Some of the most potent ingredients in the characteristically Hardyan creative situation were thus brought together – a sense of time and change, of remorse, of the intense quality of a long-distant experience surviving in memory, of loneliness, of places rendered significant by associations; the result was a group of poems, the 'Poems of 1912–13', which are among the finest of twentieth-century lyrics.

It is the name of his second wife – his former secretary, Miss Florence Emily Dugdale, whom he married in 1914 – which appears on the title-page of the official biography, *The Life of Thomas Hardy*. But the book is now recognized as almost entirely an autobiography. The circumstances of its composition, discussed elsewhere in this volume, contain many puzzling elements; but this last major work in prose seems to have occupied Hardy during his final decade, from about 1916 or 1917. However, the considerable labours it involved, including the sifting of the papers of a lifetime, seem not to have inhibited the steady flow of poetry, for, like Yeats, Hardy produced some of his finest work in his old age, and one of his most memorable poems was written on his eighty-sixth birthday. He had been born before the railway came to Dorset; he died at nine o'clock in the evening of 11 January 1928, the news was telephoned to London, and the nation heard of his death a few minutes later through the medium of broadcasting – a technological contrast which brings home the transformation of the material conditions of human life which occurred during his lifetime. (He once said that, when he first began to use the telephone, he felt like Noah walking out of the Ark and into a motor-car.) His death posed a problem, the solution to which has something of the bizarre quality of many episodes in his novels and stories. He had expressed a wish to be buried beside his wife and parents in Stinsford churchyard; but, as a national institution, he also belonged to England. By way of compromise, his heart was buried in Dorset, the remainder of his body in Westminster Abbey – a curious fate which it is, again, tempting to call symbolic.

The length of Hardy's career has few parallels in modern literature: born in the age of Dickens and Thackeray, he began writing in that of Trollope and George Eliot, continued through the 1890s and the Edwardian period, and after undergoing the metamorphosis from Victorian novelist to twentieth-century poet that has been outlined in this chapter, survived to live and write in the age of James Joyce, D. H. Lawrence and T. S. Eliot. He lived long enough to find himself, to his frequent annoyance, the subject of biographical and critical assessments, the volume of which has increased prodigiously since his death. As well as more orthodox forms of scholarly attention, on a global scale, his work has frequently been the object of curiosity of a non-literary or only partly literary kind: folklore enthusiasts, topographers, social historians and others have used his books as grist to their respective mills, and Hardy the creative artist has tended to become obscured by Hardy the chronicler of rural life and customs. There has also, from the outset, been a tendency to regard his novels and poems as offering a 'philosophy' or a system of ethics, though at the price of widespread misunderstandings and confusions. Even before the nineteenth century ended, his name had become linked with 'pessimism'; but he firmly rejected the label of pessimist, insisting that he was an 'evolutionary meliorist'. The epithet reminds us that he was a product of the age of Darwin, and his journey from youthful orthodoxy to adult scepticism has a representative quality. And yet, as so often with Hardy, the truth is too complex to be contained within a simple formula; for, while rejecting Christian doctrines and beliefs, he regarded himself as 'churchy', and retained to the end a strong emotional and aesthetic attachment to the outward manifestations of faith – church buildings and services, church music, and the language of the Bible. Hardy was indeed far from being the simple countryman or rustic story-teller that his admirers as well as his detractors have often made him out to be. If he was these things, he was also a man of wide intellectual interests and friendships, capable of moving at many social

23

levels, a serious-minded professional author and dedicated literary craftsman, and a shrewd man of business. He spent sixty years giving his thoughts and feelings to the world, but remained an intensely reticent and self-contained personality. These contrasting aspects of his mind and experience are reflected in his work, and render its interpretation and assessment a more complex task than has often been supposed.

Editors, Publishers, and Readers

Hardy's long and well-documented career would provide the subject for a fascinating detailed study of the conditions, hazards and rewards of professional authorship in the late nineteenth and early twentieth centuries. Such a study is beyond the scope of the present volume; but some aspects of the topic may be briefly touched on. As the preceding outline has suggested, it was a career that began with a marked lack of *éclat*. After his earliest, anonymous contributions to the local newspaper, Hardy had considerable difficulty in bursting into print. As a young man in the mid-1860s, during his architectural years in London, he sent poems to the magazines, only to meet with unanimous rejection. He recalled in his autobiography that he 'paid such respect' to the judgment of editors at this time 'as scarcely ever to send out a MS. twice'; and towards the end of his life he told Virginia Woolf, ' "I wrote a great many poems. I used to send them about, but they were always returned," he chuckled. "And in those days I believed in editors." ' His respect and faith were to be considerably dimmed by the experience of later years.

His first novel, *The Poor Man and the Lady*, clearly represented on Hardy's part an act of careful calculation that turned out to be based on false assumptions. His letter to Alexander Macmillan (now in the British Museum) which introduced the manuscript conveys a sense of the tyro author writing with one eye firmly fixed on the public: it sets out, frankly and somewhat naively, the 'considerations' he has borne in mind in writing the novel; and one seems to detect him estimating, from a social distance, the requirements and tolerance-level of an upper-class readership. Its unacceptability was communicated by Macmillan (in a letter now in the Dorset County Museum, and quoted from in the *Life*) with tact and an encouraging kindness; still, Hardy must have drawn the inevitable conclusion that his diagnosis of the secret of successful fiction had been inaccurate. Certainly *Desperate Remedies* shows him storming the citadel of popularity from another direction; it was published, however, on terms that must have been less than gratifying (Hardy agreed to pay £75, not all of which he recovered, towards the costs), and the modest edition of 500 copies sold only very slowly: indeed, within a few weeks of publication, Hardy had the discouraging experience of coming across it, remaindered, on a station bookstall. *Under the Greenwood Tree* was also offered to Macmillan; after an inconclusive response which he seems mistakenly to have interpreted as a refusal, it was offered to Tinsley, who paid him £40 for the English and Continental copyrights. Hardy's letter to Macmillan (dated 7 August 1871) makes it clear that in writing this novel he had taken his cue from those reviewers of *Desperate Remedies* who, while faulting the latter novel as a whole, had found something to praise in the rustic characters and settings which are a minor element therein, and had compared him to the early George Eliot. *A Pair of Blue Eyes* was the third and last of the novels to be published by Tinsley, and the first to appear in serial form. Tinsley, in his dual role as publisher of fiction in volume form and editor of *Tinsley's Magazine*, reserved the right to issue the novel as a three-decker as well as to publish it serially, all rights reverting to the author after twelve months; if sales exceeded expectations, an additional sum was to be paid over and above the £200 agreed. Tinsley's letter formally accepting Hardy's terms suggests that the latter had quickly learned to drive a harder bargain; in the event, he was to manage his literary affairs almost single-handed, and with notable success, to the end of his days.

Serialization was to cause Hardy many headaches; yet one can see why, in the literary context of the 1870s, he committed himself to a system that he was to serve for a quarter of a century. Serialization in established magazines brought regular payment which, so long as copy was forthcoming, could be depended on for a fixed period; it thus eliminated some of the financial uncertainties of authorship. Moreover, it guaranteed a wide and ready-made readership; and, rather than (as one might suppose) killing the market for the subsequent appearance of the novel in volume form, it could actually help to stimulate sales, since a book that had been enjoyed over many months would be deemed by some readers to be worth possessing, or at least borrowing from a circulating library, for perusal at one's own speed. Publication of the volumes was usually timed to anticipate by a few weeks the appearance of the final, curiosity-quenching instalment of the serial: for example, *The Return of the Native*, serialized throughout the twelve months of 1878, was available complete at the beginning of November. Simultaneous serialization on both sides of the Atlantic brought an extra fee and a considerable enlargement of the readership. The leisurely pace of publication, and the fact that readers all had their attention directed to the same portion of the story at the same time, encouraged close involvement in the vicissitudes of its characters and speculation as to its outcome: few readers nowadays (though many television-viewers) have had the experience, commonplace for the Victorians, of living with a story as a familiar companion of their lives throughout an entire year or longer. Of the dozen novels Hardy wrote for serialization, all but three appeared in monthly instalments. The three exceptions – *The Mayor of Casterbridge*, *Tess of the D'Urbervilles*, and *The Well-Beloved* – involved him in the narrative problems of the weekly serial, with its shorter, more compressed instalments. Earlier in the century, Dickens, Mrs Gaskell and others had complained of the almost intolerable pressures imposed by the straitjacket of weekly serialization; and Hardy was likewise to experience its peculiar difficulties. Of *The Mayor of Casterbridge* he later wrote in his autobiography:

> It was a story which Hardy fancied he had damaged more
> recklessly as an artistic whole, in the interest of the newspaper in
> which it appeared serially, than perhaps any other of his novels,
> his aiming to get an incident into almost every week's part
> causing him in his own judgement to add events to the narrative
> somewhat too freely.

One has to agree with Hardy that there are episodes in this novel (for example, Henchard's rescue of Lucetta from a bull) which seem to serve little purpose beyond the need to 'get an incident' into the instalment in question.

With *Far from the Madding Crowd* Hardy moved into the more distinguished ambience of the *Cornhill*, and was encouraged by his success to turn professional author. In volume form it sold markedly better than its predecessors: the first edition of 1,000 copies went quickly, and within a few weeks a second, corrected edition was called for. As a serial, it appeared anonymously; and the inevitable speculation concerning its authorship probably contributed to its success. A number of Leslie Stephen's letters to Hardy have survived; they combine judicious praise with constructive criticism, valuable as coming from one who was both a very intelligent critic and an experienced editor. As already suggested, however, Stephen was not immune from a cautiousness verging on faintheartedness whenever the slightest possibility arose of offending the susceptibilities of his most fastidious, or prudish, readers. No doubt he recalled what the first editor of the *Cornhill*, his father-in-law Thackeray, had written in its opening number: 'At our social table, we shall suppose the ladies and children always present.' The advent of Fanny Robin's illegitimate child caused Stephen particular discomfort: he confessed that he would 'somehow be glad to omit the baby'; and his refusal of *The Return of the Native* was, according to Hardy, prompted by anxieties of a similar kind. The latter novel also illustrates a familiar dilemma of the Victorian novelist over the provision of an ending that would satisfy both his artistic scruples and a conventionally minded public. Earlier, even Dickens had yielded to compromise over *Great Expectations*; now it was Hardy's turn to abandon his original intention of making Diggory Venn slip quietly away, in favour of a long-deferred union between him and Thomasin.

Editorial sensitivity was once more in evidence in relation to *The Woodlanders*. Mowbray Morris, the editor of *Macmillan's Magazine*, cautioned Hardy to exercise discretion in handling the affair between Fitzpiers and Suke Damson, and urged him 'not to bring the fair Miss Suke to too open shame'. His letter (now in the Dorset County Museum) apologizes for the excessive touchiness of his readership ('rather a queer public: pious Scottish souls who take offence wondrous easily'), but it is quite evident that, whatever his private judgment on their narrow-mindedness might be, he had no intention of giving offence. As already noted, *Tess* was also offered to *Macmillan's*, and declined by Morris, whose letter of refusal expresses disquiet at the frequent references to the heroine's physical attractions: as he put it, borrowing a term from Hardy's description of the Frome Valley, the story had 'rather too much succulence'. Earlier in his career, Hardy had contrived to allay editorial fears by making minor adjustments – in *The Trumpet-Major*, for instance, by moving a lover's meeting from a Sunday to a Saturday, and by eliminating some swear-words. But *Tess* was too radically offensive, in its central situations as well as in details, for such tinkering with the text to serve any purpose; and the version that eventually appeared in the *Graphic* was little more than a travesty of the original novel. For its appearance in volume form, however, a careful restoration of the original was made. The modern reader may find it curious that what was highly objectionable and indeed intolerable in a magazine should have been perfectly acceptable in a bound volume. The explanation of this double standard is probably that magazines were not only more readily available, but were intended for family consumption: as the editor of *Harper's* told Hardy in connection with *Jude the Obscure*, 'our rule is that the Magazine must contain nothing which could not be read aloud in any family circle'; he also insisted, however (a familiar editorial gambit), that his objections were based on 'a purism' which was 'not mine, but our readers''. *The Hand of Ethelberta* had prompted Leslie Stephen to remind Hardy to 'remember the country parson's daughters; *I* have always to remember them'; and it was later recalled that, as editor of the *Cornhill*, Stephen had remarked that the first commandment he had to enforce was, 'Thou shalt not shock a young lady'. For a novelist engaged in the exploration of problems of social and personal morality, the paralysing effects of a situation wherein 'the country parson's daughters' are taken as ideal readers need not be insisted on. To be fair to Victorian editors as a class, not all were fully committed disciples of Mrs Grundy. W. E. Henley displayed unusual courage, or rashness, in inviting Hardy to send him the most risqué of the stories in *A Group of Noble Dames* for his magazine. Leslie Stephen seems to have suffered from a genuine conflict of responsibilities: he confessed that the editorial ruling already described in connection with *Far from the Madding Crowd* was prompted by 'an excessive prudery of which I am ashamed', and seemed anxious to arrive at a viable compromise in his advice to Hardy that 'the thing must be stated, but . . . the words must be careful'. On the other hand, Edward A. Arnold, editor of *Murray's Magazine*, represents an unapologetic and uncompromising insistence on the maintenance of a 'wholesome' literary morality, in the narrowest sense in which this favourite term could be interpreted. In refusing *Tess*, Arnold wrote to Hardy:

> I know well enough that these tragedies are being played out every day in our midst, but I believe the less publicity they have the better, and that it is quite possible and very desirable for women to grow up and pass through life without the knowledge of them.

Whereas the ideal reader of a novel was, it seems, a mature adult, in periodicals the standard of the lowest common denominator had to operate so effectively that a weekly or monthly could be read aloud without preliminary censorship to a group which might certainly include those susceptible to moral infection. Podsnappery, diagnosed by Dickens in the 1860s, was still a force to be reckoned with in the 1890s and after. Even Hardy's farewell to fiction did not mark the end of his troubles with editors: as late as 1907, the *Fortnightly Review* refused to print his poem 'A Sunday Morning Tragedy', a stark narrative of seduction and abortion, on the grounds that the magazine circulated among families. Given the moral climate of the period, the refusal is of course intelligible; and perhaps Hardy was guilty of tactlessness, or a lack of realism, in submitting the poem in the first place. But such a rebuff, administered to one who was by that time widely regarded as England's foremost man of letters, cannot have been easy to stomach.

His painful experiences over *Tess* at least endowed Hardy with a measure of skill when it came to the bowdlerizing of *Jude the Obscure* for serial publication, even if that skill was somewhat cynically exercised. The manuscript shows that he first wrote the novel more or less as he wished it to be; he then went through it making alterations and deletions in ink of different colours (red and green, readily distinguishable from the black of the original text), in order that the subsequent task of restoration should be as simple a matter as possible. The changes were made in response to protests from the editor of *Harper's New Monthly Magazine* concerning the frankness with which Jude's relationship with Sue was presented; although they seriously damage the novel as an artistic structure, they appear to have satisfied the *Harper's* editor. When *Jude* appeared in volume form, Hardy contented himself with drily noting in the preface that 'the magazine version was for various reasons an abridged and modified one'. Comparison of the texts shows that some of the modifications verged on the trivial or ludicrous: 'couch', for example, was substituted for 'bed', 'affection' for 'sex' and 'shaking hands' for 'kissing'. For Hardy, there must have been something humiliating as well as irritating in all this; and it is hardly a matter for surprise that he had no patience left for a further major revision of the text, though he did go on making minor revisions as late as the definitive edition of 1912. *Jude* was the first of Hardy's novels to be published at the modest price of six shillings (*The Well-Beloved* was issued in similar fashion); it therefore broke with the nineteenth-century tradition of the expensive multi-volume novel, and its popularity as measured by sales was proportionately greater.

Hardy's long and eventful relationship with the fiction-reading public offers an interesting case-study in the problems of the late-Victorian professional author. Enough has been said to make it clear that the relationship was never a simple one of writer and reader, but was complicated by the intervening and often obstructive presences of editors and publishers – not to mention reviewers, to whose verdicts Hardy was always abnormally sensitive. Just as the Elizabethan dramatist wrote for a particular kind of playhouse, with its distinctive opportunities and limitations, the Victorian novelist's art was conditioned by publishing conventions, economic circumstances and the need to preserve accepted public standards of literature and morality. It is impossible to estimate the extent to which Hardy's novels might have been different if he had been writing in a more permissive literary climate: but it seems certain that at least some of his books, in the form in which we have them, embody suppressions and distortions, including unconscious ones, which are seriously damaging to their artistic shape as well as to their quality as realistic and responsible moral statements.

Hardy was not, of course, the only victim of Mrs Grundy and her disciples. Throughout the nineteenth century, a vigorous campaign had been waged against literary frankness, or impurity (according to the point of view taken); and although much of the campaigning zeal was directed against avowed pornography, its effects were also felt by serious literature. The Society for the Suppression of Vice, founded in 1802, for all the large claims of its title, had concerned itself mainly with 'offensive' publications; after its demise in the 1870s, it was succeeded by the National Vigilance Association, which conducted a successful and celebrated prosecution of the publisher Henry Vizetelly in 1888 for issuing English translations of some of Zola's novels. Zola became something of a byword for offensiveness in the novel, and his name was frequently evoked by the reviewers of *Tess* and *Jude*. The Obscene Publications Act of 1857 had given teeth to the law: Havelock Ellis, who praised *Jude* when it appeared, was himself prosecuted a couple of years later when he published his serious study of sexual inversion. But it was neither the law nor the organized opposition to literary candour which created the most serious and far-reaching difficulties for Hardy: publishers, editors and libraries were capable of exerting their own less obtrusive pressures with damaging and distressing results, and probably no major novelist shows better than Hardy the results of their quiet but powerful influence. As a recent historian of censorship, Donald Thomas, has said, in the Victorian period 'the most important form of moral censorship was one with which the law was not directly concerned. It was a censorship exercised ultimately by booksellers and libraries, penultimately by publishers or editors, and in the first place by authors themselves. And when all this was done there still remained the individual censorship of the buyer or the borrower.'

That 'individual censorship' was, of course, partly controlled by the reviewers in the influential periodicals, and Hardy's press, as my discussion of the reception of *Jude* has suggested, could be a very mixed one indeed; one should remember, though, that moral condemnation by a reviewer, if only drawn strongly enough, might actually promote sales among the curious and the prurient to an extent that more than compensated for the loss of virtuous purchasers. The large sales of *Jude* were a side-effect that its attackers can hardly have taken into account. There can be no doubt, however, that the combined forces of publishers, editors and subscription libraries represented a formidable discouragement to a writer who wished to deal frankly with sexual topics.

Occasionally an attack was directed at some other variety of boldness: for example, the publication of Ruskin's *Unto This Last* in the *Cornhill* in 1860 was broken off on account of its 'socialistic' tendencies; but by far the most sensitive area was that involving questions of sex and marriage. An unknown author who failed to treat such dangerous themes or situations with the requisite evasiveness might never find a publisher for his work; and even established writers could feel pressure being brought to bear upon them. John Blackwood objected to George Eliot's description of a character in *The Mill on the Floss* as a 'loosely-hung, child producing woman' (the author agreed to substitute the epithets 'prolific' and 'loving-hearted'); he even expressed his dislike of the word 'lymphatic' as applied to Mrs Tulliver; and Gordon Haight has suggested that he only allowed the vivid description of Mrs Sutton's dropsy to slip through because he had not seen the proof. Even verse was not immune from a publisher's moral veto: the firm which had originally undertaken the publication of Swinburne's *Poems and Ballads* took fright and refused to continue. Editors, anxious for their sales figures, were prepared to give offence to their authors rather than to their public: the *Cornhill*, which was to refuse *The Return of the Native*, had earlier (under Thackeray) turned down one of Trollope's stories which ventured on the dangerous ground of divorce and illegitimacy. As for the circulating libraries, such as Mudie's and Smith's, their role could be crucial to the financial success of a book, since they might purchase, or refuse to purchase, very large quantities of a new novel in its most expensive format: they were, therefore, in a strong position to express moral disapprobation in a practical form. Smith's, as Hardy recounts in his autobiography, took the step of withdrawing *Jude* from their shelves, and promised to scrutinize other books by Hardy, after the outcry by the Bishop of Wakefield and others.

Censorship and serialization were not the only factors capable of exerting an unfortunate influence on the writer of fiction: there can be little doubt that the three-volume novel, a format in which *The Return of the Native*, *The Woodlanders*, and other works appeared, encouraged a prolixity of style and an excessively slow narrative pace which Hardy would have done better to avoid. It is surely revealing that Hardy's least flawed novel, *Under the Greenwood Tree*, was not written for serialization and was published in two slim volumes, being substantially shorter than most of the others. Again, the contemporary taste, encouraged by serialization, for strong-plotted novels was one which Hardy conscientiously aimed to cater for, but which was not in harmony with his own special gifts for observation and reflection: his plots, as Richard Church has said, often creak like farm-carts.

In 1902, with his fiction-writing career behind him, Hardy was able to transfer all his copyrights to Macmillan, who also published *The Dynasts* and the verse volumes of his remaining years. The massive Macmillan Archive, consisting of 1,250 volumes of documents acquired by the British Museum in 1969, contains an interesting record of Hardy's dealings with his publishers during his final quarter-century. Some idea of his popularity at the time of the transfer may be gained from a list in his own hand of his sales figures for the year ending 30 June 1901, which he forwarded to Macmillan while negotiations were in progress: the sixpenny edition of *Tess* had sold 100,000 copies during that period, and a similar edition of *Far from the Madding Crowd* over 45,000. His correspondence during the ensuing years shows, in an elderly author of world renown, a meticulously business-like concern with the minutiae of the literary profession: though a wealthy man, he was still prepared to write, in a hand which remained admirably firm and legible to the end, a letter requiring a small fee for the anthologizing of a poem – or, where appropriate, waiving the fee. Hardy's background had taught the lesson that the labourer is worthy of his hire. At the same time he was capable of showing a complete absence of mercenary considerations in summarily disposing of his manuscripts, a large batch of which was given away to various museums and libraries, through the agency of his friend Sydney Cockerell, in 1911; others were given after his death. With genuine modesty, Hardy never seemed to entertain the notion that they might be of commercial value as well as of scholarly and sentimental interest. His proofs were always quickly and carefully corrected, and few major authors so prolific have bequeathed such a small legacy of textual problems to their editors. As the years passed, there were many requests for translations and adaptations of the novels for stage and screen. A letter of 1903 notes that the Russian translation of *Tess* has proved very popular; another, in 1919, makes the interesting suggestion that *The Mayor of Casterbridge*, *The Trumpet-Major*, and *Desperate Remedies* would be particularly suitable for filming. The Max Gate correspondence shows that, during his later years, Hardy received a large quantity, and wide diversity, of fan-mail from all over the world; much of it he replied to fully, and nearly always with great patience and courtesy.

In almost every aspect of his career, whether involving a major novel or a pot-boiling short story, Hardy was thoroughly professional, a worthy descendant of generations of craftsmen. In his later years his income from royalties and fees was substantial and he died a wealthy man: the fortune he left, over £90,000, must have been equal to something like £1,000,000 in present-day values. His books had never been instant best-sellers on the lines of many long-forgotten Victorian novels: Mrs Humphry Ward's *Robert Elsmere*, for instance, published at about the same time as *The Woodlanders*, had sold 1,000,000 copies within the year in England alone. But they enjoyed a steadily increasing popularity as, during his long lifetime, he witnessed his own transformation into a classic; as he himself remarked, near the end of his life, if he had not been a best-seller, he had at any rate been a 'long-seller'; and, fifty years later, the very large sales of recent reprints indicate no waning in his appeal to the general reader. He belongs, indeed, to the relatively small company of great writers who enjoy both an academic reputation of considerable vitality and a wide and enthusiastic following among the common readers of the world.

2

Major Novels

The existence of 'minor' as well as 'major' works in a writer's total output – assuming, for the moment, substantial agreement on the drawing of the borderline – is usually not hard to account for. Often it is a matter of early and later, immaturity and maturity: in such terms, for instance, can *Almayer's Folly* and *The White Peacock* be seen in relation to *Nostromo* and *The Rainbow*. Or 'minor' art may be a matter of scale, of the voluntary restriction of scope: thus *Hard Times* and *Silas Marner*, though they are novels of their authors' maturity, are special cases, more limited in ambition and achievement than *Little Dorrit* and *Middlemarch*. Hardy's minor novels raise problems less susceptible of easy solution. The qualitative gap between his major and minor fiction is exceptionally wide; but this is not the only difference, for the lesser novels seem to derive from motivations and interests unlike those which generated the 'novels of character and environment', and to belong to different fictional genres and sub-genres. Beside the human richness and professional confidence of the major novels, they are apt to appear imaginatively impoverished, morally evasive, incompletely engaged and awkward in execution. But even when they fail, they remain highly personal failures; to read or re-read them can be a surprising experience, affording more pleasure and interest than might have been anticipated; and each of them contributes something, and some of them a good deal, to our total understanding of Hardy.

His search, at the beginning of his career, for a personally congenial and commercially acceptable fictional mode has already been described. *The Poor Man and the Lady* was, according to his later recollections, 'a sweeping . . . satire . . . socialistic, not to say revolutionary'; but contemporary evidence suggests that it represented no mere working off of grievances, but rather a calculated attempt to write a successful book. The letter Hardy wrote to Alexander Macmillan on the same day that the manuscript of the novel was sent to him (25 July 1868) sets out the considerations which were borne in mind in its composition, and one has a sense of the young Hardy calculating, from a considerable social distance and not unerringly, the demands and the level of tolerance of an upper-class readership. *Desperate Remedies* played safer by seeking to make capital out of the recent success of the 'sensation novel'; *Under the Greenwood Tree*, less ambitious and contrived, and proportionately more fully realized, essayed humour and nostalgia, drew on personal experience rather than intellectual convictions, and represented yet another change of direction. The calculating impulse, though, was not absent, as another letter to Macmillan reveals: Hardy quotes extracts from reviews of *Desperate Remedies* which had praised the occasional rustic scenes in that novel and even invoked the impressive name of George Eliot, and it is clear that, on the strength of the implicit critical directive, he hoped to achieve greater success than hitherto by taking a pastoral setting and characters as the basis of his new novel. One has a sense at this stage of his career that Hardy is impelled by no inner conviction as to the kind of fiction he wants to write or is capable of writing. Yet another letter of the same period shows him studying reviews of his work in search of guidance, but experiencing naive bafflement at the discovery that different reviewers praised different elements.

In the novels that followed, *A Pair of Blue Eyes* used personal experience and authentic backgrounds as the foundation for a romantic and somewhat artificial tale; *Far from the Madding Crowd*, Hardy's first considerable success, returned to the pastoral novel and the influence of the early George Eliot; but *The Hand of Ethelberta* showed a perverse or defiant disinclination to be typecast as a chronicler of the countryside. Without going any further for the moment, it is evident that Hardy's first eight years as a novelist show a fundamental uncertainty on his part as to the nature of his own gifts – or possibly an unwillingness to recognize them. Whatever the writer may have proposed, however, the public disposed; and Hardy, who had by now committed himself to authorship as a career, could hardly fail to draw the obvious conclusions from the success of *Far from the Madding Crowd* and the lukewarm reception accorded to its successor.

The alternation of one or more minor novels with the production of his major fiction was a pattern which Hardy continued, fortuitously rather than deliberately, for the rest of his career as a writer of prose. *The Return of the Native* falls between the social comedy of *The Hand of Ethelberta* and the historical romance *The Trumpet-Major*; two slight novels, *A Laodicean* and *Two on a Tower*, are followed – with the significant intervention of Hardy's return to Dorset and the building of Max Gate – by *The Mayor of Casterbridge* and *The Woodlanders*; between the magnificent achievements of *Tess* and *Jude* come the feeblest of all the novels, *The Well-Beloved*, and a volume of short stories. It seems that Hardy's impressive rate of production necessitated the sacrifice of consistent quality to quantity: editorial invitations, and his own wish to secure a competence, kept his pen busy, even when creativity flagged.

Some of the contrasts which distinguish the two groups are obvious. The major novels employ a more restricted locale, usually either a rural community or a small town intimately linked with the surrounding countryside; *Tess* presents a series of different but mainly rural settings; only *Jude* quits the land after the opening section to enter the world of the urban artisan. The minor novels, on the other hand, range widely and restlessly over a variety of scenes, rural, urban, metropolitan and Continental: when his powers of invention fade, Hardy is apt to send his characters on their travels, drawing background material from his own journeyings (a particularly flagrant example is the wanderings of Ethelberta across France). The social range of the characters in the major novels is similarly circumscribed: upper-class characters, the fashionable, the worldly, and the intellectual (like Fitzpiers and Mrs Charmond in *The Woodlanders*) appear only in contrast to those for whom the countryside is more than a temporary place of residence. Another way of making the same point would be to say that the major novels are about people who work, and whose work is necessary to maintain existence: Hardy shows as much preoccupation with, and detailed knowledge of, rural occupations as Dickens and Balzac do in connection with those of the city, and his novels are full of lovingly exact information on such matters as how to plant a tree, kill a pig or perform an emergency operation on a sick sheep. But the minor fiction habitually relegates countryfolk to a minor role, often that of chorus or comic relief; and the central figures are the well-to-do, the consumers rather than the providers, or the educated professional man: architect, sculptor, musician, astronomer. A contrast of a different kind between the major and minor fiction is stylistic: no major novelist's language absents itself from felicity more quickly than Hardy's when the quickening impulse grows feeble or dies altogether. Even the best novels are not altogether free from lapses into ponderousness or banality, and some of the minor novels contain fine passages; but the different degree to which novels as close in time as *Tess* and *The Well-Beloved* utilize the resources of the language is a matter for astonishment: the contrast between the seen and felt in one and the cerebral and mechanical in the other is very evident on the stylistic level.

Hardy himself readily conceded some of the differences among his novels, not only by the afterthoughts recorded in his prefaces and elsewhere, but also by his own division of his fiction into three unequal groups, as follows:

1 'Novels of Character and Environment'
 Under the Greenwood Tree
 Far from the Madding Crowd
 The Return of the Native
 The Mayor of Casterbridge
 The Woodlanders
 Tess of the D'Urbervilles
 Jude the Obscure
 Wessex Tales (short stories)
 Life's Little Ironies (short stories)
2 'Romances and Fantasies'
 A Pair of Blue Eyes
 The Trumpet-Major
 Two on a Tower
 The Well-Beloved
 A Group of Noble Dames (short stories)
3 'Novels of Ingenuity'
 Desperate Remedies
 The Hand of Ethelberta
 A Laodicean
 A Changed Man (short stories)

This grouping was made for the collected edition of 1912, and there is evidence (in an unpublished letter) that Hardy did not set great store by the categories he devised. Although the first group contains all the major novels, they were certainly not planned as a series, and make no use (as some of Trollope's do) of the device of the reappearing character, though they are given a measure of a different kind of unity by the reappearance of environments. (I follow Hardy in classing *Under the Greenwood Tree* among the major novels: if its brevity seems to relegate it to 'minor' status, its remarkable poise and control are more than adequate compensation; and in setting, theme and tone it unmistakably belongs with the 'novels of character and environment'.)

The map of Wessex first provided by Hardy in the 1895 collected edition helped both to satisfy and to stimulate interest in the physical background of his fictional world, as well as a touristic curiosity about the correspondence between that world and the landscapes of actuality.

In this chapter and the one that follows I shall adopt different methods in examining, respectively, the major and minor fiction. Since the major novels, with some reservations, can be said to represent a relatively homogeneous group, they will be discussed *en bloc*. The minor novels, on the other hand, present greater diversity and call for individual treatment; they are therefore examined in Chapter 3 in chronological order of composition.

Hardy's description of his major fiction as 'novels of character and environment' certainly does not take us very far towards discerning a common purpose or a common method. The phrase firmly relegates plot or story to second place – an account which does not altogether square with our experience of reading these narratives, and is not entirely consistent with his more fully declared belief that 'The real if unavowed purpose of fiction is to give pleasure by gratifying the love of the uncommon in human experience, mental or corporeal . . . The uncommonness must be in the events not in the characters.' A large part of Hardy's contemporary and continuing popularity is owed, it seems worth insisting, to his skill as a story-teller. But the phrase is less open to attack in so far as it encourages us to attend to the developing role and significance of the 'environment' in these books, and the topic is one that this chapter will return to.

Beyond this, certain recurring features can be traced throughout the group of novels. Most obviously, they are all love stories, treating, at various levels of seriousness, the problems and vicissitudes of sex-relationships inside and outside marriage. At first the situations are of the simplest. In *Under the Greenwood Tree* the heroine, Fancy Day (the hint of fickleness as well as freshness in her name is ominous), is loved by Dick Dewy, the first of a line of honest, open-hearted countrymen whose lack of guile makes them easy victims for the calculating, the faithless, the ingrate and the usurper. The introduction of Parson Maybold as a rival to Dick, and a socially attractive proposition for the ambitious young schoolmistress, was a late notion of Hardy's: there is manuscript evidence that Maybold's interest in her originated only when more than half the book was written; but it has the effect of modulating the latter portion of the story into a minor key – most strikingly in the wistful cadence of its conclusion, when the newly married Dick and Fancy (for at this stage Hardy is still prepared to give us a happy ending) lay down the basis of their lifelong relationship:

'We'll have no secrets from each other, darling, will we ever? – no secret at all.'
'None from to-day,' said Fancy. 'Hark! What's that? . . . '
'O, 'tis the nightingale,' murmured she, and thought of a secret she would never tell.

Later heroines are to resist temptation less successfully, but already the discordant undertone is present beneath the reassuring surface of marital harmony: Fancy's very promise conceals a deception. (Hardy gives us another version of this situation in *Tess of the D'Urbervilles* when Tess, a more scrupulous wife than Fancy, decides to have 'no secret at all' from Angel Clare, and sees her honesty bring about the destruction of her marriage.) The ending of this early novel often seems to be overlooked by readers and critics who speak of it as a pastoral idyll of undisturbed serenity: starting out as a portrait of the pre-industrial organic community basking in golden sunshine (the novel is set in the period of Hardy's parents' youth), it nevertheless introduces, almost in spite of itself, hints of change and disillusion.

In *Far from the Madding Crowd* the simple triangle of lovers is replaced by a slightly more complex figure; and that last term, with its dual associations with geometry and the dance, is doubly relevant to Hardy's notions of plot-making. Three men of different temperaments aspire to Bathsheba's hand: Gabriel Oak, the shepherd, whose names are a guarantee of his heroic combination of goodness and strength; Troy, traditional soldier-philanderer, who does not belong to the rural community (he is, ominously, of upper-class origins) and does not share its values, manners, or occupations; and Farmer Boldwood, whose stolidity has been purchased at the price of repression and whose feelings, once accidentally released, drive him to obsession, crime and madness. Again, Hardy felt constrained to provide his readers with a happy ending; but this time it is reached only by way of suffering and tragedy, including two deaths. In both of these novels, the sexual problem – specifically the hesitations of a woman who undervalues the worth of unspectacular integrity, loyalty and devotion – is complicated by a social problem. Fancy Day is tempted by Maybold's status in the community (in which she herself stands somewhere between the parson who tempts her and the tranter's son she eventually marries). Bathsheba is dazzled by Troy's flamboyant sexuality, but it is relevant too that Gabriel's chances of success have been minimized by the financial disaster which, early in the story, has reduced him from independence to the status of one of her employees. Social differentiation between rivals in love recurs throughout the major novels, and is not confined to them. There can be little doubt that Hardy's portrayal of the emotional life at the mercy of economic circumstances derives some of its strength from his own experiences, though the theme is admittedly a dominant one in nineteenth-century fiction. Dick and Gabriel, like Giles Winterbourne and Diggory Venn a little later, may also owe something to that lost prototype, the hero of *The Poor Man and the Lady*.

In subsequent novels the complications produced by the workings of different varieties of love, ranging from romantic adoration to carnal appetite, become more intricate, and the havoc wreaked in human lives by blind passion or unwise marriage becomes more extreme. In *The Return of the Native*, Diggory loves Thomasin, who marries Damon Wildeve, who is loved by Eustacia, who nevertheless marries Clym Yeobright. The pattern embodies disappointment, frustrated desire, infidelity, ambition, unrequited love: there is no shortage of marriages, but they signally fail to accommodate the existing love-relationships. Hardy fights shy in this novel, however, of following through the situations he has created: at this stage in his career he lacks the courage – or, to put it more tolerantly, cannot afford – to explore at all adequately the results of violation of the marriage-tie; and Eustacia's flight with Wildeve ends not in adultery but in death. As for Thomasin and Diggory Venn, Hardy's original bold notion of having the latter slip quietly away at the end of the story was abandoned in deference to the expectations of his readership, and a more conventional ending substituted.

It is in *The Woodlanders* that Hardy's treatment of the marriage question becomes more explicit and his rejection of the happy ending is asserted. Later he was to deplore the moral timidity of this novel; but it seems fairer to regard it as representing an advance in courage and honesty, for there is now no way to a happy ending, and it is the patient and faithful Giles who must suffer and die, not, as in earlier stories, the wrongdoer (Troy, Eustacia). The patterning of relationships in this novel resembles three triangles touching at certain points. The union of Grace Melbury and Giles Winterbourne, which originally possessed a certain natural rightness, is prevented by her father's uneasy ambitions and by the education she has received; substituting town-bred standards and expectations for those of her girlhood (her expensive education has been crowned by a tour of Bath, Chelten-ham and Continental watering-places), she has 'fallen from the good old Hintock ways'. (As we shall note later, there is an unconscious irony in the autodidactic author of such novels as *The Hand of Ethelberta* observing that 'cultivation had so far advanced in the soil of Miss Melbury's mind as to lead her to talk of anything save of that she knew well'.) The arrival of the outsider Fitzpiers ('like a tropical plant in a hedgerow') provides a successful rival to Giles; but Fitzpiers in turn dallies with two other women, the village girl Suke Damson and the wealthy parvenue Felice Charmond. Fitzpiers's infidelity, and Grace's belated recognition of Giles's true worth, raise the question of divorce; and Hardy touchingly renders the hope succeeded by frustration with which Melbury and his daughter pursue the will-o'-the-wisp of rumoured legislation making divorce more readily accessible. Simple natures and decent moral impulses are shown caught in the trap of archaic and irrelevant legal, social and religious sanctions. The heroic gesture of Eustacia's flight with Wildeve is not the kind of course of action open to a woman of limited imagination such as Grace, who belongs to the tradition of fickleness inaugurated by Fancy Day: Giles has to die, a victim of hollow conventions and empty proprieties; and, since Suke Damson is made to emigrate and Mrs Charmond is melodramatically disposed of by an earlier lover who turns up oppor-tunely from South Carolina, Grace is left to return, not unwillingly, to her husband. The last word, and the ultimate loyalty to Giles's memory, remain with the country girl Marty South, who, with Giles and Grace, forms a third triangle of forces. Dignity and integrity, though not happiness, belong to such characters as Giles and Marty: one of the finest moments in the book is the scene in which they plant young trees together, Giles absorbed in a task he is performing with an expert's skill, Marty finding a mute though imperfect satisfaction in being with him, even though he is virtually unconscious of her sex, which is indeed played down by the narrator in accordance with a common Victorian convention of idealized femininity. In contrast, the courtship and marriage of Fitzpiers and Grace, against a background of comfortable hotels and other scenes of bourgeois affluence, seems superficial and insubstantial. Hardy has reached a point in his fiction – and it is to prove a point of no return – at which true love is inseparable from disappointment and heartache.

In *Tess of the D'Urbervilles*, Hardy returns to the strong but simple triangle of relationships: his heroine dominates this novel even more than Eustacia Vye dominates *The Return of the Native*, while the contrast between Alec and Angel seems to be of the starkest variety – at the outset, indeed, almost allegorical in its presentation of the two men as stereotypes. Alec, consistently bogus whether he is posing as the scion of an ancient house or as a convert and preacher, is one of Hardy's diabolic characters: he actually tells Tess at one point that he is 'the old Other One come to tempt you', and he frequently assumes a disguise and unpleasantly disconcerts her by turning up unexpectedly. At the same time, as Ian Gregor has pointed out, he is the stock-in-trade villain of Victorian melodrama and the familiar seducer of popular songs and ballads: with his smart clothes, his 'black moustache with curled points', his 'bold rolling eye', and (a period danger-signal) the 'cigar between his teeth', he is a standard contemporary portrait of the well-to-do cad or experienced seducer. Angel's background is as superficially impeccable as his name: his somewhat oppressively pious home (perhaps based on Horace Moule's), and his Muscular-Christian brothers, seem to guarantee integrity, or at least innocence; but this Angel dwells in a fallen world and, when demands are made upon his charity, fails to rise to the occasion. His betrayal is of a different order from Alec's, but no less devastating in its effect upon Tess. Angel's Brazilian ordeal produces enlightenment but, as so often in Hardy's fictional world, the unconscious timing of events is grimly unlike that of romantic fiction: rather than bringing rescue in the nick of time, he arrives too late. ('Too Late, Beloved!' was the novel's original title; and Tess tells Angel at Sandbourne, after she has returned to Alec, '"I say it is too late".')

As for Tess herself, to say, as I said above, that her presence dominates the novel is not to overlook her extraordinary passivity. As a creature of flesh and blood she is rendered more fully than any other character in Hardy's fiction – indeed, beside her, such allegedly 'physical' characters as Tom Jones or Hetty Sorrel seem relatively unrealized; when we read, for instance (in Chapter 27), that 'her arm, from her dabbling in the curds, was as cold and damp to his mouth as a new-gathered mushroom, and tasted of the whey', we encounter writing of an extraordinary sensuousness and even eroticism, not easy to parallel in nineteenth-century fiction, though Lawrence was to achieve similar effects twenty years later in Sons and Lovers. Yet, as a mind or a consciousness, Tess makes remarkably little impact: one sees why Henry James spoke so patronizingly of this novel, for Hardy has grappled with, without altogether solving, a version of the problem James had set himself a decade earlier in The Portrait of a Lady – that of making a 'mere . . . girl' a rich enough centre of interest for a novel. Hardy's novel, of course, draws its strength from other directions; but the personality of Tess, as distinct from her surroundings or experiences or her representative quality, is of a distinctly limited depth and complexity: she speaks much less than most fictional heroines, and even when she is driven to express her feelings they seem to spring spontaneously from instinct and intuition rather than resulting from inner conflict and mental drama. The reiterated imagery of the shy and vulnerable wild creature (she is compared at least three times, for instance, to a trapped bird) perhaps offers an unintended clue to Tess's limitations as protagonist.

As Lawrence noted, *Jude* reverses the sexual roles, but otherwise reproduces the situation, of *Tess*: whereas Hardy's heroine was caught between two men representing (at least at first glance) spirit and flesh, the hero of Hardy's last novel is caught between two antithetically presented women. Sue Bridehead's Christian name, as Hardy reminds us means 'lily', and her surname recalls 'maidenhead' and may suggest a conflict between marriage and virginity; while Arabella is a Circe-like enchantress who is repeatedly associated with swine, recurrently threatens to pull Jude down to a level of animality, and embodies the sensuousness of Tess Durbeyfield without her innocence and simplicity. In a sense, the real subject of the novel (though not Hardy's point of departure) is the destructive power of sexuality, which is referred to somewhat obliquely in the 1895 preface as 'the strongest passion known to humanity'. In *Far from the Madding Crowd* twenty years earlier, that destructive power had been shown at work in Boldwood; but, in spite of his tragic obsession, it was still possible for the novel to end serenely, and even cosily, with Gabriel Oak's winning of Bathsheba as the delayed reward for his steadfastness; and certainly Gabriel's manliness had never included a strong sexual component. A member of the rustic chorus comments that ' "I never heerd a skilful old married feller of twenty years' standing pipe 'my wife' in a more used note than 'a did" ', and there is indeed something precociously middle-aged and unimpassioned about such patient lovers as Gabriel Oak and Diggory Venn. Jude has his share of patience and steadfastness, but he is a more physical creature than Giles: we are permitted to see him through the eyes of Arabella as a desirable sexual object. And, in the world of the later novel, his sterling qualities are no longer of avail. Just as his educational yearnings and genuine intellectual passion are spurned or ignored by the academic establishment, his search for a love-relationship which will satisfy his physical needs without leading to self-disgust is frustrated by the two women with whom he becomes involved. Ultimately, the two themes of the novel – Jude the scholar, Jude the lover – intertwine, and the search for love involves the abandonment of his ideals and aspirations. Hardy's presentation of love and sex has travelled all the way from the romantic idyll of *Under the Greenwood Tree* to a realistic diagnosis of animality, frustration and disillusion (within, of course, the permitted limits of late-Victorian magazine fiction: Hardy later admitted that he would have wished to have dealt more explicitly with Sue's denial of her sexual favours to Jude). It is worth noting that, prominent and even dominant though the account of Jude's sexual life is in the novel as we have it, Hardy's preoccupation with the themes of love and marriage seems to have forced itself into the story against the current of his original intentions: as his diary records, the book took its origin from the conception of a short story about a young man 'who could not go to Oxford'; and as John Paterson has shown, the manuscript reveals that 'what was undertaken as a critical examination of the educational system in Hardy's time came inadvertently, in its working out, to take in an equally critical examination of the sacrament and institution of marriage'.

Though all Hardy's novels are love stories, then, there are considerable variations of tone and emphasis in their handling of this theme. All but the most resolute opponents of biographical criticism are likely to detect a correlation between the changing attitudes to love and marriage expressed in Hardy's fiction and the deterioration of his own marriage. At the same time his fiction responds, if only to a limited extent, to contemporary pressures: behind *Jude*, for example, with its radical questioning of the basis of marriage, lies not only personal bitterness and disillusion but a public debate which had gained fresh impetus from the Parnell case. Moreover, Hardy's lovers are not, even in *Under the Greenwood Tree*, the timeless youths and maidens of pastoral tradition, but creatures firmly set in a carefully delineated landscape, in a more or less specific period of time, and in a society which is involved in a process of change that is not always dramatic (there is, for instance, nothing in Hardy's work comparable to the account given by Dickens in *Dombey and Son* of the impact of the railway), but remains inexorable. These three determinants of individual destiny, the topographical, the historical and the sociological, need to be exemplified at some length.

The arena in which Hardy's dramas take place is, at any rate until the last two novels, geographically very limited; but he is prepared to insist that the restriction of locale involves no diminution of the possibilities of human interest or universal significance. In *The Woodlanders*, for example, Little Hintock is 'one of those sequestered spots outside the gates of the world', but 'the concentrated passions and closely-knit interdependence of the lives therein' are capable of producing 'dramas of a grandeur and unity truly Sophoclean'. (If the plotting of this novel hardly fulfils the Aristotelian prescription for unity of action, there is a notable unity of place, nearly all the events of the story taking place in a very confined area.) The invention of Hardy's Wessex seems to have been a happy accident. For self-evident reasons, he began by writing about the landscapes and communities he knew most intimately; when he leaves Wessex, it is usually to make a brief excursion to some other neighbourhood he had explored as a visitor (Cornwall in *A Pair of Blue Eyes*, the Continental scenes of *A Laodicean*) or, in the case of London, as a resident. The success of the novels of country life left him, as a professional novelist, with little choice: the relative failure of the society-novel *The Hand of Ethelberta* after the triumph of *Far from the Madding Crowd* carried an unmistakable message, and in spite of Henry James's tart comment on the latter novel that the 'only things we believe in are the sheep and the dogs', the reading public was clearly anxious to hear more about Wessex. Certainly by the time he settled at Max Gate Hardy seems to have accepted the role of chronicler of folk-life and painter of the local scene. As already noted, for the collected edition of 1895 he prepared a map of Wessex to satisfy the demands of those who admired the novels for their evocation of a region at once particularly beautiful and peculiarly rich in associations of the past; on more than one occasion he added a warning, however – not always heeded by his admirers – that he had freely adapted landscapes and buildings for his purposes rather than simply transcribing them from life.

In most of the novels the locale is remarkably small and self-contained. When a young man in *The Mayor of Casterbridge* tells his sweetheart he has taken a job thirty-five miles away, she replies, ' "I shall never see 'ee again!" ' Distances are often measured in terms of a man's capacity to walk, a journey from one village to another involves a significant shift of scene, and the normal life of the community is enclosed by the surrounding hills or woods, and controlled by the natural rhythms of the day and the year. One of Hardy's favourite devices for opening a story, as in *The Woodlanders* and *The Mayor of Casterbridge*, is to show a stranger entering an unfamiliar neighbourhood: the stranger is normally on foot, and evidently has not come far, but there is a sense conveyed of a venturing into new scenes. In such conditions, differences imperceptible to a stranger take on importance: as one of the rustic characters remarks of Little Hintock, ' "I wouldn't live there if they'd pay me to. Now at Abbot's Cernel you do see the world a bit." ' One result of this proximity of lives is to justify to some degree the coincidental encounters which are so frequent in Hardy's novels, and have so often been treated as a blemish on his plot-making: in a world so circumscribed, where even itinerant figures such as Diggory Venn and Physician Vilbert pursue their regular beats, accidental meetings are less an occasion for surprise than they would be on a more extensive setting. It is true that co-incidence can seem to be driven hard at times: in *The Mayor of Caster-bridge*, for instance, the furmity-woman turns up to confront Henchard after twenty years when he is serving as magistrate; the accidental witness of Lucetta's secret marriage to Farfrae also happens to be Henchard's principal creditor; Joff, in asking a favour of Lucetta, indicates that he, like her, has previously lived in Jersey and has known of her there – and the list might be lengthened without difficulty. The responsibility for this overworking of chance probably rests partly with the contemporary demand that serial fiction be strongly plotted, with secrets and mysteries, surprises and revelations, in abundance. Hardy is certainly not the only Victorian novelist whose plotting is open to this kind of criticism: even such a conscientious realist as George Eliot is capable of resorting to similar devices. In his defence, it can be argued that coincidence of the type which involves the intrusion of one set of circumstances upon another over a long period of time dramatizes Hardy's preoccupation with the inescapable nature of the past. A man like Henchard is never entitled to believe that he has left a phase of his life behind him for good and all, since the quirks of chance may bring it before him again when he least expects it.

The search for unity through consistency of setting already noted in *The Woodlanders* is equally true of several other novels: the action of *The Return of the Native* is played out on the heath and the adjacent communities; Casterbridge and its environs dominate *The Mayor*; and in *Far from the Madding Crowd*, as C. J. Beatty has shown, a small number of buildings (church, homestead, barn, malt-house) serve as focal points for most of the important scenes. Often, indeed, Hardy makes significant dramatic and contrastive use of the principal buildings and institutions of a community – manor-house, church, school, farm, mill, and so forth; and they can be evoked with an affectionate as well as a professional particularity, so that the reader has a sense of knowing his way about them almost as intimately as the characters, and of sharing their feelings for the physical texture of their lives. What Arnold Bennett was to do for the industrial town and the working-class area of London, Hardy did for the market-town and the village. Buildings can even be credited with eccentric individuality in a manner reminiscent of Dickens:

> Farmer Shiner's was a queer lump of a house, standing at the corner of a lane that ran into the principal thoroughfare. The upper windows were much wider than they were high, and this feature, together with a broad bay-window where the door might have been expected, gave it by day the aspect of a human countenance turned askance, and wearing a sly and wicked leer.
>
> *Under the Greenwood Tree* (Chapter 5)

In the account of Elizabeth's first sight of High-Place Hall in *The Mayor of Casterbridge* (Chapter 21), animism serves a more important function:

> Looking round at the door which had given her egress, by the light of the solitary lamp fixed in the alley, she saw that it was arched and old – older even than the house itself. The door was studded, and the keystone of the arch was a mask. Originally the mask had exhibited a comic leer, as could still be discerned; but generations of Casterbridge boys had thrown stones at the mask, aiming at its open mouth; and the blows thereon had chipped off the lips and jaws as if they had been eaten away by disease. The appearance was so ghastly by the weakly lamp-glimmer that she could not bear to look at it – the first unpleasant feature of her visit.

The over-explicitness of the final phrase of this paragraph is as characteristic of Hardy's narrative art as the exactness of the physical description.

If the settled inhabitants of these localities are ignorant of the world at large, it is the touching ignorance of innocence (witness Mrs Dollery's complacency about Abbot's Cernel as a centre of activity); and by way of compensation they stand to gain an enriching security and stability from their association with their environment – an association often extending beyond the individual life and over generations. Hardy himself was born in the house built by his grandfather; and some of his most poignant scenes involve the uprooting from, or destruction of, a family home. In *The Woodlanders*, Giles's former dwelling is demolished: 'the walls were levelled, according to the landlords' principle at this date of getting rid of cottages whenever possible'. Giles does precisely what Hardy himself would have done in the circumstances, returning in the twilight and rambling over 'the patch of ground on which he had first seen the day'; and the sense of loss and waste is characteristically brought home by a detailed observation sensuously apprehended: 'Apples bobbed against his head, and in the grass beneath he crunched scores of them as he walked. There was nobody to gather them now.' The destruction of the ancient, harmonious way of life with its seasonal tasks and delights is brought home with the image of the fallen (not gathered) apples. And there is the memorable account in *Tess of the D'Urbervilles* of the former cottage which Mrs Stoke-d'Urberville has converted to a fowl-house:

> The lower rooms were entirely given over to the birds, who walked about them with a proprietary air, as though the place had been built by themselves, and not by certain dusty copyholders who now lay east and west in the churchyard. . . . . The rooms wherein dozens of infants had wailed at their nursing now resounded with the tapping of nascent chicks.
>
> (Chapter 9)

In turn, churches and barns and houses derive most of their interest from the lives that have been associated with them. For a professional architect, Hardy had surprisingly little time for the formal beauty or intrinsic interest of buildings, preferring to regard them as documents relating the history of a family or community.

In the last two novels, however, there is a deliberate disruption of the pattern of connections between people and places: the uprooting of individuals and families, and the invasion of stable communities by alien elements, which plays a minor role in the earlier novels, comes in *Tess* and *Jude* to determine the shape of the action. The former traces the heroine's wanderings through a geographically restricted but very varied world – varied socially, economically and even climatically, as well as in landscape. From her home at the suggestively named Marlott she goes to the Stoke-d'Urberville home at Trantbridge, and thence to Talbothays, Wellbridge, 'near Port-Bredy', Flintcomb-Ash, Kingsbere, Sandbourne, Stonehenge, and finally to execution at Wintoncester. The scenes at Talbothays and Flintcomb-Ash in particular are rendered with greater visual and sensuous fullness than the others, and also contrast sharply and almost allegorically with each other. The *Saturday Review*, in judging this novel unfavourably, grudgingly conceded the effectiveness of 'the few hours spent with cows', and Henry James no less patronizingly noted that 'there are indeed some pretty smells and sights and sounds'; but some other readers of this novel have responded more enthusiastically and have regarded the chapters covering Tess's life at Talbothays dairy as among Hardy's highest achievements. Their power derives partly from the way in which the summer season, the fertile landscape and the ripe physical qualities of the heroine all unite to form part of a densely evoked atmosphere. Hardy's descriptions prevent even the town-dwelling reader from forgetting that the central activity in question, the regular milking of the cows, involves a close physical contact between human and non-human (compare the 'yellow sheepskin gloves with gauntlets' worn by the girls for 'swede-grubbing' at Flintcomb-Ash, and the steam-powered threshing-machine there which turns the traditional rural activity into a modern ordeal); and the powerful sense of physicality overflows into the development of Tess's relationship with Angel Clare. Some of Hardy's best prose – not only least marred by his habitual affectations and misjudgments, but positively admirable in the economical sureness with which a precisely observed object or phenomenon is conveyed – is to be found in this section of the novel. Take, for example, the magnificent passage in Chapter 20, too long to quote, describing Tess and Angel out of doors in the 'spectral, half-compounded, aqueous light' of a midsummer dawn, 'as if they were Adam and Eve' in a newly created world. The Talbothays section is dominated by the summer sun, a motif which takes its place in a wider pattern of allusions throughout the novel, from the early reference to 'old-time heliolatries' to the ray that wakes Tess at sunrise as she lies on the 'oblong slab' at Stonehenge. The motif of sun-worship ('One could feel that a saner religion had never prevailed under the sky': Chapter 14) is set in contrast with the role of organized religion – in, for example, the burial of Tess's baby in unconsecrated ground. Flintcomb-Ash, on the other hand, is associated with winter imagery: it is a fit setting for Tess's sufferings, and one to which its infertile soil and the uncharitableness of her employer also naturally belong. Where Talbothays had stood for a Keatsian sense of burgeoning life and full awareness of the body, Flintcomb-Ash (as its unyielding and funereal name sufficiently conveys) stands for the coldness of death: even the turnips are stored in 'a long mound or grave'. Revealingly, though, Hardy is not content to express his sense of these opposing forces only through poetic symbols, but proceeds to offer a sociological and historical explanation of the starve-acre nature of this community: the village belongs to an absentee landlord whose concern for the community is limited to its profitability. The penalty of Adam is given due weight (and Chapter 43 contains a fine description of severe winter conditions), but is compounded by the forces of man-made history.

In *Jude the Obscure*, disruption and dislocation come to dominate the structure of the novel, as its section-titles ('At Marygreen', 'At Christminster', etc.) indicate: the orphan Jude, and his fellow-orphan Sue, have never had and never succeed in finding a home in the fullest sense of the word. Tess lives to see her family home dismantled, and her last dwelling-places are the seaside boarding-house where she lives with, and kills, Alec, and the unoccupied house which she briefly occupies as a retreat from the world with Angel; but at least she has started from a parental home. Jude's first appearances are solitary and wistful, placed in a landscape to which he has no sense of belonging: 'The brown surface of the field went right up towards the sky all round, where it was lost by degrees in the mist that shut out the actual verge and accentuated the solitude . . . ."How ugly it is here!" he murmured' (Chapter 2). His wanderings take him to a series of mean furnished lodgings and temporary residences, but he never finds a home. It is no accident that the opening words of the novel record that 'The schoolmaster was leaving the village', and that the first picture offered in this strongly visual novel is the sad one of a cottage piano and a packing-case of books perched on a cart. (There had been earlier house-moving scenes in *Far from the Madding Crowd* and *Tess of the D'Urbervilles*, and a detailed description of the 'day of removal' in the essay 'The Dorsetshire Labourer': the image of familiar objects taken from their accustomed private places and nakedly exposed to the public gaze while in transit was evidently a potent one for Hardy.) As in *Tess*, landscapes and townscapes are used not merely as realistic backgrounds but as projections of the emotions of the characters. Christminster is a university city seen in authentic detail and with the professional precision of a trained architect: we can be sure that Hardy, like Jude, had actually touched the crumbling stonework of the colleges and assessed the need for 'restoration'. But Christminster also has a less literal role in its changing relationship to Jude's waning illusions: it is first a 'heavenly Jerusalem' seen mirage-like from a distance, then perceived close at hand, eventually understood for what it really is, but always loved and yearned after even as he lies dying. Sue's observation that it is the railway station and not the cathedral which should be reckoned the centre of the city in their generation is a good example of Hardy's use of physical locations as metaphors for the ideas and feelings underlying the story. Hardy took unusual pains over what might be called topographical 'research', revisiting (as his 1895 preface notes) the scenes in which it is set; and the action is presented as a series of episodes in carefully specified settings, from the early pictures of Jude looking down the village well or standing alone in Farmer Troutham's field, to his death in a lodging-house in the shadow of the Christminster colleges.

The self-imposed limitations evident in Hardy's choice of settings are also evident in his presentation of society: although the depicted segment of English society is not identical throughout his fiction, it is usually restricted – severely so, indeed, in comparison with some of his predecessors in the Victorian novel. Within the relatively narrow range, however, sharp differentiations can be made. The interest of the closing portion of *Under the Greenwood Tree* turns on Fancy Day's social misgivings at the prospect of marriage to Dick Dewy, temptation taking the form of Parson Maybold. (Fancy, being, like two of Hardy's sisters, a schoolmistress, would have been especially sensitive to status and to the precariousness of her own social position.) Similar situations recur in *Far from the Madding Crowd*, and in *The Return of the Native*, where it is the glamour of Clym Yeobright's residence in Paris and his occupation as a jeweller, rather than his personal qualities, which attract Eustacia to him. With *The Mayor of Casterbridge* the fortunes and misfortunes of the protagonist are intimately related to the esteem in which he is held in the small provincial market-town; and the graph of his public career is traced by a series of scenes depicting Henchard in various social situations: presiding over the banquet at the King's Arms in his heyday, attempting to rival Farfrae in providing a holiday entertainment for the townsfolk, or disastrously and self-laceratingly pushing himself forward to offer a clumsy greeting to visiting royalty. Farfrae, as his name suggests, is the outsider, the new man, who represents the younger generation knocking at the door. (The parallel between Henchard and Ibsen's Solness is an interesting one; within a few years of writing this novel, Hardy was to take a keen interest in Ibsen's dramas, translated into English by his friend Edmund Gosse, and Ibsen's dramatic debates on the marriage question were to leave their mark on *Jude the Obscure*.) Specialized skills and unmistak-able talent compensate for Farfrae's classlessness; while as a Scot – Hardy took pains to make his speech as authentic as possible – he can bypass the problem of accent as a badge of class-membership. Hardy, who took a scholarly and personal interest in the question of 'standard' speech versus dialect, and was to return to it in *Tess*, must have had his own reactions to this aspect of social behaviour sensitized by his friendship with Horace Moule and by his years in London, if not earlier. One of Henchard's most savage outbursts is sparked off by Elizabeth's use of dialect words, 'those terrible marks of the beast to the truly genteel', as the narrator drily comments: to her innocent phrase 'bide where you be', he retorts: ' "Bide where you be, . . . Good God, are you only fit to carry wash to a pig-trough, that ye use such words as those?" ' The irony of his own slipping from the standard 'you' to the dialectal 'ye' passes without comment, but can hardly be unintended.

With *The Woodlanders* the interloper or detached stranger takes a different form in the person of Edred Fitzpiers, the physician-playboy or research-scientist-cum-dilettante who destroys the simple contentment of Little Hintock. But the sources of the trouble begin much earlier than Fitzpiers's arrival, with Melbury's decision to educate his daughter and to send her into the fashionable world. For all his passion for knowledge and his laborious self-education, Hardy holds no brief for education at *any* price. When Grace returns from boarding-school there is a very characteristic passage behind which it is hard not to sense the pressure of the autobiographical impulse: when she returns to her old home,

> The chambers seemed lower than they had appeared on any previous occasion of her return, the surfaces of both walls and ceilings standing in such near relations to the eye that it could not avoid taking microscopic note of their irregularities and old fashion. Her own bedroom wore at once a look more familiar than when she had left it, and yet a face estranged. The world of little things therein gazed at her in helpless stationariness, as though they had tried and been unable to make any progress without her presence. Over the place where her candle had been accustomed to stand, when she had used to read in bed till the midnight hour, there was still the brown spot of smoke.
>
> (Chapter 6)

As so often in Hardy, the visible scene is here used metonymically to express Grace's experience: the 'irregularities' of the plasterwork are both physical flaws in the fabric of the old house and ingredients in Grace's disappointment with her home and her family; and the 'brown spot of smoke' (carefully preserved, we learn, by her father) speaks as eloquently as any verbal statement of the contented girlhood she has left behind her. The sense of communion with 'the world of little things', objects forming an intimate part of the individual life and yet seeming to possess their own independent being and separate existence (the room is capable of looking 'estranged'), can be found in many passages of Hardy's prose and verse. Grace's conflict, which leads her to vacillate in her actions and relationships, is between the world of Little Hintock and that wider world of her recent experience, of which Fitzpiers and Mrs Charmond have brought disconcerting reminders into the rural community. The world of Little Hintock has not only tradition, loyalty and decency on its side, but also morality, even judged in the most conventional terms. Hardy loads the scales against the intruders by making them not merely un-productive and indifferent to the life and welfare of the community, but loose-living.

By a touch of architectural irony, Mrs Charmond lives in an Elizabethan manor-house, but has no real *human* connection with the neighbourhood or the local people: one of the earlier references to her is Mr Melbury's comment, ' "I wish she took more interest in the place" '; and later Grammer Oliver opines more uncompromisingly that ' "she's the wrong sort of woman for Hintock – hardly knowing a beech from a woak." ' She is a rootless and restless woman, capable of quitting the village at short notice for 'foreign lands'; she has been a 'play-actress', an occupation significant, perhaps, for its nomadic as well as its morally dubious associations, and is the widow of a 'rich man engaged in the iron trade in the north' who has retired with his fortune to Wessex. The social phenomenon in question is the now familiar one of the invasion of rural society by wealthy migrants from alien regions who bring nothing in the way of attachment or commit-ment to the neighbourhood in which they choose, for no doubt superficial reasons, to settle.

A parallel situation obtains in *Tess*, where the genuine but decayed Durbeyfields are set in contrast with the bogus claimants to the ancient name. Again, Hardy uses architectural styles (as, throughout this novel, he uses landscapes) as metaphors: the affluent Stoke-d'Urbervilles occupy a modern red-brick mansion with 'acres of glass-houses': 'everything looked like money'. At Alec's first encounter with Tess (Chapter 5) he forces a hothouse strawberry between her lips: not only is the sexual symbolism potent, and the fruit an element in an extensive pattern of references to the colour red associated with Tess (and admirably analysed in an essay by Tony Tanner), but there is a disquieting sense of disturbance of the natural and fitting order of things in Alec's casual production of the fruit out of season. The natural rhythm of the year helps to determine the structure of the novel: when Tess revisits Talbothays, for instance, she sees a scene that has changed as dramatically as her own life: 'The gold of the summer picture was now gray, the colours mean, the rich soil mud, and the river cold.' But the upstart d'Urbervilles, though living in the country, dwell outside the seasonal processes and pursuits which control the lives of the countryfolk. Tess's reaction to the offer of the fruit underlines the simplicity which is already prompting Alec to mark her out as a victim: 'he asked her if she liked strawberries. "Yes," said Tess, "when they come".' This tiny incident is echoed in two later passages: in Chapter 8, when Alec 'nipped his cigar with the tips of his large white centre-teeth', his aggressive masculinity directed towards a manufactured object contrasts with Tess's gentle acceptance of the soft ripe fruit; and in Chapter 30, when Angel Clare picks blackberries for Tess, rather than forcing them upon her in the manner of Alec, he simply offers them to her.

Like the Charmonds, the so-called d'Urbervilles come from the north of England, and from the tradesman or merchant class. For Hardy the invasion of Wessex by such as these constitutes a threat to its social stability and to the harmonious relationship between the natural setting and its human inhabitants. In both novels the action is set against a background of rural activities: the invaders are conspicuous by their lack of connection with these activities, and by the separation of their lives from the natural rhythms of the countryfolk. The light shining through the rural darkness which indicates Fitzpiers's nocturnal studies in Chapter 6 of *The Woodlanders* has something dramatically unnatural about it:

> Almost every diurnal and nocturnal effect in that woodland
> place had hitherto been the direct result of the regular
> terrestrial roll which produced the season's changes; but here
> was something dissociated from these normal sequences, and
> foreign to local knowledge.

'The season's changes' provide the natural rhythm against which the syncopation of these alien lives appears so disturbing and disruptive. No English novelist is more fascinated than Hardy by the work men do with their hands in a rural community, and some of his most sharply observed descriptions are of manual processes. His account of Giles Winterbourne during the cider-making season, for instance, lends fresh force to traditional claims for the dignity of labour.

> He looked and smelt like Autumn's very brother, his face being sunburnt to wheat-colour, his eyes blue as corn-flowers, his sleeves and leggings dyed with fruit-stains, his hands clammy with the sweet juice of apples, his hat sprinkled with pips, and everywhere about him that atmosphere of cider which at its first return each season has such an indescribable fascination for those who have been born and bred among the orchards. Her heart rose from its late sadness like a released bough; her senses revelled in the sudden lapse back to Nature unadorned. The consciousness of having to be genteel because of her husband's profession, the veneer of artificiality which she had acquired at the fashionable schools, were thrown off, and she became the crude country girl of her latent early instincts.

The overflowing ripeness of the description recalls Keats's 'To Autumn'; but Hardy is concerned not only to give us a personification of the earth's bounty but to show, dramatically, the effect of this vision upon Grace: the image of the 'released bough', and the heady sensuous pleasure which accompanies the reappearance of Giles, reinforces Hardy's insistence throughout this novel upon the superiority of 'Nature unadorned' to 'the veneer of artificiality'; of instinct, and even crudity, to self-conscious gentility. Beside Giles's vigour and skill, exercised upon the fruits of the earth, Fitzpiers seems merely effete and his scientific 'work' trivial: one might even accuse Hardy of anti-intellectualism were it not that Fitzpiers's scientific investigations hardly merit being taken very seriously. There is, one might add, a curious paradox in that, while Giles indubitably stands for manliness, it is of a chaste and almost sexless kind; as for Fitzpiers, although in character and spirit he is a nullity, he leaves us in no doubt about his sexual potency. If Hardy shows his sympathetically presented characters as close to the sources of life, he also endows them with a childlike or prelapsarian innocence.

Education, especially in Hardy's last two novels, is presented as an instrument of social change; yet it is worth noting his far from complacent attitude towards its effects upon the individual. His own life offers an exemplary instance of the material benefits of education, and especially of intellectual self-help: his own progress from country builder's son to professional author, and from the Bockhampton cottage to the imposing gentleman's residence at Max Gate with its indoor and outdoor servants, is a notable Victorian success-story. Of its immaterial benefits he may have felt less sure: in one of his poems, recalling his childhood church-going, he writes:

> So mindless were those outpourings! –
> Though I am not aware
> That I have gained by subtle thought on things
> Since we stood psalming there.
>
> ('Afternoon Service at Mellstock (About 1850)')

and in the novels, most notably in *Tess* and *Jude*, education is usually shown as generating unhappiness, or at least serving to unsettle the placid acceptance of one's worldly lot, and to intrude disturbing ambiguities concerning the roles one is to play. Tess has 'passed the Sixth Standard in the National School under a London-trained mistress', an experience which has brought the questionable advantage of enabling her to speak two languages, 'the dialect at home, more or less, ordinary English abroad and to persons of quality'. As with Richardson's Pamela, her superiority in education to the average girl of her class renders her especially vulnerable to a gentleman-seducer. Her education has also erected a barrier between herself and the mother whose guidance she so badly needs:

> Between the mother, with her fast-perishing lumber of
> superstitions, folk-lore dialect, and orally transmitted ballads,
> and the daughter, with her trained National teachings and Standard
> knowledge under an infinitely Revised Code, there was a
> gap of two hundred years as ordinarily understood.
>
> (Chapter 3)

Tess herself has been made aware of a world of promise – though also of peril – beyond her Marlott home: after her first glimpse of Angel Clare, the young men of the village suffer by comparison with his gentility ('but, ah! they did not speak so nicely as the strange young man had done').

In *Jude* education becomes a major theme – indeed, initially, it is *the* theme of the novel, though soon ousted by the sexual topics to which Hardy evidently responded with greater intensity. Although the hero's self-education follows a course unlike Hardy's in some respects – Hardy, for instance, had not had to struggle single-handed with the mysteries of Latin grammar – there are clearly, in spite of his disavowals, strong autobiographical elements; and one tiny detail is suggestive of his readiness to turn to his own experience:

as W. R. Rutland has pointed out, Jude's catalogue of favourite passages in Homer exactly corresponds to a list in Hardy's own copy of Clark's Homer. If Jude has the makings of a fine scholar, motivated by a disinterested intellectual passion, he is also an at least averagely sensual man; and his frustrations stem partly from the lack of provision for working-class boys to enter the universities, but also from the very different kinds of problem represented by Arabella and Sue – different from each other, as well as different from his intellectual disappointments. The result of the directions taken by the novel is to obscure the original pattern of Jude's attempts to storm the walls of Christminster with no other weapon than merit; and the novel as we have it merges two very different orders of predicament. If some philanthropist had handed Jude, say, £1,000, his educational problems might have been over; but under no circumstances, we feel – not even a wholesale reform of the marriage laws – could his relationships with Arabella and Sue have been anything but deeply unsatisfying. Hardy's diagnosis of the injustices of the social order runs the risk of being overwhelmed by his handling – in some respects timid, but also strikingly original for its date – of the theme of sexual incompatibility; what begins as a novel of social protest becomes, almost in spite of itself, a powerful analysis of the workings of the sexual impulse.

As well as being set in the contexts of an intimately known region and a particular social order, Hardy's novels are all, to a greater or lesser degree, localized in time; they present a society structured on fairly well-defined lines and standing at a particular point in its history. But time, one of the normal preoccupations of the novelist, takes on unusual dimensions of significance in Hardy's work. For the history of individual lives, the history of a given society, and human history itself, are habitually placed in the Victorian perspective of a newly acquired sense of geological time, conveyed by Hardy most famously in one of the minor novels, *A Pair of Blue Eyes*. The individual life, so important at short range and depicted with such meticulous circumstantiality by the fiction-writer's art, is also seen as occupying an infinitesimal portion of the life of the universe, and judged at least partly in these terms. In another minor novel, *Two on a Tower*, Hardy expresses his sense of the physical minuteness of our world of people and objects in relation to the immensity of space unrolling before the astronomer (cf. also the early sonnet 'At a Lunar Eclipse'); but it is man's relation to time rather than to space which seizes his imagination more persistently. Human history is shown as stretching back into the prehistoric mists, with a consequent dwarfing of the particular epoch or life. The historian – and that term can include the narrator of Hardy's fictions – is continually made conscious of lives in the present being in close (if usually unconscious) association with innumerable anonymous and unrecorded lives in the past; the fact that the locale of the novels is an area which has been continuously occupied since prehistoric times intensifies this sense of the dead pressing upon the living. And even if characters in the novels are usually unaware of the place of their own all-absorbing joys and sorrows in the pattern of indefinitely repeated experiences, the narrator is ever ready to point it out to the reader.

When Jude, for instance, stands alone in Farmer Troutham's field, he is struck by its ugliness, and the narrator's initial comment on the newly harrowed land, with its uniform brown surface, is that it seems deprived 'of all history beyond that of the few recent months', and possesses a 'meanly utilitarian air'. But the corrective comment quickly follows that

> to every clod and stone there really attached associations enough and to spare – echoes of songs from ancient harvest-days, of spoken words, and of sturdy deeds. Every inch of ground had been the site, first or last, of energy, gaiety, horse-play, bickering, weariness. Groups of gleaners had squatted in the sun on every square yard. Love-matches that had populated the adjoining hamlet had been made up there between reaping and carrying. Under the hedge which divided the field from a distant plantation girls had given themselves to lovers who would not turn their heads to look at them by the next harvest; and in that ancient cornfield many a man had made promises to a woman at whose voice he had trembled by the next seed-time after fulfilling them in the church adjoining. But this neither Jude nor the rooks around him considered.

> (Chapter 2)

Hardy's repopulating imagination crowds the empty landscape with the ghosts of the past: nothing moved him so effectively to recreate the lives of the dead as a silent and desolate scene such as a churchyard or an archaeological site. And, in this instance, what may seem like a digression, a brief excursion on a familiar Hardyan hobby-horse, is in fact one of a series of episodes in which Jude is shown as seeing without understanding, or as misinterpreting, the scene before him. Moreover, the love-matches which have so quickly turned sour are to provide the unconscious model for Jude's own experience.

As the individual destiny takes its place in the pattern of lives formed by uncounted generations, and its convictions of the uniqueness of personal experience are exposed as unfounded, its illusions of freedom drop away; but its insignificance can also be endowed with dignity and solemnity (as in Gray's 'Elegy') by its identification with the common lot. Mrs Henchard, so ineffectual in her lifetime, is laid in 'the still-used burial-ground of the old Roman-British city', and her dust mingles there 'with the dust of women who lay ornamented with glass hair-pins and amber necklaces, and men who held in their mouths coins of Hadrian, Posthumus, and the Constantines' (*The Mayor of Casterbridge*, Chapter 20). (Roman graves had been uncovered during the digging of the foundations for Max Gate, not long before Hardy wrote this account of Mrs Henchard's burial.) This double perspective on the individual event – Mrs Henchard dead in her insignificance at a certain point in time, Mrs Henchard solemnly taking her place with the dead of the ages – lends an ambiguous resonance to the human act: dying, like loving, links men in a universal timeless association with each other, but also reduces individual experience to a unit in an endlessly repeated process.

But if the living in Hardy's novels are surrounded by the dead, and find themselves re-enacting scenes and reliving emotions that have been indefinitely repeated, this does not mean that they are not also, in the nineteenth century, confronted by problems different from those of their ancestors, and even their immediate forebears. Hardy writes, in the opening chapter of *The Return of the Native*, of 'the mind adrift on change, and harassed by the irrepressible New'; and the phrase might serve as the epigraph for much of his work, and certainly for all the major novels. Victorian science had given not only an awareness of the extent of geological time ('the very finger-touches of the last geological change' can be detected on Egdon Heath), but, during Hardy's youth, an understanding of Darwinian concepts of evolution, adaptation and extinction. The extension of these concepts from organisms to human society is not difficult; so that Hardy can write, of the 'reddleman' Diggory Venn, that 'he was one of a class rapidly becoming extinct in Wessex, filling at present in the rural world the place which, during the last century, the dodo occupied in the world of animals. He is a curious, interesting, and nearly perished link between obsolete forms of life and those which generally prevail.' To describe the dodo in action before it is too late is, in a sense, a large part of Hardy's purpose: not simply for the historical or senti-mental value of the record (though it is as such that Hardy's novels have often been widely read and admired), but because human problems are expressed with a peculiar intensity and poignancy in situations wherein the sense of impermanence or approaching and irreversible change is strong. Christopher Ricks has noted that Tennyson, in, for instance, *The Idylls of the King*, repeatedly resorts to 'the art of the penultimate', invoking a plangent and permeating notion of the end being close at hand; and Hardy's fiction conveys a similar Victorian feeling that an epoch is in the process of passing away, and that change, whatever it may bring, is not likely to be for the better. In the later novels the rate of change seems to accelerate: between Tess and her mother, Hardy tells us, is a gap of centuries rather than a single generation ('When they were together the Jacobean and the Victorian ages were juxtaposed'); and Jude, like Arnold's scholar-gipsy, finds his yearnings at odds with an alien world. Even in the earlier novels, although the old world can still claim a stability and solidarity that have gone for ever from the world of *Tess* and *Jude*, there are discords beneath the ancient harmonies. The musical metaphor is especially appropriate for *Under the Greenwood Tree*, where the church-band, of the kind of which Hardy's father had been a lifelong member, is in process of being rendered redundant and thus driven into extinction by the new organ. The darker implications of such a change are not explored in this novel, which ends with a time-defying reassertion of traditional folk-life, with 'music, dancing, and the singing of songs' as part of the wedding celebrations under the 'ancient tree'. Even here, though, the note of change is not altogether silenced; for the age-old customs are touched by Victorian self-consciousness:

> The propriety of every one was intense, by reason of the
> influence of Fancy, who, as an additional precaution in this
> direction, had strictly charged her father and the tranter to
> carefully avoid saying 'thee' and 'thou' in their conversation,
> on the plea that those ancient words sounded so very humiliating
> to persons of newer taste; also that they were never to be seen
> drawing the back of the hand across the mouth after drinking –
> a local English custom of extraordinary antiquity, but stated
> by Fancy to be decidedly dying out among the better classes of
> society.

The tone seems to rule out any intensity of concern, and both the 'local English custom of extraordinary antiquity' and the invading 'newer taste' are seen with a measure of ironic detachment. Henchard's views on local speech, already quoted, are to be infused with much more bitterness. Nevertheless, in the face of such passages, it will hardly do to characterize *Under the Greenwood Tree* as a simple tale of bygone rural felicity: paradise has not yet been lost, but the warning signs are beginning to appear, and can be read in retrospect.

Some of the later novels move the time of their action closer to the time of composition, and express more insistently what Hardy called 'the ache of modernism'. By the time we reach *Tess*, the village customs have not altogether disappeared, but they have suffered a radical change; and if the form has survived, the spirit has gone. The 'club-walking' in the second chapter of the novel is a debased relic of the ancient May-day dance; 'the banded ones were all dressed in white gowns – a gay survival from Old Style days, when cheerfulness and May-time were synonyms – days before the habit of taking long views had reduced emotions to a monotonous average'. Even as late as *The Mayor of Casterbridge*, Hardy had been intent upon recreating the world of his father's youth, just (though only just) in the pre-railway age: 'the railway had stretched out an arm towards Caster-bridge at this time, but had not reached it by several miles as yet' (Chapter 37). But Tess's story takes place in the 1880s: Hardy is no longer looking backward, lovingly and (a potent source of his popularity) nostalgically recalling the past, but forces himself and his heroine to confront the new order. At one point Tess and the railway are brought together: 'no object could have looked more foreign to the gleaming cranks and wheels than this unsophisticated girl, with the round bare arms, the rainy face and hair, the suspended attitude of a friendly leopard at pause, the print gown of no date or fashion, and the cotton bonnet drooping on her brow' (Chapter 30). Tess's comment to Angel about the 'cans of new milk' they have brought from the dairy is tinged with regret as well as wonder:

> 'Londoners will drink it at their breakfast tomorrow, won't
> they?' she asked. 'Strange people that we have never seen.'
> 'Yes – I suppose they will. Though not as we send it. When its
> strength has been lowered, so that it may not get up into their
> heads.'
> 'Noble men and noble women, ambassadors and centurions,
> ladies and tradeswomen, and babies who have never seen a cow.'

Hardy perhaps intends us to see that Tess's world, though linked with the metropolis by train, is nevertheless as remote from it as another planet; and that the baby who has never seen a cow is no less alien a

phenomenon than a centurion. Yet Tess, through Alec and Angel, is
to be seduced by the manners, and judged by the morals, of the world
beyond her ken.

In other respects *Tess* is a novel of contemporary life. Its account of
rural depopulation is relevant to the Dorset of the 1880s, as may be
seen from a comparison between the description of the 'mutations so
increasingly discernible in village life' in Chapter 51, and Hardy's
non-fictional account of the 'increasingly nomadic habit of the labourer'
in his essay 'The Dorsetshire Labourer' a few years earlier. Another
episode, Angel Clare's brief emigration to Brazil, shows him dealing
more cavalierly with contemporary fact when it involves scenes and
events remote from Wessex. Angel's Brazilian adventures are not a
transcription of recent historical events, but appear to be largely based
on the experiences of a group of English emigrants who left Liverpool
for Rio in 1872 – a date, that is, well in advance of the supposed
period of the action. Unlike Dickens, whose transcription of the
emigrants' experiences in *David Copperfield* is close to contemporary
fact, Hardy has little interest in rendering events in the larger world:
Angel's departure is frankly a plot-device intended to remove him
temporarily but effectively from the scene of action.

As for Jude Fawley (and his earlier surname, 'England', in Hardy's
manuscript, perhaps suggests that he was intended to be to some
degree representative), he is more severely 'harassed by the irrepressible
New' than any other protagonist. It is ironic that his early efforts are
concentrated on the ancient classics and on traditional theological
studies, and that he should select the venerable institutions of Christminster as his heart's desire; for he is brought to feel, with bitterness,
the irrelevance and inefficacy of all these in the modern world (as
when, self-laceratingly, he recites the Latin creed in a Christminster
public house). Robert Gittings has argued persuasively that Sue
Bridehead, with her enthusiasm for John Stuart Mill, is essentially a
girl of the 1860s – of Hardy's own youth, that is – rather than of the
1890s; but the novel as a whole has the feel of a contemporary document. Questions of marriage and divorce had, by the time this novel
was written, not only acquired a deep personal interest for Hardy but
were more widely topical. A possible source for the novel which seems
not to have been previously noted is a work of popular anthropology
and sociology, E. Westermarck's *History of Human Marriage*, published
in 1891, just at the time Hardy had begun to think about his new novel:
it was widely read, ran through several editions, and has a comment
on marriages between first cousins that is highly pertinent to the

situation of Jude and Sue ('Several writers . . . believe that there are no injurious results at all from those marriages, unless the parents are afflicted with the same hereditary morbid tendencies . . . '). Hardy's cousin, Tryphena Sparks, who appears to be referred to in the first preface to *Jude*, had died in 1890; and although there have been some unwarrantably wild surmises about the significance of Tryphena in Hardy's life, it looks as if this novel may well have originated in a fusion of Hardy's memories of the distant past, his private griefs of the moment, and questions which were being agitated in the public domain, in the theatre (Hardy saw *Hedda Gabler* in 1893) as well as in the newspapers and journals.

A further irony which Hardy may not have foreseen is that, though Jude's time is out of joint, it was only by the narrowest margin that things missed being very different. Only a few years after the novel was first published, Ruskin College, Oxford, was established (in 1899) with the intention of providing higher education for working-class men at a reasonable cost. As the subsequent report *Oxford and Working-Class Education* (1909) shows, this was a natural development of the Adult School movement which had begun at the end of the eighteenth century and the Mechanics' Institutes and Working Men's Colleges of the nineteenth century. Jude's problem was not a new one; and if he had been a little younger, he might have been one of Ruskin College's first students.

If, as seems reasonably clear, Hardy's last two major novels are stories of contemporary life, there is a certain inevitability about his career as a writer of fiction terminating at this point. Without apparently planning his novels according to any premeditated scheme of chronological coverage, he had in fact by 1895 given an account of Wessex life, its past and its present, and how its changes came about, throughout almost the whole of the nineteenth century.

Most discussions of Hardy's novels, including my own up to this point, have centred on his themes, characters and settings, and the degree of effectiveness with which they are communicated, rather than on the quality of the novels as individual solutions to the problems of narrative art. It has to be conceded that Hardy offers much less grist to the mill of the student of fictional technique than most other major novelists. Though he read novels in his earlier years, he was not a critical student of the art of fiction; and there is nothing in his prefaces, notebooks or diaries to suggest that he gave much thought to its peculiar problems and possibilities. Comparison with his contemporary Henry James shows at once that his conception of the novel was traditional rather than innovative; the suggestion that he abandoned fiction because developments in the criticism and practice of the novel in the nineties had left him behind may be well-founded. Technique and experiment, he would probably have maintained, were matters for the poet; and his verse shows an extraordinary preoccupation, well beyond the call of duty, with self-imposed difficulties of metre and rhyme. But a novel, he might equally have insisted, is a straightforward matter of construction, like building a dwelling-house or a barn: that his fellow-novelists should have concerned themselves with the subtle potentialities of point of view or time-shift would, one suspects, have struck him as puzzling and disproportionate. Style he recognized as a problem in both prose and verse; but structure and technique, except in their broadest practical applications, were hardly taken into account. If Hardy ever made detailed plans or time-schemes for his novels, they have not survived; and there is little internal evidence of forethought – indeed, there are sometimes unmistakable signs of radical changes of direction during the course of composition. The preface to *Jude the Obscure*, which seems to have occupied him for longer than any other novel, speaks of the 'scheme' being 'jotted down' a couple of years before composition began; since, however, the story certainly underwent drastic modification and expansion as writing proceeded, that 'scheme' can have been only the barest outline or germ. All the novels employ a third-person narrator and pursue a straightforward chronological narrative, with occasional awkward jumps in time ('a long procession of years', for instance, passes between the second and third chapters of *The Mayor of Casterbridge*).

In only one respect, I believe, does Hardy's narrative technique display a marked originality and individuality; but that is so prominent throughout his work, and especially in the major novels, that it calls for detailed analysis. I refer to what may be loosely termed his pictorialism – the use of sharply visualized situations verbally rendered, not merely as a means of evoking character or scene, but as a method of telling a story. I would not suggest that this technique was always consciously used by Hardy; I believe that it proceeded from his habitual and idiosyncratic mode of vision, evidence for which can be found not only in his fiction and poetry but in his autobiography and diaries. It seems undeniable that Hardy's visual sense was exceptionally acute, and his visual memory remarkably tenacious. The autobiography, in many parts so primly and conventionally trivial, now and then recreates, in prose that suddenly quickens into life, an instant of brief but intense visual experience from the distant past. For example: one summer morning of his youth, as he is about to sit down to breakfast, Hardy remembers that a man is due to be hanged outside Dorchester gaol, some three miles away: he hurries to a spot of rising ground, and puts to his eye the 'big brass telescope' which is a family heirloom. At the precise moment that he focuses the image of the malefactor on the gallows, the figure drops down and the town clock faintly strikes the hour. The whole episode is narrated in a dozen lines, but it has the ingredients of many an incident in the fiction: the stark contrast of the figures – the murderer in white fustian, the officials in dark suits – like a sketch by Goya or Daumier, the sun reflected on 'the white stone façade of the gaol', the sudden, piercing glimpse by a solitary observer, distant and unseen, of a moment of decisive action or revelation. And the effect on the young Hardy lends to this brief and freakish experience the kind of weight we associate with certain passages in Wordsworth's *Prelude*: 'He seemed alone on the heath with the hanged man [he recalls], and crept homeward wishing he had not been so curious.' Again, thirty years later, Hardy visits Paris with his brother, and these two respectable middle-aged provincials take in the Moulin Rouge, where Hardy happens to stand among the audience at the precise point at which he sees the cancan dancers whirling and grinning against a macabre back cloth – the view through the windows behind the stage of the tombs and monuments of the adjoining Montmartre cemetery. Hardy's daily vision has a knack of superimposing images in this way, and of observing scenes in close-up or from an unfamiliar angle: he listens to John Stuart Mill addressing an open-air meeting, and notes the 'vast pale brow, so thin-skinned as to show the blue veins'; he is fascinated by the microscopic life of insects as well as by the immensity of the universe revealed by the telescope; and he records in his diary, after visiting an art exhibition, 'If I were a painter, I would paint a picture of a room as viewed by a mouse from a chink under the skirting.'

An anecdote very early in the *Life* suggests both that he was very sensitive to visual impressions and that he instinctively sought an outlet through verbal expression for the emotion produced in him by the visible world: the staircase in the Hardy cottage, he relates,

> had its walls coloured Venetian red by his father, and was so situated that the evening sun shone into it, adding to its colour

a great intensity for a quarter of an hour or more. Tommy used to wait for this chromatic effect, and sitting alone there, would recite to himself 'And now another day is gone' from Dr. Watts's Hymns, with great fervency, though perhaps not for any religious reason, but from a sense that the scene suited the lines.

The emotional power of the visual experience, the sense of its impermanence, the solitary, self-contained world of the observer – we have in such a moment the prototype of many a lyric, and many a passage in the Wessex novels.

If Dickens's greatest natural gift was his ear, as Angus Wilson has said, Hardy's was surely his eye; and his keen response to the visible world was of course sharpened and disciplined by his training and practice as an architect, which left its mark on his writings – directly, in the many precise descriptions of buildings, and in his architect- and artist-heroes; indirectly, perhaps, in the symmetry of his plots and (as W. H. Auden once suggested) in his preoccupation as a poet with metrical design and experiment. His language is seasoned by what must be a stronger flavouring of architectural terms than that of any other major novelist: who but Hardy would have described a woman's seductive posture on a couch as a 'cyma-recta curve'? He was a meticulous draughtsman, illustrated his first volume of verse, Wessex Poems, in a fastidious and highly idiosyncratic style, and carefully preserved the notebook in which he had made architectural sketches as a young man, adding to it as late as 1920.

His youthful frequenting of the National Gallery, already recounted, gave him (in C. J. Weber's words) an 'expert and detailed knowledge' of European art of many periods. It also set a pattern for his later life, for he continued to visit galleries and collections in England and on the Continent for the next half-century; in 1895, for instance, we find him saying in a letter to a friend, 'I feel I want to look at some pictures'. His taste and his expertise are manifested on several levels in the fiction. At the lowest level, there are frequent allusions to painters and paintings which seem to do little more than testify to the author's standing as a man of culture – except in so far as they also produce in the reader a sense of cultural inferiority. Sometimes the reference represents only a vague gesture: as Eustacia gazes at Clym Yeobright's face, for example, it is described as being 'in Rembrandt's intensest manner' – and all well and good, for the imprecise allusion causes no embarrassment. Many of these allusions spring from the attempt to compensate for the inadequacy of our language to describe colour, and Hardy regularly resorts to such indications as 'the greenish shades of Correggio's nudes', 'the angry crimson of a Danby sunset', eyebrows in 'Vandyke brown', and so forth. But what are we to make of the description of an old woman in *Jude the Obscure*, who has 'a countenance like of Sebastiano's Lazarus'? Hardy had seen Sebastiano del Piombo's *Raising of Lazarus* in the National Gallery, and it seems to have been one of his favourite pictures, for he refers to it at least twice elsewhere. But in the highly probable event that the reader is less familiar with the painting than Hardy, the reference seems frustrating and pointless. And unless we believe that novelists exist in order to provide employment for the writers of footnotes, it is hard to see what force such a passage can be intended to have. (In fairness to Hardy, it must be said that he is not the only Victorian novelist to tease and baffle the reader in this way: a very curious passage in *Daniel Deronda* hints at Titian's *Tribute-Money*, which George Eliot had seen in Dresden and greatly admired: it is, as it later turns out, a reference of some importance in the novel, but hardly explicit as it stands.)

At a more important level, Hardy's study of the painter's art is manifested in his fondness for grouping figures and for creating special effects of lighting and shadows, scale and perspective. More than any other English novelist, I think, he is addicted to placing his characters in doorways or windows, reflecting them in mirrors and pools, making them peer down wells or into barrels or through telescopes – in other words, 'framing' them: cutting off a portion of his fictional world for special scrutiny like the view-finder of a camera. This was, in various forms, a cliché of the nineteenth-century painter's art: Whistler's 'white girl', for instance, stands before a mirror, and there are dozens of pictures in which an interior scene is given an extra dimension by the provision of a contrasting or reinforcing glimpse of the outside world – as in *The Young Photographers* by Hardy's namesake, Frederick Daniel Hardy. One of Thomas Hardy's trademarks, too, is to let a scene be viewed through an open door or a chink in the wall (a visual analogue of the overheard conversations with which his novels also abound); another is to reduce the physical mass and solidity of human existence to a silhouette or a tiny speck seen from afar – one recalls the Mellstock villagers at the beginning of *Under the Greenwood Tree* outlined against the sky like figures on 'Greek or Etruscan pottery', and Tess moving across the distant landscape like a fly.

Discussions of Hardy's affinities with graphic art have tended to concentrate on his relationship to the old masters, and it is true that most of his explicit *references* to painters and paintings are to major and minor artists from the early Italians to Reynolds and Turner. I want first to consider a single important example of this relationship; and then to suggest that this is not the whole truth about Hardy's debt to painting, and that his response to the art of his own time ought not to be overlooked.

Without Hardy's familiarity with the Dutch and Flemish schools of realistic genre painters, his early novels would not have been what they are, though it may be that the influence was mediated through an important nineteenth-century literary tradition as well as being derived directly from his frequenting of the galleries. There is, of course, a long novelistic and critical tradition which links the realistic novel with this kind of painting. One of the earliest examples is in Sir Walter Scott's famous review of Jane Austen's *Emma* in the *Quarterly*: it recalls, he says, 'the merits of the Flemish school of painting', and when later reviewers sought analogies for the novel of everyday settings and close observation, it was to the Dutch masters, and to such later exemplars of the same tradition as Chardin and Wilkie, that they habitually turned. The early Dickens, for instance, was called by one reviewer 'the literary Teniers of the metropolis', and that kind of parallel reappears unfailingly throughout the period. In mid-century it is given authoritative endorsement by the early novels of George Eliot: the well-known passage in *Adam Bede*, praising the 'rare, precious quality of truthfulness . . . in many Dutch paintings', is a kind of manifesto of domestic realism in fiction, and there is evidence that Hardy had pondered such passages carefully. The guesswork of the *Spectator* reviewer that the first instalment of the anonymously published serial *Far from the Madding Crowd* was by George Eliot was not entirely preposterous. The *Adam Bede* passage includes a reference to a 'village wedding . . . where an awkward bridegroom opens the dance . . . while elderly and middle-aged friends look on'; and it is with just such a scene that *Under the Greenwood Tree* concludes. It comes as no surprise that this novel should be subtitled 'A Rural Painting of the Dutch School'. If Hardy had a particular painting in mind, it may well have been not Dutch but English – Thomas Webster's *Village Choir*, which he must have seen in what is now the Victoria and Albert Museum. Most of the critics of this novel have taken their cue from its subtitle, rather than from the Shakespearean main title with its hints of pastoral and escapism; and it has been faulted for failing (notably in some of the dialogue) to live up to its realistic promises. But this may be to underestimate the flexibility of Hardy's art, to miss the range of his allusions to the visual arts, and to do less than justice to the novel's delicacy of tone. The pictorial mode of presentation is extensively used, but the parallel with realistic painting does not provide a completely adequate analogy to the kind of narrative and descriptive techniques that are in question.

It is perfectly true, of course, that there are many 'Dutch' pictures of minutely observed scenes and characters. In the gamekeeper's cottage is a 'large nail, used solely and constantly as a peg for Geoffrey's hat; the nail was arched by a rainbow-shaped stain, imprinted by the brim of the said hat when it was hung there dripping wet'. Such passages enact verbally the mental responses of one who examines a realistic painting, 'reading' the visual signs in such a way as to reconstruct imaginatively a way of life. A static *object*, that is (in this case the stain on the wall), suggests a *story*, or at least the notion of human action in a social environment; and, as we shall see, this became one of Hardy's descriptive mannerisms. But such gambits do not by any means exhaust his repertoire of modes of visual presentation in this novel. The description already cited which compares the Mellstock villagers to the figures on a painted vase is clearly allied to a different genre of representation; so are the other scenes of dramatic chiaroscuro effects – the novel opens in starlight and ends in moonlight, and the nocturnal lighting effects produce shadows and silhouettes and lend unexpected forms to familiar objects. Quite different again is the presentation of the heroine, Fancy Day: when she first appears to the choir members, who are standing in the outer darkness, she is framed by a lighted upper window; holding a candle in one hand, and extending the other 'to the side of the window', she is wrapped in a white robe; her 'bright eyes' look 'into the gray world outside with an uncertain expression', and she displays 'a twining confusion of marvellously rich hair'. The whole passage not only reads like a careful description of a painting, but strongly recalls the type of female beauty that Hardy must have encountered both on the canvases of the Pre-Raphaelite Brotherhood and in Dante Gabriel Rossetti's poem 'The Blessed Damozel', in the opening lines of which (as in Hardy's description) attention is successively focused on eyes, hair and robe. With Eustacia Vye in *The Return of the Native* Hardy develops the same type even further: Eustacia very closely resembles those tall, long-faced, heavy-lidded maidens to whom the P.R.B. were so addicted, and who are summed up in Henry James's description of Mrs William Morris as a 'grand synthesis of all the Pre-Raphaelite pictures ever made . . . a mass of crisp black hair heaped into great wavy projections on either side of her temples, a thin pale face, a pair of strange sad, deep dark Swinburnian eyes . . . '. Eustacia is 'tall', 'full-limbed', with dark hair 'clos[ing] over her forehead', dark eyes with 'oppressive lids and lashes', and Italianate lips forming (once again) 'the curve so well known in the arts of design as the cima-recta, or ogee'; and her description might be applied with little change to many a Pre-Raphaelite canvas. Fifteen years later, Hardy returns again to the Pre-Raphaelite style of beauty in the heroine of his fantasy-novel *The Well-Beloved* – a tall maiden whose 'hair was massed low upon her brow, the colour of the thick tresses being . . . repeated in the irises of her large, deep eyes'. In his portrait of Eustacia, as so often, Hardy seems to be describing not a woman but a picture; and, correspondingly, to be inviting the reader to make a mental construction of a picture according to his specifications, and then to contemplate it with the kind of techniques of interpretation and association that he might bring to a painting in a gallery.

Nor were the Pre-Raphaelites the only artists of Hardy's own time to provide suggestive models for the rendering of character and incident in fiction. It is surely no coincidence that the two bourgeois arts of fiction and genre painting flourished in England during the same period; and the Victorian genre painters have many affinities with Hardy's art. Their canvases are sometimes referred to as 'narrative paintings', and the hybrid term neatly complements the kind of 'verbal picture-making' towards which Hardy so often aspires. In Trollope's *Last Chronicle of Barset* – published as Hardy was at work on his first novel – Mrs Dobbs Broughton tells the fashionable artist Conway Dalrymple: 'No painter living tells a story so well as you do' – the function evidently strikes her as entirely appropriate and desirable; and the nature of these mutually indebted arts is crystallized in Aubrey Beardsley's phrase, 'story painters and picture writers'.

This mutual interdependence of the genres involved a confusion of critical terms; and there was, and is, a well-established and fairly extensive terminology which refers to literary qualities by means of analogies with the visual arts. Nineteenth-century reviewers used these terms extensively: to take an instance at random, when one of Trollope's novels was discussed in the *Spectator* in 1872, it was described as 'full of good painting', there were references to one character as 'a striking picture' and to the 'coarse painting' of another, and several other allusions to pictures and portraiture – even though Trollope is not in fact a writer in whom the visual sense seems to be particularly

highly developed. And the nineteenth-century habit of speaking of a
writer presenting a 'picture' (or 'word-picture') or a 'portrait';
'painting' or 'etching' or 'engraving' a scene; executing a 'sketch' or
'caricature'; using 'light and shade' or 'colour' in his descriptions, and
so forth, is by no means extinct.

Hardy, however, goes well beyond most other novelists in presenting his scenes with minute attention to their visual qualities, and
in requiring of his readers that they engage with energy and precision
in the act of imaginative picture-making. If we compare Hardy with,
for example, Sir Walter Scott, one sees the difference immediately.
Most people, if not pressed too hard, might grant such epithets as
'colourful' and 'picturesque' to the Waverley Novels; but if we look
at what Scott actually does when he wants to give us a 'picture' of
(for instance) a pretty girl (Effie Deans in *The Heart of Midlothian*),
we find only the most approximate stereotype: she is a 'beautiful and
blooming girl' with 'ringlets of brown hair' and 'a laughing Hebe
countenance' – and that classical allusion surely betrays the portraitist
as working not from any real or precisely imagined model but from
a generalized and traditional notion of female pulchritude. Hardy,
on the other hand, is likely to place his subject with some precision
in relation to other persons and objects, to place the viewer with
equal precision, to indicate the source and strength of the light and
the nature of shadows, to evoke colour and texture as exactly as
language permits, and where necessary to eke out the imperfections
of language with comparisons to actual pictures or styles of painting.
Which is not to say that he always succeeds: only that 'pictorialism'
perhaps means more in relation to Hardy than to almost any other
English novelist.

But let me return to my earlier claim that, for relevant parallels to
Hardy's verbal picture-making, we must look not only at the old
masters, to whom he explicitly and somewhat self-consciously refers,
but also at contemporary artists, whose work he certainly knew but
who scarcely formed part of the traditionally venerated culture.
Hardy refers in his autobiography to 'the solidarity of all the arts';
and certainly, in mid-nineteenth-century England, the arts of prose
fiction and painting entered into a relationship of common purpose,
comparable techniques and mutual influence that was by no means
new in kind but which (I do not think it is extravagant to claim) has
no parallel in degree either before or since. Many of the most popular
works in both media sought to represent with scrupulous attention
to detail the surface of life, especially the life of the bourgeoisie.

The Royal Academy moved to Burlington House in 1869, just at the time Hardy began to write fiction; and the summer exhibitions were very popular from that year onward, with average attendances of some 300,000. We know from his autobiography that Hardy was there in May of the following year, when he no doubt saw Millais's popular *Boyhood of Raleigh*; and the *Life* contains a string of references to other Academy functions – exhibitions, dinners, private views, soirées – which Hardy attended conscientiously during the next half-century. His enthusiasm seems to have been genuine as well as durable, and in 1919, at the age of almost eighty, he was still turning up for the annual Academy dinner. There would seem to be at the very least a strong *prima facie* case for supposing that prolonged exposure to so many acres of canvas – a large proportion of which belonged to the category of genre painting – might have had its effect upon a novelist's visual perceptions; and I believe it can be claimed that, whereas nearly all the pictorial *allusions* in Hardy's novels are to the earlier, classic schools of painting, the unacknowledged influence of this distinctive and immensely popular variety of contemporary painting is at least equally pervasive.

What are the characteristics of these 'narrative paintings', which have been described as 'visual literature'? The *OED* records the appearance of the term 'genre painting' in 1873 – almost precisely, that is, when Hardy began to write fiction; but the commodity had been in vigorous circulation for at least a generation before this date. These paintings draw on a strong tradition of book-illustration, they are frequently literary in theme (with Shakespeare and the Romantic poets as favourite sources), and many of the Academy painters were also prominent as illustrators of fiction. They have, very prominently, their own verbal dimension: their titles tend to be full and informative, like those of nineteenth-century programme music, and sometimes incorporate a quotation or literary reference; and they were often supplemented by lengthy catalogue entries.

Within the frame of the typical narrative painting, figures and objects are used to convey information or suggestion in a manner which recalls the storyteller's use of material objects. Some of the most prominent types of 'message' transmitted through pictorial devices are: indications of time and place (through costumes, buildings, weather phenomena, etc.); social, occupational and other attributes of the figures represented (through dress, furnishings, tools, etc.); emotional states (through facial expression, gesture and posture, all frequently depicted in an exaggerated and stylized manner); actions performed, in progress or impending; and implicit moral, social or psychological comment. All these, of course, have their counterparts in the techniques of Victorian fiction in general and in Hardy's work in particular. One of his favourite devices is to 'show' the reader an object and to leave him to draw his own conclusions from it; and the ideal reader of a Hardy novel is expected to share this skill with some of his characters – the countryman's ability to observe the world around him and interpret visual evidence that might be overlooked by a less attentive viewer. Mr Melbury in *The Woodlanders*, for instance, is a man of limited education and imagination, but he is a veritable Sherlock Holmes in his powers of reconstructing an incident from a horse's hoof-marks or a splash of unfamiliar mud. And the narrator of the novels is often himself a close observer and interpreter of signs: he is apt to indicate a character's social or occupational status, for instance, not from the standpoint of omniscience but by noting details of his appearance or the way he walks, as with Michael Henchard, who has 'the walk of the skilled countryman as distinct from the desultory shamble of the general labourer'. I have cited already Hardy's use of such signs as the stain made by a hat which hangs habitually on the same nail, or the thumb-marks on an old pack of playing-cards – details which evoke a whole way of life, snapshots which convey a sense of long stretches of time; and Victorian genre painting is full of such visual signs.

In the Victorian period, then, not only did nearly every picture tell a story, but many stories carried on their business through a kind of picture-making; and Hardy's approach to the task of describing, for instance, the human face gives a new meaning to the cliché 'a speaking likeness'. Of Clym Yeobright, in *The Return of the Native*, he writes as follows:

> The observer's eye was arrested, not by his face as a picture, but by his face as a page; not by what it was, but by what it recorded. His features were attractive in the light of symbols, as sounds intrinsically common become attractive in language, and as shapes intrinsically simple become interesting in writing.

This is a curious passage which seems to involve a circular process, of words generating pictures which in turn generate words.

Visual signs abound in the art of the Victorian genre painter. In the last of Frith's famous *Road to Ruin* series, the unmade bed, the abandoned toys and cradle, the empty cupboard with its door ajar, tell their silent tale; so does the poison phial lying on the floor in

Wallis's *Death of Chatterton*, and the concertina, butterfly, harebell and rainbows in Millais's *Blind Girl*. An almost inevitable reaction to viewing such pictures is to formulate, silently or otherwise, a verbal response on the lines of 'Ah, yes, I *see* what has happened – or what is about to happen'; and this complements the imaginative picture-making which the reader of Hardy's fiction finds himself required to perform. To turn to these pictures after reading Hardy is to find many echoes and parallels. In *The Mayor of Casterbridge*, Elizabeth-Jane is shown carrying a black-bordered mourning card as a silent message of her father's death; and this is a cliché of the Victorian genre painter. In, for example, George Hicks's *Woman's Mission – Bad News*, painted during Hardy's years in London, the husband, one hand covering his face in a stylized gesture of grief, holds in the other a black-bordered sheet of note-paper. Letters are almost as prominent in Victorian paintings as in Victorian novels, including Hardy's. The situation of Redgrave's governess, for example – that favourite fictional character-type – is focused on the letter she holds. In all of these pictures the viewer is prompted by a visual sign to construct the 'story' or situation represented by the picture. In one of those groups of three narrative paintings which so strongly recall the three-volume novel or the three-act drama, Augustus Egg's *Past and Present*, we find a half-eaten apple and a house of cards built by children at play, used as symbols of sexual temptation and imminent domestic catastrophe. We can match this with the kind of visual symbolism or allusiveness to which Hardy was so addicted: Tess, for example (in the manuscript, though not in the final version), being seduced in white muslin on a red rug, Sergeant Troy performing his sword-exercise, or Jude and Arabella drinking beer beneath a crude illustration of Samson and Delilah – this last one in turn recalling the Victorian painter's device of the picture-within-a-picture. Another picture, Martineau's *The Last Day in the Old Home* – and its title might well be a chapter-heading in a Victorian novel – was exhibited in 1862, the year in which Hardy went to London as a rising young architect. It is packed with informative and suggestive detail, and we have no difficulty in extracting from it both a narrative situation (comprising the imagined past and future as well as the instant of time seized by the picture), and an element of social and moral comment.

It may not be too wild an exaggeration to suggest that to read a typical Hardy novel is like visiting the Royal Academy in the mid-Victorian period. For Hardy, like Hamlet, is constantly exhorting us to look here upon this picture and on this; and these 'pictures' are not

merely descriptive set-pieces, dropped into the text as a backcloth
to the action; they are, rather, an idiosyncratic mode of story-telling.
One of Hardy's most characteristic *narrative* devices is to invite the
reader to contemplate a number of verbal 'pictures': the narrator
describes their components and draws our attention to features of
special interest, as if he were a guide or a well-informed companion
in a picture-gallery, but his own knowledge is incomplete – he is
himself a spectator, not the artist – and, like us, he seems to be driven
to make what deductions he can from the visible evidence. The
omniscient narrator recording a sequence of events for the ordering of
which he is responsible has disappeared in favour of a watcher or spy,
catching occasional and sometimes baffling glimpses of a central
situation from the angle of his place of concealment.

Let us glance, by way of illustration, at the opening pages of *The
Woodlanders*. Like most of Hardy's novels, it begins with the estab-
lishing of a local context for the action, specified with the kind of
precision that recalls the biography or the guide-book as much as a
work of fiction. The scene at first is empty, but this does not mean
that it is without interest: we are treated to some reflections on 'the
physiognomy of a deserted highway', and the metaphor is a revealing
one: we can read the character of an empty road, Hardy tells us, as
readily as that of a human face. A solitary figure then appears: he is
nameless, and we know of him only what his appearance reveals
('It could be seen by a glance at his rather finical style of dress that he
did not belong to the country proper'). Soon a carrier's van comes
into sight, 'half full of passengers, mostly women': the deserted
highway is now populated, but the narrator sees the new arrivals as
strangers, learning no more of them than is revealed by their brief
dialogue. As the van rumbles along, the spectator who stands behind
it (like Hardy at the Moulin Rouge) sees a picture formed by the
superimposing of images: through the windows he sees 'a square
piece of . . . sky and landscape', against which are placed 'the profiles
of the seated passengers . . . their lips moving and heads nodding in
animated private converse . . . in cheerful unconsciousness that their
mannerisms and facial peculiarities were sharply defined to the public
eye'. The careful composition of the picture, the effect, as in a silent
film, of image without speech, the thoughtful scrutiny of an unseen
observer – these are all familiar ingredients in Hardy's presentation of
human behaviour.

The next scene offers some equally typical elements. The barber
stands in the darkness outside Marty South's cottage, the interior of

which is illuminated by the light of her fire. Marty (at this stage she
is identified only as 'a girl', of course, for the narrator seems to know
no more of her than the barber or the reader) wears a leather apron
and holds a bill-hook: her palm is 'red and blistering': she has a pile
of 'finished articles' beside her – we are given, in short, the kind of
rustic interior that might have appealed to certain Academy painters;
and from such details as these we begin to build up a picture of Marty's
way of life. As we scan other details in the scene apart from the single
human figure, we draw conclusions that go beyond the immediate
present: 'a little round table' is 'curiously formed of an old coffin-stool',
and, with the assistance of the narrator – who sees no more than we do
at this point, but who is better versed in the folk-life of Wessex – we
are enabled to deduce with some precision 'the social position of the
household', which is 'almost as definitively shown by the presence of
this article as that of an esquire or nobleman by his old helmets or
shields'. To convey information in this way, not by direct statement
but through the suggestive quality of a material object, is a favourite
trick of Hardy's: a few pages later, the description of an old man,
Creedle, itemizes his jacket, his boots and his pocket-knife, and
describes them as 'silent testimonies of war, sport, and adventure' –
articles, that is, from which conclusions can be drawn concerning the
owner's life and experiences; and the use of such 'silent testimonies' –
commonplace objects with a communicative power which transcends
the immediate time and place – is of course a favourite characteristic
of the kind of painter I have been referring to. As for the 'silence' that
the phrase insists on, this is indeed an ingredient of many of Hardy's
most powerful scenes. Later in *The Woodlanders*, when Fitzpiers
hurries to a rendezvous in the woods with Mrs Charmond, he is
followed by Grace's father, who is anxious for his daughter's happiness
and reputation: while Melbury watches the two of them, and the
narrator watches all three, they enact an expressive pantomime:

> Mrs. Charmond had come up with the doctor, . . . who was
> standing immediately behind the carriage. She had turned to him,
> her arm being thrown carelessly over the back of the seat.
>   They looked in each other's faces without uttering a word,
> an arch yet gloomy smile wreathing her lips. Fitzpiers clasped
> her hanging hand, and, while she still remained in the same
> listless attitude, looking volumes into his eyes, he stealthily
> unbuttoned her glove, and stripped her hand of it by rolling
> back the gauntlet over the fingers. . . . He then raised her hand

to his mouth, she still reclining passively, watching him as she
might have watched a fly upon her dress.

The theatrical postures, the intense expressions, the external actions
which signify a relationship – all these recall the art of the genre
painter; and the passage I have quoted might well be a description of
an Academy canvas – entitled, perhaps, 'The Meeting in the Woods'.
At moments, indeed, the characters seem to behave almost like
artists' models, as they strike their poses: in a later scene Fitzpiers, once
again in the woods, sees Grace approaching him:

> [He] continued to regard the nearing picture, till at length
> their glances met for a moment, when she demurely sent off
> hers at a tangent and gave him the benefit of her three-quarter
> face, while with courteous completeness of conduct he lifted his
> hat in a large arc . . . when Fitzpiers held out his hand Grace
> touched it with her fingers.

They behave like figures in a painting of contemporary life; and
usually there is a figure present (in this case Marty South) who is both
part of the visible scene and a watcher of the central actors.

To return for a moment to Marty's coffin-stool: for Hardy this is
the kind of humble object which speaks volumes and, as he says of
the expression of Marty's face, can be interpreted 'as readily as a
printed word'. As already noted, the power of such objects to evoke
associations with human life and emotions takes precedence for Hardy
over their aesthetic qualities. He once noted in his diary that 'the
beauty of association is entirely superior to the beauty of aspect, and
a beloved relative's old battered tankard to the finest Greek vase'. Both
the genre painting and the typically Hardyan description habitually
offer the equivalent of the battered tankard – the simple object rendered
poignant by its association with humanity.

Again, in *The Mayor of Casterbridge*, both a vocabulary of seeing
(such words as *sight*, *view*, *picture*, *scene*, occurring with exceptional
frequency) and an imagery of seeing are also prominent: Elizabeth
looks at Lucetta 'as a critic eyes a doubtful painting'; Henchard stares
at his wife's letter 'as if it were a window-pane through which he saw
for miles'; and towards the end of his life, we are told, the world
had become 'a mere painted scene to him'. On the opening page of
the novel, taking up Douglas Brown's hint that 'the interests of a
portrait artist seem to be at work', we may note Hardy's intense
preoccupation with the visual aspect of his as yet unnamed characters:

they are visible phenomena whose background and history are only capable of being deduced from the evidence of their appearance, and only later do they become identified as individuals with special claims on the reader's attention and of whom the narrator has special knowledge. At first it is their representative quality which is stressed; and in spite of the carefully placed historical reference ('before the nineteenth century had reached one-third of its span'), the figures wear an aspect of timelessness. The trio of man, woman and child could have appeared, with only trivial differences, in any epoch; and if the parallel of the Holy Family and the Flight into Egypt (that favourite subject of classical painting) comes into the reader's mind, it is soon reinforced by the appearance of the word *nimbus*, characteristically ironic in its context, in the fifth paragraph. Like many paintings on religious subjects, the description offers much precise and realistic detail of a homely kind: the white horn waistcoat buttons, the glazed canvas (implying the play of light) of the hat, the tools peeping out of the rush basket; some of it, indeed, is so scrupulously and even pedantically described as to suggest that the writer is working (as, in a sense, he is) with a picture before him. The reference, for instance, to the man's face showing in profile an angle 'so slightly inclined as to be almost perpendicular' smacks of the language of the life-drawing class. As in a painting, too, these figures are silent; and though movement is implied, the descriptive details catch them in an instant of rest. The point of view is that of an interested but ignorant observer, who first surveys the figures from a distance and then moves (in a typical phrase) into a 'closer view'; that is to say, the omniscient narrator who is to be charged with most of the story-telling has not yet assumed his full functions, and the observer, like the reader, must draw what conclusions he can from the dust on their shoes and clothes, their facial expressions, and the man's manner of walking. From all this, and prompted by the more percipient narrator, we reach certain conclusions concerning the man's calling and character and his relationship with the woman; but all our knowledge is based on observation, even the folds in his clothing yielding their quantum of understanding of his 'dogged and cynical' nature, and we scrutinize this verbally drawn picture as we might search a realistic painting by one of Hardy's contemporaries for significant hints embodied in tiny visual details.

Hardy begins *The Mayor of Casterbridge*, then, holding up for the reader's contemplation a picture which contains much and suggests more. This same picture is recalled to the reader in two passages near the end of the novel. The first is when Elizabeth-Jane watches Henchard leave the town for ever: 'Though she did not know it Henchard formed at this moment much the same picture as he had presented when entering Casterbridge for the first time nearly a quarter of a century before, . . . ' It is again, we note, a *picture* that is in question, and its similarity to the earlier one is stressed through visual details as well as by the general statement: as before, he carries a rush-basket, and once again the attention is focused on the precisely observed 'creases behind his knees coming and going alternatively'. Secondly, Henchard himself recalls the earlier scene in soliloquy: ' "Yes, we came up that way, . . . She was carrying the baby, and I was reading a ballet-sheet. . . . " ' In this way the opening scene performs a function in the novel that is not merely local. But it has also been evoked much earlier, in the parallel description which opens the third chapter (and which was, in the original serial version in the *Graphic*, also the opening passage of the second instalment). Here there is similarity and contrast, for the scene this time contains two figures instead of three, Susan Henchard and her daughter (now 'grown-up' but readily – though as it turns out erroneously – identified by the reader with the baby of Chapter 1). As before, the narrator restricts himself to drawing what conclusions seem legitimate from the visible evidence afforded by the scene, which, externally at least, has altered so little:

> The scene in its broad aspect had so much of its previous character, even to the voices and rattle from the neighbouring village down, that it might for that matter have been the afternoon following the previously recorded episode. Change was only to be observed in details. . . .

The figures in the landscape in their different ways both show signs of the passing of time, and as so often the presentation of the scene dwells on appearances and limits analysis of character to what can be inferred from them. Characteristic phrases are: '*A glance was sufficient to inform the eye* that this was Susan Henchard's grown-up daughter'; 'They walked with joined hands, and it could be *perceived* that this was the act of simple affection' (my italics). The parallel to the earlier scene includes the figure of the furmity-woman, much changed but still stirring her pot.

At the outset of his novel, therefore, Hardy is attuning his reader's response to a narrative art that makes use of scenes presented in sharply realized visual detail and in which commonplace objects can assume unusual importance. Before we have read much further in the novel, we encounter an example of one of his favourite descriptive devices, the 'framing' of a scene within the larger scene by so disposing his characters that one of them is in a position to view others through an open door or an uncurtained window. In this way a portion of the external world is cut off from the rest for the special attention of the observer, and the reader. After years of separation, Mrs Henchard first sees her husband again through the window of the King's Arms hotel in Casterbridge, where Henchard, as Mayor, is presiding over a 'great public dinner'. The reader, who knows nothing at this stage of how Henchard has spent the last eighteen years, is enabled to stand in Susan Henchard's shoes as, an unrecognized outsider, she surveys the brilliantly lighted scene within. The method is similar to that of the opening scene: details perceived by the watchers outside enable us to deduce what changes have taken place in Henchard (" '. . . how his diamond studs shine!' " exclaims Elizabeth-Jane, and she observes that the Mayor drinks only water). The difference is that the task of observation is now performed by two of the characters, and the narrator's share of the narrative burden is correspondingly lighter. Many Victorian authors might at this point have seen fit to summarize the vicissitudes of Henchard's life since the 'sale' of his wife, or to contrive matters so that he should tell his tale at length to an auditor. Hardy does neither, and, as often elsewhere, it is less a narrative that he invites us to listen to than a picture he holds up before us. It is noteworthy that in passages such as this his fondness for the general moral reflection and the philosophic epigram undergoes a temporary self-denial: his creative mind seems fully engaged in depicting the visualized scene in terms of which the episode has been conceived.

Two points already briefly made call for further comment. One is the use of a character in the novel as observer, whose eyes can take in a given scene and whose mind can seek to interpret it. Mrs Henchard's view of the Mayor's public dinner is a case in point. A simpler example is the impression made on Elizabeth-Jane by the 'Scotch gentleman', later identified as Farfrae:

> she looked at him quite coolly, and saw how his forehead
> shone where the light caught it, and how nicely his hair was
> cut, and the sort of velvet-pile or down that was on the skin
> at the back of his neck, and how his cheek was so truly curved
> as to be part of a globe, and how clearly drawn were the lids
> and lashes which hid his bent eyes.

The description of Farfrae at this point is limited to what the girl is supposed to have observed, though it must be said that she looks at him as if she proposed to draw his picture. This temporary shift of vantage-point is in effect accompanied by a shift in the narrative point of view; and the impersonal narrator's momentary relinquishing of his role in favour of a participant in the scene produces an effect of dramatic immediacy which a fuller description, with benefit of the former's omniscience, would not give. In the example quoted, the shift to the girl's point of view is accompanied by stylistic modification or 'colouring' ('how *nicely* his hair was cut', 'the *sort of* velvet-pile or down') which, by its deliberate triteness and awkwardness, seems to reflect the thoughts of this unsophisticated girl. This method of presenting a scene through an observer's eyes is widespread in the Wessex novels. In *Far from the Madding Crowd*, for instance, Gabriel Oak watches Bathsheba through a hole in the wall of a cowshed, and in *The Return of the Native* the reddleman watches Eustacia's silhouette come and go on the barrow on Egdon Heath. Such examples might be multiplied many times over.

In the second half of *The Mayor*, a single building occupies a role of some importance in the action. High-Place Hall, which becomes the home of the newly rich Lucetta, is a Palladian country mansion set down in the centre of Casterbridge. 'Some of its rooms overlooked the market-place', and its situation as a grandstand for discreetly viewing the goings-on of the community is fully exploited by Hardy. Its external face is the first one presented to the reader, again through the agency of Elizabeth: 'Elizabeth's eyes sought the upper rooms, and saw lights there'; but quickly we are taken inside, to share the prospect enjoyed by the two women, who sit 'looking out upon the market, which formed an animated scene'. Like two latter-day ladies of Shalott, they are able to watch – and the reader with them – the comings and goings of Henchard and Farfrae. (Elizabeth has had some previous experience of watching the younger man through windows, having in her father's house occupied a 'back room affording a view of the yard', which she exchanged for 'a front chamber overlooking the street' after his dismissal.) The peculiar advantages of High-Place Hall as an observation post are stressed: it is described as 'a gazebo over the centre and arena of the town' and the market-place is like 'the regulation Open Place in spectacular dramas, where the incidents that occur always happen to bear on the lives of the adjoining residents'. This passing scene, which might well have occupied a large and crowded canvas by Frith, is viewed from a distance and with apparent detachment by the two women, yet it impinges closely on their lives, for the two men to whom their fates are linked both frequent the market-place. Detachment and involvement are both implied in a dialogue between Lucetta and Farfrae in which the pictorial motif recurs:

> 'Your numerous fairs and markets keep me interested. How many things I think of while I watch from here!'
> ... 'Do you look out often?' he asked.
> 'Yes – very often.'
> 'Do you look for any one you know?'
> Why should she have answered as she did?
> 'I look as at a picture merely. But,' she went on, turning pleasantly to him, 'I may do so now – I may look for you.'

Observers, vantage-point and the 'framing' of the busy scene outside by the window are all brought together in Hardy's use of High-Place Hall, which helps to give unity to the latter part of the book by serving as the location for several important scenes.

The metaphorical function of vision and blindness, modes of seeing and failing to see, interpretation and misinterpretation of the visible, is nowhere more evident than in *Jude the Obscure*. When Hardy wants to show a character drawing nourishment from an illusion, he habitually shows him as seeing incompletely or imperfectly, as Jude over and again sees an ideal and not a real Christminster. For an example of the opposite – the sudden perception of a truth conveyed in terms of a clearing of vision – we can turn to *Far from the Madding Crowd*: when Bathsheba announces that Boldwood has shot Troy, the announcement has 'somewhat the effect of setting the distorted images in each mind present into proper focus'. The observers and non-participants who are such familiar Hardyan character-types, as they contemplate life from the periphery of the sphere of action, are enabled to see with unusual clarity; but if detachment brings discovery and revelation, involvement can entail a loss of vision.

The early pages of *Jude the Obscure* recall Dickens's account in *Great Expectations* of his hero's gaining his 'first most vivid and broad impression of the identity of things'. As a child, Jude is exceptionally sensitive to his surroundings, and unusually observant of small things as well as large: the opening chapter shows him looking down a well, as if straining to see what the future holds, and soon he is walking carefully down a damp path to avoid crushing the earthworms that most boys would not even have noticed. In the third chapter, he climbs to the roof of a barn under repair and from that vantage-point strains his eyes (the expression is Hardy's and is used twice in this passage) to see the distant city of Christminster. A friendly workman tells him

'Christminster is out across there, by that clump. You can see it – at least you can on a clear day. Ah, no, you can't now.'
The other tiler . . . had also turned to look towards the quarter designated. 'You can't often see it in weather like this,' he said. 'The time I've noticed it is when the sun is going down in a blaze of flame, and it looks like – I don't know what.'
'The heavenly Jerusalem,' suggested the serious urchin.

Christminster is there, but invisible; it is a real city, but also, to Jude, a city of the mind and spirit; he knows its geographical location, but simultaneously it belongs to the same order of existence as the heavenly city of 'the Apocalyptic writer' (in the New Testament, the Epistle of Jude is immediately followed by the Revelation). Later in the evening he returns, reascends the ladder, and again scans the horizon; this time he sees, or seems to see, Christminster, but the experience is curiously equivocal:

It was Christminster, unquestionably; either directly seen,
or miraged in the peculiar atmosphere.
The spectator gazed on and on. . . .

The force of that 'unquestionably' seems weakened by the unusual epithet 'miraged', itself a somewhat ambiguous term. A mirage may be an optical illusion produced by certain atmospheric conditions and explicable in scientific terms, while in emotional terms acting as a source of false hopes and subsequent disappointment – and of such a nature Jude's experience of Christminster turns out to be; or it can be, in the words of the *OED*, 'the appearance in the sky of a reflected image of a distant object', permitting a visual experience different from the customary one afforded by an object or scene substantial enough in itself. The reader is thus prepared for the paradoxical role of Christminster, as both an actual city and the city of Jude's dreams. Indeed, in the passage under discussion, 'dreams' is a significant and recurring word; already the sharpness of the hero's perception of reality is blunted, and he has now begun to see things through a glass darkly. (An interesting parallel is offered in the same passage by the 'old woman's "shop" window, with its twenty-four little panes set in lead-work, the glass of some of them oxidized with age, so that you could hardly see the poor penny articles exhibited within . . .'.)

D

The spectacle, or vision, of the 'far-off city' is the first of three views of Christminster sought by Jude as, over a period of years, he draws steadily nearer to his goal of reaching the city; and the three incidents form a progressive pattern in the novel that can hardly be accidental. The first of them is the boyish experience already referred to. The first part of the story, following Hardy's own division, ends with Jude perceiving 'the faint halo, a small dim nebulousness, hardly recognizable save by the eye of faith', and resolving to set off for Christminster: again the language of Hardy's prose, with the associations of *halo*, spiritual as well as pictorial, thrown into question by the reiteration of 'faint . . . dim . . .', and the characteristic phrase 'the *eye* of faith' is worth close attention. At the beginning of the second part, with marriage to Arabella and separation from her behind him, Jude is found walking towards the city 'at a point a mile or two to the southwest of it', and from there he obtains 'his first near view of the city'. Seen from this second and much closer vantage-point it no longer has the remote and magical quality of the earlier vision, though the time of day is the same and the rays of the setting sun are still reflected by the buildings of the medieval city, which 'now lay quiet in the sunset, a vane here and there on their many spires and domes giving sparkle to a picture of sober secondary and tertiary hues'. However, once within the city, Jude's perceptions are seen to be modified and distorted by his preconceptions: setting out after nightfall and wandering in its 'dark corners which no lamplight reached', he sees only those aspects of the city which appear to harmonize with the Christminster of his dreams: 'When he passed objects out of harmony with its general expression he allowed his eyes to slip over them as if he did not see them.' Again, the obscurity, like the 'rottenness of the stones' of the ancient buildings, is symbolic as well as realistic and pictorial; and the vocabulary of seeing is persistent. Jude's absorption in a world of his own imagining – almost as remote from the real Christminster as from the earthy *milieu* of Arabella – is made plain to the reader by his sense of isolation, of being what Hardy calls 'a self-spectre', 'almost his own ghost', experiencing the sensation 'of one who walked but could not make himself seen or heard'. (The theme recurs in the poem 'Wessex Heights', written shortly afterwards.)

Jude's third view of Oxford, somewhat later, is obtained from within its heart – more precisely, from the lantern of the Sheldonian Theatre. It represents a turning-point in his mental life and the onset of disillusion: the time is characterized as 'the afternoon on which he awoke from his dream', and the panoramic view afforded by the

Sheldonian provides a vision of reality, as the dark corners of the city glimpsed at night had nurtured his groundless ambitions: 'it had windows all round, from which an outlook over the whole town and its edifices could be gained'. As often, a clear view of physical objects is accompanied by mental or emotional insights – in this case, that 'those buildings . . . were not for him'. The experience is quickly reinforced by the curt letter from the head of a college, advising him to abandon his notions of a scholar's career and to stick to his trade.

These three views of Christminster thus trace the graph of Jude's hopes and disappointments in the early part of the novel. After the third, he still believes that Christminster is worth attaining, though compelled to accept that it is not for such as he. What Hardy seems to have presented in this earlier portion of his novel is a pattern of three related stages of experience: Jude's initial clear-sightedness is followed by blindness or blinkered vision under the temporary but powerful influence of an outside agency, the loss of sight being itself followed by an eventual realization of the truth and a regaining of accurate perceptions, or at least perceptions which have shed some of the grosser elements of self-deception. Of this kind is Jude's changing consciousness of Christminster in relation to his own life. His idealistic notion of what the city stands for produces a temporary blindness to the reality around him in the intensity of his attention to the inward vision: the observant boy of the opening chapters becomes the youth who hardly notices the 'peeps of country' as he walks along, preoccupied as he is by his dreams of Christminster. At another such moment of abstraction from his material surroundings, however, reality asserts itself abruptly and shockingly:

> In his deep concentration on these transactions of the future Jude's walk had slackened, and he was now standing quite still, looking at the ground as though the future were thrown thereon by a magic lantern. On a sudden something smacked him sharply in the ear, and he became aware that a soft cold substance had been flung at him, and had fallen at his feet. A glance told him what it was. . . . (Chapter 6)

The transition from an inward 'looking' at what does not exist to the actual seeing of a physical object thrust into the foreground of his attention is significant. The pig's pizzle thrown by Arabella – one of Hardy's most effective symbols, both bold and apt – shatters his contemplative mood as Arabella herself is to shatter the 'future' which Jude is envisaging; and under the spell of her sexual attractiveness he undergoes a second and parallel experience of the vision–blindness–vision pattern already described. At first he sees clearly enough: 'A glance told him' what the unconventional missile was, and the description of the scene observed by Jude from the other side of the fence (the small homestead and the country girls washing the pigs' chitterlings in the running water) is vividly realistic. But the Circe-like power of Arabella operates quickly, and his clear vision, after a final brief moment of illumination, is lost:

> It had been no vestal who chose *that* missile for opening her attack on him. He saw this with his intellectual eye, just for a short fleeting while, as by the light of a falling lamp one might momentarily see an inscription on a wall before being enshrouded in darkness.

By way of partial (though unsatisfactory) compensation for this loss of vision, his love for Arabella casts its own peculiar light upon the real world and modifies the appearances of objects thereby. When Jude revisits the spot where they have kissed for the first time, he sees the scene not in its objective reality but coloured by his infatuation ('a pollard willow stood close to the place, and that willow was different from all other willows in the world'); and when, in her company, he climbs a summit from which the region around Christminster can be seen, he is blind to the existence of the city for a glimpse of which he has formerly strained his eyes. Hence the repeated references to Samson (Jude twice sees a picture of Samson and Delilah): for Jude too, love is a folly leading to blindness.

Seeing, then, in its various literal and metaphoric forms and in its absence, pervades the novel at the levels of both narrative and style. For Jude it is an activity executed with varying degrees of success at different stages in his history. But he is, as well as being an observer, a doer and a maker; and Jude Fawley's commitment, in the earlier part of the novel, to ecclesiastical architecture and to the Gothic and Neo-Gothic styles is intimately related to some of its major themes. He comes to Christminster at a moment when the extensive repair and restoration of medieval buildings is in progress: specifically, 'the Cathedral repairs' involve the overhauling of 'the whole interior stonework . . . , to be largely replaced by new'. In the stoneyard where he seeks employment, he observes the contrast between old and new in masonry:

> He asked for the foreman, and looked round among the new

traceries, mullions, transoms, shafts, pinnacles, and battlements standing on the bankers half worked, or waiting to be removed. They were marked by precision, mathematical straightness, smoothness, exactitude: there in the old walls were the broken lines of the original idea; jagged curves, disdain of precision, irregularity, disarray.

In such passages symbolic meanings seem to be thrusting rather vigorously through the literal statements. In the language of the previous paragraph, the new stone represents 'ideas in modern prose' – nineteenth-century rationalism – in contrast to the 'old poetry' of the college buildings, survivors of an age of mental obfuscation. The whole passage is, however, somewhat puzzling. Hardy's attitude to Gothic seems ambiguous at this point: Gothic charm is dismissed as an accidental by-product of time (the 'lichened colleges . . . had done nothing but wait, and had become poetical'); moreover, the symbolism of the paragraph quoted above is weakened by the fact that the purpose of modern restoration is to replace the 'original idea' of ancient architectural features, not to improve on it. His attitude to Neo-Gothic is, however, quite unambiguous, as the following comment makes clear:

[Jude] did not at that time see that mediævalism was as dead as a fern-leaf in a lump of coal; that other developments were shaping in the world around him, in which Gothic architecture and its associations had no place.

The embodiment of those 'other developments' is Sue Bridehead; and the notion of the irrelevance of medievalism – in the teaching of Christminster and its habits of thought and belief no less than in the physical fabric of its buildings – is central in the development of Jude's relationship with Sue, in which the instinctive championing of contrasting artistic styles is a symptom of a basic difference of temperaments. When Jude proposes a visit to Wardour Castle, she objects that it is ' "Gothic ruins – and I hate Gothic!" '; and later she tells Jude that he should ' "have learnt Classic. Gothic is barbaric art, after all. Pugin was wrong, and Wren was right." ' Unconsciously Sue arouses Greek rather than Christian associations by her appearance: at various times she is compared to 'the figures in the Parthenon frieze' and 'a Ganymedes'; and in one of those improbable but not impossible episodes characteristic of Hardy's instinct for finding a precise visual counterpart to an abstract idea, on a solitary walk she comes across a group of plaster statuettes, 'reduced copies of ancient marbles', placed on the grass 'almost in a line between herself and the church towers' of Christminster. While Sue rejects Gothic and all it stands for, Jude retains a love of medieval architecture as exemplified by Christminster even when his disillusion with the city as a satisfactory intellectual and spiritual home is complete. Even when he is unable to work at his craft, he expresses his commitment to the city of his dreams and visions by making 'Christminster cakes'. As Sue explains to Arabella:

'. . . They are reminiscences of the Christminster Colleges. Traceried windows, and cloisters, you see. It was a whim of his to do them in pastry.'
    'Still harping on Christminster – even in his cakes!' laughed Arabella. 'Just like Jude. A ruling passion. . . .'

But by this time the attachment is sentimental and nostalgic rather than deriving from a deep conviction of the reality of Christminster values.

Jude, then, is one for whom the visible world powerfully exists, one endowed by nature with an exceptional capacity 'to notice such things', as Hardy wrote of himself in a much-anthologized poem ('Afterwards'). His vision is, however, obscured by two separate causes which appear to be working in opposition to each other, but which unite in inducing a disastrous blindness to truth and reality. One is the power of the sex-urge, represented by the Delilah-like Arabella; the other his youthful dreams of Christminster as an earthly Jerusalem. He is a worker in stone, a maker of churches and houses; yet he also builds castles in the air (his old great-aunt observes that, as a child, he had a trick 'of seeming to see things in the air'), and his yearning to forsake substantial buildings for ethereal ones is at the root of his misfortunes. The bitterness of his defeat resides in his belated recognition that Christminster is a sham, less a home of godliness and good learning than a bulwark of complacent archaism and irrelevance: it is as unworthy of his longings and his efforts as Sue is (as he tells her in his agony the last time he sees her) 'not worth a man's love'.

Jude, like most of Hardy's other novels, was illustrated on its first appearance before the public; but the illustrations were in a sense superfluous, for Hardy – whose 'quizzical bright eyes' Virginia Woolf noted even near the end of his life – has provided his own 'pictures' within the text, and indeed conducts the business of story-telling, here and elsewhere, largely by their means. That the pictorial element is so much more evident in the major than in the minor novels may well be an index of the extent to which the former embody a much fuller involvement of Hardy's imaginative (image-making) powers.

3
Minor Novels

The 'minor' half of Hardy's fiction – somewhat more than half, if we include the short stories – has always been overshadowed by the major novels; and it would be foolish to suggest that things should be otherwise. One striking discrepancy between these two groups is that, whereas Hardy shows an increasing density and complexity in his major fiction from *Under the Greenwood Tree* to *Jude the Obscure*, there are almost no signs of a similar development in his minor fiction: *Tess* and *Jude* are arguably his finest achievements in prose, but *The Well-Beloved*, which falls between them, represents no significant advance in maturity on *A Pair of Blue Eyes* twenty years earlier. What seems clear is that the minor novels somehow failed to engage Hardy's full creative interests and energies: either the problems they raised did not sufficiently challenge him; or their particular modes and settings did not call forth a full response from his sensibility and experience; or, perhaps for extraneous reasons (most obviously, in the case of *A Laodicean*, serious illness), he shirked, or was driven to shirk, the deeper issues they were capable of raising.

It seems worth insisting, though, that the minor fiction has some claim not to be ignored, not only by the serious student of Hardy but by anyone who enjoys his work. Hardy can indeed be bad, but he is not uniformly bad; and he contrives to be bad in a manner that is often interesting and nearly always individual; so that he is hardly ever boring. Sometimes, and not always in their big scenes, these novels are capable of coming unexpectedly to life and lingering in the memory long after their contrivances, their absurdities and their verbal infelicities are forgotten. His lesser fiction does not tap the rich themes which make his major novels so substantial and satisfying; with a few exceptions, it lacks the sense of place, solidly specified in itself and vivid in its vital relationship with humanity; it is for the most part unhaunted by the aching sense of time and transience that is part of the full and fine Hardyan manner; but it is recognizably the work of the same man, and ought not to be overlooked in any full account of his achievement.

Desperate Remedies

For the reader who comes to *Desperate Remedies* with a knowledge of the shape of Hardy's subsequent career, it is tempting to dismiss this earliest surviving novel as a false start, a venture into fictional territory remote from his true talents and interests. Its weaknesses are only too apparent; but it is still very readable, and the signs of potential strength are recognizably there. One of its most obvious and irritating manner-isms is the tendency – which Hardy was to learn to control, if not completely to overcome – to display his knowledge of life and litera-ture too ostentatiously. The first half of the novel in particular is clogged with epigrams, presumably intended to inspire confidence in the anonymous author's breadth of worldly experience. Some are brief ('The chief pleasure connected with asking an opinion lies in not adopting it'; 'Social definitions are all made relatively: an absolute datum is only imagined', etc.); others are so laboured in manner as to make Mr Micawber sound like a model of terse simplicity:

> Adherence to a course with persistence sufficient to ensure success is possible to widely appreciative minds only when there is also found in them a power – commonplace in its nature, but rare in such combination – the power of assuming to conviction that in the outlying paths which appear so much more brilliant than their own, there are bitternesses equally great – unperceived simply on account of their remoteness.

Sometimes these undigested and indigestible lumps of reflection turn up in the dialogue, with wholly unconvincing results. Bookish references, the fruits of Hardy's conscientious reading and note-taking, have a similar effect of slowing down the pace of his narrative and blurring the outlines of his descriptions. A vivid interior scene, for instance – a London slum-dwelling, with drunken parents, neglected children, 'a roll of baby-linen . . . on the floor; beside it a pap-clogged spoon and an overturned tin pap-cup' – is marred by the extravagant description of a clock:

> Against the wall a Dutch clock was fixed out of level, and ticked wildly in longs and shorts, its entrails hanging down beneath its white face and wiry hands, like the faeces of a Harpy

('foedissima ventris proluvies, uncaeque manus, et pallida
semper ora').

This starts well enough, and the Dickensian touch ('in longs and shorts')
is felicitous; but Hardy is unable to resist the show-off classical parallel
suggested by 'entrails', and his description degenerates into pedantic
absurdity. At such times his misguided notions of 'good style' work
against the natural inclinations of his literary gifts.

The other gross defect of *Desperate Remedies* is the superabundance
of plot: the young Hardy seems to have taken only too thoroughly to
heart the advice to write a novel with a strong narrative interest, and
the book is chockful of secrets and mysteries, plots and counterplots,
coincidences, impersonations and disguises. We have to read no further
than the third page to find a young lady rejecting a suitor with the
intriguing words: ' "Good-bye!; good-bye forever. As recognized
lovers something divides us eternally." ' Later she is shown a locket
by her employer, whom she has apparently met as a total stranger,
only to discover that 'the face in the miniature was the face of her own
father'; and she marvels (as well she might) 'at the strange confluence
of circumstances which had brought herself into contact with the one
woman in the world whose history was so romantically intertwined
with her own'. Although the sensation novel of the school of Wilkie
Collins and Miss Braddon was Hardy's model here, he demonstrates
that the presentation of external action is not his forte; for when he
tries to make his narrative exciting through a rapid sequence of
events, he is apt only to make it unconvincing or preposterous, as in
the climax in which the villain pursues the heroine round a table:

The panting and maddened desperado – blind to everything
but the capture of his wife – went with a rush under the table:
she went over it like a bird. He went heavily over it: she flew
under it, and was out at the other side.

On the credit side, there are a few pages in the novel which, among
so much flat or pretentious writing, come suddenly to life and are a
portent of one of the main strengths Hardy was later to develop.
The description of the Three Tranters Inn shows an engagement of
his genuine interests and sympathies, and the cider-making scene
which follows is a foretaste of many similar rustic episodes, with its
unaffectedly accurate descriptions (the farmer 'packing the pomace
into horsehair bags with a rammer') and the humour of its rustic
dialogue (' "Yes, matrimony do begin wi' 'Dearly beloved', and ends

wi' 'Amazement', as the prayer-book says" '). The *Spectator*, whose review of the novel caused Hardy such intense distress, was perceptive enough to praise this element ('an unusual and very happy facility in catching and fixing phases of peasant life'). For a brief space, Hardy's prose sheds its abstractions and he forgets to be clumsily didactic or knowing, as his attention is for the moment fixed not on his commonplace books but on his first-hand experience of rural life and speech.

Another striking achievement of *Desperate Remedies* is the power with which, especially in a few passages dealing with the villain Manston, it succeeds in conveying a sense of suppressed sexuality. For its period, the novel shows unconventionality and even courage in its handling of sexual situations: it would hardly, one suspects, have won acceptance by the magazines, and some of its reviewers found it 'unpleasant' and 'disagreeable' (favourite epithets of Mrs Grundy's Victorian disciples). In this respect too the book, which can scarcely be regarded as a successful work of fiction as a whole, is prophetic of an element which was to be of importance in Hardy's major fiction.

The third way in which this early experiment shows something more than a commonplace imitative talent is the strong and sometimes highly individual powers of visualization revealed in many scenes and episodes. Here again, we can see, at a fairly crude stage of development, evidence of a faculty that was to become both a mannerism of Hardy's method and style and, in its most effective manifestations, one of the hallmarks of his idiosyncratic vision. From the nightmare-like early scene in which the heroine looks through a window at the spectacle of her father falling to his death from a high scaffolding, the novel is full of passages wherein the reader is encouraged to share the character's or narrator's role as viewer or *voyeur*; and Hardy's fiction from this point on was to be full of scenes glimpsed through windows or open doors, through peepholes or up chimneys or down wells or in mirrors – not only static scenes but snapshots, as it were, of a revealing action 'frozen' for an instant and captured by the writer as it might have been caught by the genre painter so popular in the mid-Victorian period, or by the new art of photography.

Although Hardy was later to discourage attempts to trace autobiographical elements in his fiction, it is quite clear that in this early novel (as in others) he draws on his own recent knowledge and experience of the world. His hero, Springrove, is an architect who goes to London 'to endeavour to advance a little in my profession' and who has 'loved verse passionately', 'read it continually', and written it himself 'on emotional subjects'; in all this he bears obvious resemblance to the young Thomas Hardy.

A Pair of Blue Eyes

A Pair of Blue Eyes also opens in a manner which strongly recalls a turning-point in the author's own life. He had gone down to St Juliot, Cornwall, in 1870 on architectural business, and had there met Emma Lavinia Gifford, whom he was to court and marry. In the novel his hero, who bears the socially unpretentious name of Smith, encounters his heroine Elfride (whose uncommon name begins with the initials of Miss Gifford's Christian names) under precisely similar circumstances. As Michael Millgate has pointed out, the fact that Hardy had recourse to autobiography in this novel ought not to surprise us if we remember that it was written at short notice and under the pressure of serialization; but Professor Millgate's description of it as 'a kind of rag-bag of information, ideas, descriptive vignettes, personal experiences, fragments of the author's brief literary past' is somewhat unfair to a book which contains a simple but strong plot and at least two characters which are more than merely conventional. It is true that Hardy's epigrams still lie more thickly upon the ground than is desirable: there are, in particular, some very laboured dialogues between Elfride and Knight, in which Hardy seems to be striving after conversational brilliance but achieves only a stilted dreariness; and it is true also that the use of coincidence is forced – it is surely improbable that Knight, as Smith's friend, should happen also to be both a distant relation of Elfride's stepmother *and* the anonymous reviewer of Elfride's novel (which Smith chances to stumble upon during a visit to Knight's chambers). The grotesquely long arm of coincidence also contrives that Smith should be sent on church-restoration business to, of all the villages in England, precisely that in which his humble parents dwell; and that, in the final macabre episode, Smith and Knight should travel to Cornwall by the very train which also carries Elfride's coffin. Coincidences which do no violence to our credulity in the restricted topography of the major novels are less acceptable when they are made to operate across the map of a more extensive territory. Throughout this novel, characters have a knack of turning up, or disappearing, more conveniently than plausibly: one senses that Hardy is experiencing considerable difficulties in manoeuvring his cast so as to have the right people, and only the right people, where he wants them at a given moment. Smith, for instance, is whisked off to Bombay (as Angel Clare was later to be despatched to Brazil and Arabella to Australia) somewhat summarily.

But when all its weaknesses have been conceded, *A Pair of Blue Eyes* represents a considerable advance on *Desperate Remedies*, and it is a more ambitious book, though a less complete artistic success, than *Under the Greenwood Tree*. Elfride is Fancy Day writ large – a heroine who not only contemplates the desertion of her naive and youthful lover for a man of greater intellectual powers and higher social status, but actually goes ahead with it. (In her mixture of intellectual precocity, emotional immaturity and unpractical idealism, she also anticipates Sue Bridehead: as her stepmother shrewdly comments, 'she will say things worthy of a French epigrammatist, and act like a robin in a greenhouse'.) She is, however, far from being mercenary or a mere heartless coquette, and the novel traces with some subtlety the change in her personality from her immature love for Stephen, over whom she takes pleasure in exercising her sexual power, to her pathetic subjection to Knight's inflexible demands upon her.

Smith, who describes himself as 'a rural builder's son' – an exact description of the author – has a crushing sense of social inferiority: he has his way to make in the world, without the advantages of wealth, education or connections. Since he loves Elfride, the daughter of a snobbish clergyman with aristocratic connections, we have once again the theme of the poor man and the lady. Smith has been much influenced by Knight, an older man who writes for the reviews and has assisted him with his programme of self-education (whatever the biographical significance of the fact may be, the parallel with Horace Moule is unmistakable). Knight is an unsympathetic character, and on the whole a less convincing one than Stephen or Elfride; perhaps Hardy at this stage was simply not qualified by experience to portray a metropolitan intellectual. The obsessive side of his nature possesses more interest: a member of fashionable London society whose journalistic essays exhibit a rather cynical worldly wisdom, he is wholly without sexual experience and has (like Angel Clare) an almost pathological yearning for an inexperienced bride (' "I *hate* the fact that you have been caressed before," ' he tells Elfride). In the event he treats Elfride so badly that readers are likely to forgive *her* heartless behaviour towards Smith, whom she has jilted without a word of explanation or remorse, and to find themselves readjusting their attitude towards her in the latter part of the novel. The main action turns on a secret: Elfride dare not disclose to Knight that, during her infatuation with Smith, she has not only been engaged to him but has spent the night away from home with him (though perfectly innocently: they have travelled by train from Devon to London, changed platforms, and immediately returned). Unlike the secrets in *Desperate Remedies*, though, which merely provide a somewhat factitious atmosphere of suspense and mystery, Elfride's secret is linked to a genuinely interesting study in feminine psychology; and in at least two respects – her conscious use of sexual power to compensate for the social disadvantages of being a woman, and her entanglement in a destructive web of social conventions and prejudices – she anticipates the later heroines.

Hardy's use of coincidence has been referred to, and related to it is the ill-luck which seems to dog so many of his protagonists, from Elfride onward. At worst, this can become an irritating mannerism on the novelist's part: one sometimes feels, callously, that his heroine has only to place herself in a compromising situation to meet the enemy who has sworn revenge upon her, only to write a letter to have it turn up as damaging evidence against her, and only to venture on a metaphorical description of her lover as 'a strong tower for me against the enemy' to have an actual tower collapse promptly before her eyes. Such a device may produce telling episodes, but can clearly be overdone; however, Hardy also uses such circumstantial accidents more impressively, to show how trivial events may have far-reaching effects upon human existence. In *Desperate Remedies*, Manston's misreading of a railway time-table proves a turning-point in the action; and in *A Pair of Blue Eyes* Stephen's failure to realize that a marriage licence obtained in London cannot be used in Plymouth changes the course of several lives. The ironic notion of human happiness and welfare at the mercy of such trifling lapses of efficiency recurs throughout Hardy's work; and, to be quite fair, they are something more than a plot-device resorted to by the harassed writer of serials.

The example cited above of the convenient collapse of a church tower is characteristic of another recurrent type of episode in Hardy's fiction: the bizarre, highly improbable (though not strictly impossible), weightily symbolic incident, of which the most notable example in *A Pair of Blue Eyes* is the famous episode on the 'Cliff without a Name' in Chapters 21-2. Elfride and Knight go on a cliff-walk; far out to sea can be observed the approach of the boat bringing Smith, to whom she has pledged herself, back from India. Trying to retrieve his hat, which has blown from his head, Knight finds himself unable to reascend the slippery slope, and, endeavouring to assist him, Elfride finds herself in similar difficulties; thanks to his efforts, she is able to regain solid ground, but only at the cost of his slipping further down. The nearest help is far away, and he cannot possibly hold on for more than a few minutes. This is indeed a classic cliff-hanging situation, for it is at this juncture that the sixth instalment of the novel, as originally published, breaks off; there is further evidence elsewhere in the book that Hardy was mindful, in his first effort at serial fiction, of the importance of keeping the audience in suspense from month to month. Elfride saves Knight, of course; but the means are less predictable than the outcome, for she does so by making a rope out of the only materials on hand – her underclothes. Ironically, this defiance of the proprieties which enables her to save his life is the same quality which has prompted the indiscretion which he is later unable to forgive. After the rescue, intense relief prompts their first embrace: 'At the moment of embracing, Elfride's eyes involuntarily flashed towards the *Puffin* steamboat. It had doubled the point, and was no longer to be seen.' And in the same moment Stephen has, effectively, disappeared from her emotional horizons. Throughout the whole episode, Hardy's keen powers of visualization compel acceptance of what is in some respects a contrived and implausible episode. The most memorable moment occurs when Knight, suspended in space, feels himself entirely alone in the universe (Elfride is busy disrobing, unknown to him and out of sight):

> opposite Knight's eyes was an imbedded fossil, standing forth in low relief from the rock. It was a creature with eyes. The eyes, dead and turned to stone, were even now regarding him. It was one of the early crustaceans called Trilobites. Separated by millions of years in their lives, Knight and this underling seemed to have met in their place of death.

The vivid apprehension of a visual experience as an accompaniment to intense emotion or a moment of crisis, and the sense of the infinitesimal extent of human life in relation to the history of the earth as revealed by nineteenth-century science: these are to be characteristic features of Hardy's literary technique and thought throughout the next half-century.

The Hand of Ethelberta

The contrast between *The Hand of Ethelberta* and its immediate predecessor, *Far from the Madding Crowd*, is vividly brought home by a comparison of the illustrations which accompanied these novels on their first appearance before the public. *Far from the Madding Crowd* was illustrated by Helen Paterson, who, like Hardy, married during the course of its serialization (her husband was William Allingham, the minor poet). Hardy admired her work, and was not blind to her personal attractions: she is the 'H.P.' of his poem 'The Opportunity', written many years later. Her reputation had been made as a water-colourist specializing in such subjects as milkmaids and rustic cottages; and her drawings for Hardy's novel are in a familiar Victorian vein of idealized rusticity, though in the later numbers her pictorial style modulates from the sentimental-pastoral to the sentimental-melodramatic. *The Hand of Ethelberta* was illustrated by George Du Maurier, who had been contributing to *Punch* for some fifteen years and had already worked for such established novelists as Thackeray and Mrs Gaskell. That he should have been selected to work for Hardy, and should have agreed to do so, may be interpreted as a tribute to the latter's growing reputation. His drawings have an elegance worlds removed from the *simplesse* of Helen Paterson's work: they present the characters, and especially the heroine, in a diversity of costumes, with an effect not unlike a series of fashion-plates. The barn has been quitted for the drawing-room, smock-frocks and gaiters have been shed in favour of the contemporary dress of the metropolitan upper class; and the change in Hardy's setting, theme and style from one novel to the other is hardly less abrupt.

The novel is subtitled 'A Comedy in Chapters'; but in spite of some resolute attempts at witty dialogue, humorous situation and epigrammatic comment, one's reflection on closing the book is that Hardy's pursuit of the comic spirit is somewhat less than half-hearted. Again, the novel seems to hark back to *The Poor Man and the Lady*, and specifically recalls Hardy's description of that lost work as 'a sweeping dramatic satire of the squirearchy and nobility, London society, . . . and political and domestic morals in general'. In spite of its local (and not always happy) excursions into comedy, its central themes are serious and even tragic; and although there are some memorable passages, its general unsatisfactoriness stems from a shirking of the implications of the issues that are raised.

Ethelberta is one of a family of ten; their mother is a bedridden invalid, their father 'in service' as a butler and therefore living outside the family home. When the story opens the heroine's career has been a paradigm of Victorian social mobility: a combination of intelligence and education has qualified her for employment as a governess, and her beauty has involved her in a runaway marriage with the son of the household, who has promptly died and left her a penniless widow while still hardly more than a girl. In these circumstances she is driven to live on her wits, which are considerable; but if her situation is somewhat reminiscent of that of Thackeray's Becky Sharp, it is also quite different in the crucial respect that her motives are not at all self-seeking, for she is devoted to her family and feels a moral responsibility to ensure their present and future welfare. Her personal qualities qualify her to move in high society, and her widowed status gives her a mobility that would be denied to an unwed girl; but her humble background, and the peculiarly humiliating nature of her father's occupation, are shameful secrets that must be kept hidden at all costs but which continually threaten social disaster. (At one point, as a guest in the house where he is employed, she finds herself being served by him at dinner.) Hardy, as Robert Gittings has demonstrated, was something of a specialist in the emotions arising from socially embarrassing family circumstances; and the situation is handled with tact and delicacy. Ethelberta publishes a book of poems which is enthusiastically received by the fashionable world; she also enjoys a brief and remunerative vogue as a *diseuse*, or professional story-teller. It becomes apparent, though, that marriage represents the only permanent form of security for herself and her family. There are four candidates for her hand. One, Christopher Julian, is a familiar type of Hardy hero: a composer and church-organist, gentle and reserved in nature and without worldly prospects, he loves her devotedly but finds his longings inevitably doomed to disappointment. Two others, Ladywell and Neigh, are fine gentlemen whose candidacy she takes more seriously, but who are likewise rejected. Eventually she marries Lord Mountclere, a dissipated landowner old enough to be her grandfather. At this point Hardy seems to lose his sense of direction, suffering perhaps from a sense of constraint produced by the fictional genre of social comedy to which he had committed himself. The genuinely interesting human problem of Ethelberta's happiness is abandoned in favour of a comic battle of wits between the heroine and her husband, as they intrigue and counter-intrigue for control; an epilogue makes it clear that she is the winner, and that she has settled down to a workable if unromantic marriage-relationship with a reformed Mountclere, and is devoting her energies to running his estate and writing an epic poem.

On the way to this conclusion, some of the potentially fruitful elements of the early situations have inevitably been suppressed or distorted. There are, for instance, hints of the psychological strain to which Ethelberta is subjected in her quest for her family's material well-being: she tells her father, ' "I sleep at night as if I had committed a murder: I start up and see processions of people, audiences, battalions of lovers obtained under false pretences – all denouncing me with the finger of ridicule . . . I don't want to marry a second time among people who would regard me as an upstart or intruder" ' (Chapter 36). But we do not see her sufficiently from the inside for this aspect of her predicament to be more than sketched in outline; and the tragic dimensions of her marriage to Mountclere remain unexplored. Hardy's presentation of his heroine's inner life and of the full implications of her choice seems quite insubstantial in comparison with what, for example, George Eliot and Trollope had already achieved in fiction by this date. Again, the rejection of Julian which necessity demands is too cursorily dealt with, and its effects are scarcely glanced at: the pattern of Ethelberta's emotional life involves the denial of genuine feelings, the pursuit of the most eligible lover for her purpose, and the entering into what may be called an immoral marriage – yet she is shown at the end of the book as, to all appearances, tolerably satisfied with her lot. She has achieved her heart's desire of providing for her family, but the sense of a tragic sacrifice, of a price having to be paid for ignoring the demands of the heart, is signally absent. Hardy's comic formula is seen to be a disastrously limiting and damaging one.

Much of the writing is stilted and pretentious:

> Had not Ethelberta's affection for Christopher partaken less of lover's passion than of old-established tutelary tenderness, she might have been reminded by this reflection of the transcendent fidelity he had shown under that trial – as severe a trial, considering the abnormal, almost morbid, development of the passion for position in present-day society, as can be prepared for men who move in the ordinary, unheroic channels of life.
>
> (Chapter 25)

The stiff syntax and abstract vocabulary remind us of Hardy's early use of the prose of *The Times* as a model in his quest for a style; he never completely outgrew this juvenile manner, but was prone to revert to it whenever his eye was no longer on the object. His epigrammatism, both in dialogue and in commentary, sets out to be 'brilliant' and worldly-wise; but is too often merely gauche, trite and literary in the worst sense. The themes of this novel have something in common with those of G. B. Shaw's early plays, but a comparison of their styles is very much to Hardy's disadvantage. On the other hand, there are some vivid passages of descriptive writing, particularly when a contrast between urban and rural life is in question. Here is a city sunset:

> just at the hour of the sun's lowest decline, when it was fading away, yellow and mild as candle-light, and when upper windows facing north-west reflected to persons in the street dissolving views of tawny cloud with brazen edges, the original picture of the same being hidden from sight by soiled walls and slaty slopes. (Chapter 29)

and its companion-piece, a London sunrise:

> Tall and swarthy columns of smoke were now soaring up from the kitchen chimneys around, spreading horizontally when at a great height, and forming a roof of haze which was turning the sun to a copper colour, and by degrees spoiling the sweetness of the new atmosphere that had rolled in from the country during the night, giving it the usual city smell. (Chapter 30)

As these examples suggest, Hardy nearly always writes well when his object is to enable the reader to visualize a scene with some precision; this novel also contains some powerful moments of visual symbolism, including the opening scene, in which Ethelberta observes a duck pursued by a hawk – a Darwinian episode which foreshadows her own struggle for survival. The most memorable episode in the book describes a surreptitious visit of inspection by the heroine and her sister to the property of one of her suitors. (Her sister, Picotee, who quietly endures the spectacle of the man she loves single-mindedly devoted to another, is an early sketch for Marty South of *The Woodlanders*: unlike Marty, though, she finds her patience is rewarded.) This dandified London gentleman's 'country estate' turns out to consist of a kennels where the dogs are fed on horseflesh: revolting lumps of putrefying carrion hang from the trees, while emaciated horses stand bleakly waiting their turn to be slaughtered. Hardy wrote few scenes more haunting, or with a stronger physical impact, than this symbolic revelation of the rottenness on which metropolitan leisure and elegance are based.

The Trumpet-Major

The Trumpet-Major is a historical novel and a love story; it is set in Hardy's favourite period of history, that of the Napoleonic wars, and in a Dorset coastal area in which daily life is interrupted by the call to arms, and love and courtship proceed under the daily threat of invasion and conquest. The central characters of the book – the eponymous John Loveday, his brother Bob the sailor, the heroine Anne Garland, and others – move on a stage which also accommodates such historical figures as King George and Captain Hardy; and in certain scenes (when Anne accidentally meets the King, for example, and when Bob calls on Captain Hardy) the invented world of Hardy's fiction mingles with the world recreated by his studies, both enthusiastic and painstaking, in the history of the period ('the stream of recorded history'). For this is the most carefully researched of all the novels: the 'Trumpet-Major Notebook', containing notes made by Hardy in the British Museum in the summers of 1878 and 1879, and now in the Dorset County Museum, includes a mass of material, not all of it used in the novel, drawn from contemporary sources – material relating both to public events and to such background details as ladies' fashions and types of vehicles. Perhaps for this reason, Hardy seems to keep a greater distance (in more than just the temporal sense) between himself and his story than in any other novel. Instead of deep involvement in its issues and in the fates of his characters, we have an often playful irony:

> It was also ascertained that Mr. Loveday's great-grandparents had been eight in number, and his great-great-grandparents sixteen, every one of whom reached to years of discretion: at every stage backwards his sires and gammers thus doubled and doubled till they became a vast body of Gothic ladies and gentlemen of the rank known as ceorls or villeins, full of importance to the country at large, and ramifying throughout the unwritten history of England.

Instead of tragedy, we have a wistful poignancy such as that of the novel's concluding sentence:

> The candle held by his father shed its waving light upon John's face and uniform as with a farewell smile he turned on the doorstone, backed by the black night; and in another moment he had plunged into the darkness, the ring of his smart step dying

away upon the bridge as he joined his companions-at-arms, and went off to blow his trumpet till silenced forever upon one of the bloody battle-fields of Spain.

The temporal stance of the narrator, some three generations after the period in question (it is seen 'through the mists of . . . seventy or eighty years'), enables him to present a kind of double perspective which looks back at the events of the action, but also forwards from those events to the subsequent fates of the characters at a point in time later than that at which the novel's action terminates. The effect of this time-shifting device is to stress the pastness of the past, and to underline the fragility of human existence and human happiness – recurring themes of Hardy's prose and verse. He is writing of a generation preoccupied with its own pleasures and problems, but soon to be torn apart by war and, in some instances, to be slaughtered on the battlefields of Europe. But the tone is pathetic rather than tragic: the attitudes to these themes are not the characteristically Hardyan bitterness or despondency, but something more tender and compassionate. A good example occurs in the third chapter, in the idyllic scene where the soldiers riding by the millstream are offered freshly picked cherries by the miller; the scene concludes with the comment:

It was a cheerful, careless, unpremeditated half-hour, which returned like the scent of a flower to the memories of some of those who enjoyed it, even at a distance of many years after, when they lay wounded and weak in foreign lands.

Sergeant Stanner's boisterous song in Chapter 5 has this postscript:

Poor Stanner! In spite of his satire, he fell at the bloody battle of Albuera a few years after this pleasantly spent summer at the Georgian watering-place, being mortally wounded and trampled down by a French hussar when the brigade was deploying into line under Beresford.

And after the King has reviewed the troops in Chapter 12, and the crowd has dispersed, leaving the downs empty:

They still spread their grassy surface to the sun as on that beautiful morning not, historically speaking, so very long ago; but the King and his fifteen thousand armed men, the horses, the bands of music, the princesses, the cream-coloured teams – the gorgeous centre-piece, in short, to which the downs were but the mere

mount or margin – how entirely have they all passed and gone!
– lying scattered about the world as military and other dust,
some at Talavera, Albuera, Salamanca, Vittoria, Toulouse, and
Waterloo; some in home churchyards; and a few small handfuls
in royal vaults.

But *The Trumpet-Major* is also based on sources the British Museum
could not provide, and Hardy's role is that of the antiquarian and
folklorist, utilizing monuments, artefacts and oral tradition, as much
as it is that of the historian working from documents. The 1895
preface declares that 'the present tale is founded more largely on
testimony – oral and written – than any other in this series', and the
avowed sources include 'the recollections of old persons well known to
the author in childhood, but now long dead, who were eye-witnesses
of those scenes', as well as his study of 'casual relics of the circumstances amid which the action moves'. Hardy's belief in the superior
interest of objects hallowed by human associations, compared with
those possessing only a formal beauty – his preference for the
'associative' over the 'aesthetic' – is repeatedly illustrated: he can
imaginatively reconstruct a chapter of human experience from 'an
outhouse door riddled with bullet-holes, which had been extemporized
by a solitary man as a target for firelock practice when the landing
was hourly expected, a heap of bricks and clods on a beacon-hill,
which had formed the chimney and walls of the hut occupied by the
beacon-keeper, . . . and other such lingering remains', familiarity
with all of which antedates his study of written history. For although
Hardy is in this novel going back well beyond his own lifetime, he
is not going so far back that he does not preserve childhood memories
of listening to the survivors of the period; and the sense of *felt* history,
apprehended through physical objects, has preceded the more deliberate and systematic study of records.

The 'private' world of the novel has at its centre a girl and three
men. Anne Garland has some of the self-centred wilfulness and
inconstancy of Fancy Day and Grace Melbury, and like Grace she
destroys the happiness of a noble but unassertive man; John Loveday,
like Giles Winterbourne, is the faithful lover ('his determined steadfastness to his lodestar') who sacrifices his own chance of happiness
to ensure that of those for whom he feels a protective love; his brother
Bob is a womanizing sailor, emotionally shallow and fickle (his father
calls him a 'weathercock') and blind to the real feelings of others;
Festus Derriman is a cowardly braggart, lustful and irascible, a comic

villain. Reading this novel, one is repeatedly struck by the way in which emotions or situations which would be likely to take on a tragic dimension in a major Hardy novel are here softened and muted, their full potential being left unexplored. A minor instance occurs in Chapter 10, where the romantic and sexual impact of the soldiery on a rural neighbourhood is described:

> Every belle in the village soon had a lover, and when the belles were all allotted those who scarcely deserved that title had their turn, many of the soldiers being not at all particular about half-an-inch of nose more or less, a trifling deficiency of teeth, or a larger crop of freckles than is customary in the Saxon race. Thus, with one and another, courtship began to be practised in Overcombe on rather a large scale, and the dispossessed young men who had been born in the place were left to take their walks alone, where, instead of studying the works of nature, they meditated gross outrages on the brave men who had been so good as to visit their village.

The evasiveness of 'courtship' and the casual dismissal of the plight of the 'dispossessed young men' are noteworthy: what might elsewhere have turned into melodrama or tragedy here merely furnishes ironic comedy. More importantly, the contrast between the idealized devotion of John Loveday and the different kinds of sexuality represented by Bob and Festus – the one amiably philandering, the other aggressively masculine and crudely concupiscent – though hinted at, is never fully developed. It is true that Hardy comes close (probably as close as his editor, who insisted on the elimination of such martial oaths as 'O Lord!', would permit) to depicting Festus as a would-be rapist in Chapter 27: when Anne locks herself in a lonely cottage to escape his attentions, he first threatens her with violent love-making (' "One kiss would have been enough that day in the mead; now I'll have forty, whether you will or no!" '), next tries to break the door down, and then, 'brimful of suppressed passion', goes for a ladder to climb in at her window – at which interesting point the *Good Words* instalment breaks off. It is hard to take Festus seriously, however: for all his 'colossal' physique, he remains something of an over-grown schoolboy, selfish, insensitive and dirty-minded. But, more seriously, what is almost entirely lacking is any probing of the complexities of the heroine's feelings about her various lovers: apart from one throw-away phrase alluding to 'the not altogether un-relished fear and excitement that [Festus] always caused', her behaviour and her shifts of inclination seem to lack adequate motivation, and though she is obviously intended to be charming, she remains rather uninteresting.

It is hard not to close the book with a sense of opportunities missed, as well as with a sense of something of a distinctly minor kind having been accomplished. Perhaps the most rewarding aspect of the book is its portrayal of a fragment of English society at a certain moment in history: a society narrowly circumscribed but depicted with considerable delicacy of social nuance, from the position of Anne's mother, widow of an artist, in 'a twilight rank between the benighted villagers and the well-informed gentry', and the grotesque miser Squire Derriman, personally ludicrous but commanding respect by virtue of his hereditary status, down to the engaging comedy of the rustics caught up in the excitements and perils of war.

A Laodicean

Hardy classified *A Laodicean* as a 'novel of ingenuity'. With less charity, one might observe that the intolerably protracted contrivances of its action at times indicate something closer to desperation. It starts, however, with some promising ideas, and the painful circumstances of its composition must be blamed at least in part for its failure to develop satisfactorily, though the exigencies of serialization are doubtless also responsible for its prolixity. Yet it remains an interesting, and in some respects a highly individual, failure.

The principal characters are an architect-hero and an heiress-heroine – yet another version, in fact, of 'the poor man and the lady', though there are some variations on the familiar theme. When the novel opens, George Somerset is found sketching a church doorway: he is (as Hardy himself had been) in the rural community but not of it, a 'pale face' among the 'brown skins' of the field-labourers. We learn that he has undergone periods of enthusiasm for various styles of architecture in turn, but has not yet found his 'true point of departure'; it is with Gothic, however, that he is initially associated ('sketching medieval details in these neo-Pagan days'). Leaving the church, he encounters a very different edifice in the same neighbourhood: a recently erected red-brick nonconformist chapel with a blue slate roof; and he witnesses there a curious scene, a refusal on the part of a young lady of striking appearance to accept baptism by total immersion. This is the local heiress, Paula Power, whose father has made a fortune out of railway-construction (he 'made half the railways in Europe'). In refusing the ceremony she is going against his dying wish; she represents, we are told, 'a modern type of maidenhood', and she is, with her unstable nature, vacillating between conformity and unconventionality, another early sketch for Sue Bridehead. Paula inhabits Stancy Castle, purchased by her father from the modern representative of an ancient family who himself now lives in a brick villa symptomatic of 'mushroom modernism'. His daughter, Paula's closest friend, therefore goes to the castle of her ancestors as a visitor. The castle itself is 'half ruin, half residence', and Paula lives there as a 'modern flower in a mediaeval flower-pot'. The habitable part is linked to urban civilization by telegraph wires, the telegraph apparatus being placed in an 'old tapestried chamber'; with a characteristic touch, Hardy notes that the electric wire has been passed through an arrow-slit. A new clock has also been installed, indicating the seconds whereas the old one indicated only the hours; for in the nineteenth century human notions of time itself have changed: ' "Paula says that time, being so much more valuable now, must of course be cut up into smaller pieces." ' Paula intends to spend part of her fortune in renovating the ruined portion of the castle: her problem is over the right choice of architectural style. Should it be imitation Gothic, or a classical style which rejects all associations with the middle ages? (Again, there is a foreshadowing of *Jude the Obscure*, where the medieval–classical antithesis is a dominant motif on both literal and metaphorical levels.) Paula inclines towards the Greek rather than the Gothic: she contemplates turning part of the castle into a colonnaded court, and also plans a model town nearby with an industry for the manufacture of imitation Hellenic pottery.

Hardy uses the two styles as metaphors for two sets of values and two kinds of attitude towards the past. Paula and Somerset (who quickly falls in love with her) are divided by their architectural predilections as well as by the contrast between her inherited wealth and his need to pursue a profession. She tells him, when she commissions him to draw up plans for the restoration, ' "I am not a mediaevalist myself . . . I am Greek" ', and she seems (again like Sue Bridehead) to have the social and intellectual independence of a free spirit, unfettered by orthodoxy. Yet the situation is more complex than it appears. She wishes at moments that she were a de Stancy, 'romantic and historical', rather than an upstart interloper, and it is left to Somerset to remind her of 'that other nobility – the nobility of talent and enterprise'. At one point she poses the crucial question:

' "Do you think it a thing more to be proud of that one's father should have made a great tunnel and railway like that, than that one's remote ancestor should have built a great castle like this?" ' Although her wealth makes Somerset feel at a disadvantage, his ancestry is more distinguished than hers: his great-uncle was 'the well-known vice-admiral' (Hardy, we recall, claimed kinship with the famous Admiral Hardy), and he comes of 'an old stock . . . though not a rich one'. His father is an Academician, enjoying social prestige but far from rich. Yet in the late-nineteenth-century world of this novel (it is subtitled 'A Story of To-day') economic factors are decisive, over-riding considerations of birth in the eyes of all save a few senti-mentalists like Paula – and even she is ready enough to wield the power which her fortune gives her and her name suggests. Another contrast is drawn between Paula's family and that of the de Stancys, the son of that decayed line becoming Somerset's rival for her hand. These 'antipodean families', the Powers and the de Stancys, represent the new and the old: the railway-builder has not only transformed the landscape but has helped to reform the social hierarchy. Hardy was himself conscious of belonging to a family which had come down in the world; in *Tess of the D'Urbervilles* he was to return to the theme of the two families who pass each other on the stairs of social and economic history.

A Laodicean evidently expresses some of its author's own long-standing personal preoccupations. (Possibly one of the reasons for the artistic unsatisfactoriness of the minor novels in general is the extent to which they are called on to accommodate untransposed personal experiences and preoccupations.) The hero's quest for a career open to his talents, his concern with the ethics of architectural restoration, his enthusiasm for theological argument – in these and other respects we can find close parallels in Hardy's early life. Like Somerset, he had been a young man of eclectic intellectual interests, and there may be autobiographical elements in the hero's reflections on 'the years when poetry, theology, and the reorganization of society had seemed matters of more importance to him than a profession which should help him to a big house and income . . .', and in his account of his early intellectual adventures:

> Born, so to speak, a High-Church infant, in his youth he had
> been of a thoughtful turn, till at one time an idea of his entering
> the Church had been entertained by his parents. He had formed
> acquaintance with men of almost every variety of doctrinal

practice in this country; and, as the pleadings of each assailed him before he had arrived at an age of sufficient mental stability to resist new impressions, however badly substantiated, he inclined to each denomination as it presented itself . . . till he had travelled through a great many beliefs and doctrines without feeling himself much better than when he set out.

Somerset's expertise in the doctrines of Paedobaptism, exhibited at his first meeting with Paula, recalls Hardy's discussions (recounted in the *Life*) with his fellow-pupils at Hicks's office in Dorchester. The hero's verse-writing 'in every conceivable metre, and on every conceivable subject', and 'his discovery at the age of five-and-twenty that these inspired works were not jumped at by the publishers with all the eagerness they deserved', also have a strong personal flavour.

The adaptation of first-hand experience and the airing of deeply felt issues were in any case insufficient, however, to fill a three-volume novel; and Hardy found himself reduced to the desperate remedy of stock characters and contrived incidents. There is in this novel an abundance of plotting, in both senses of the word, to delay to inordinate lengths the eventual union of hero and heroine: intrigue, accident and coincidence are supplied in abundance. An architectural rival thickens the plot; a ruthless uncle of Paula's is produced from abroad at short notice and makes the course of true love even rougher; and the tireless machinations of the villain of the piece, the Mephistophelean 'cosmopolite' Dare, who turns out to be Captain de Stancy's illegitimate son (conveniently for the novelist's purposes, he has his real name tattooed on his chest) – all these seek to lend the narrative a factitious interest. The fourth and fifth books are, however, irredeemably clumsy in execution: the lovers, kept apart by a series of misunderstandings engineered by Dare, trail across Europe from one fashionable centre to another, the heroine followed at a distance by the hero. These episodes are tediously protracted, and one has the sense of feeble material being stretched like elastic. The latter part of the novel involves a huddle of arrivals and departures, telegrams and eavesdroppings, guilty secrets, blackmail and unexpected encounters: Hardy indeed returns, briefly and unsuccessfully, to the sensation novel as his model. In the final chapter, after the couple are at last united, the castle burns down (Dare's final appearance is as arsonist); they resolve to leave it as a ruin and to build a new house beside it, both now being prepared to accept 'the modern spirit' in its architectural embodiments.

The defects of *A Laodicean* are difficult, if not impossible, to excuse. It suffers from an excess of plot, and its haughty and self-centred heroine is neither very attractive nor very convincing, though her fickleness and frigidity are interesting as an anticipation of the more penetrating portraiture of Sue Bridehead, as is a curious voyeuristic scene in a gymnasium, in which Paula's boyishness is stressed. Stylistically, too, the novel is open to attack in many places. One of Hardy's earliest critics, Annie MacDonell, quotes some egregious instances from this novel, and makes the following shrewd observation:

> Other writers have fits of carelessness, when they are slipshod and vapid. When Mr. Hardy nods, he seems to sit particularly bolt upright, to pick his words and construct his sentences with more than ordinary elaboration. When he is bored he becomes formal, not listless.

Hardy was never very happy about dictating, though in this instance he had no choice; perhaps for that reason, and because revision was difficult to carry out, the language is more often clumsy, and verges more often on the downright ludicrous, than is usual in his work. A kiss is a 'long-drawn osculation'; the gaming-room at Monte Carlo is the 'negative pole of industry' and 'a heated phantasmagoria of tainted splendour'; and there are some absurdities in the dialogue, as when a character observes ' "I suffer from attacks of perspiration whenever I sit in a consecrated edifice".' Of *conscious* humour there is virtually none, and the almost unvarying dignity and solemnity of even the young lovers render them less than human and their fate less than absorbing. *A Laodicean* is not a novel that many are likely to feel enthusiastic about rereading; yet, as with some of Hardy's other failures, even its defects are apt to be interesting in a highly idiosyncratic way, and there is a clear continuity of themes, character-types and situations between it and the major fiction. Captain de Stancy's consciousness of his family's decadence, and his despairing wish that he were 'behind the iron door of our old vault', are to be echoed, more memorably, by Tess Durbeyfield. The book's most original feature is the almost allegorical use of contrasting architectural styles. Hardy had already touched on this theme in an early poem (dated 1867), 'Heiress and Architect', which may in turn have owed something to Tennyson's 'The Palace of Art'; but he also anticipates in an interesting way Ibsen's *The Master Builder*, which he was not to see for another dozen years.

Two on a Tower

For the intellectual background of *Two on a Tower*, Hardy turned from architecture to astronomy. His aim in this novel was, according to the 1895 preface, 'to set the emotional history of two infinitesimal lives against the stupendous background of the stellar universe', and he undertook a certain amount of technical research for this purpose, corresponded with at least one astronomer, and, as he recalls in the *Life*, contrived under false pretences a visit of inspection to Greenwich Observatory. Swithin St Cleeve is a beautiful youth who combines a passion for astronomy (he aspires to be a 'new Copernicus') with worldly innocence. He is the son of a socially unfortunate marriage between a curate and a farmer's daughter, both dead; he has received a good education but lives in his grandmother's humble cottage. (The recurring pattern of modest or equivocal origins combined with talent and ambition to produce social self-consciousness in the heroes of these novels will by now have become apparent.) His position in the community is therefore somewhat ambiguous. Lady Constantine is the lady of the manor and inhabits the Great House; she is unhappily married to a husband who has ill-used her and has set off to hunt lions in Africa, having first made her promise not to go into society during his absence. When the novel opens, she is, like a Tennysonian high-born lady, consumed by 'an almost killing *ennui*', which contrasts with the ardently questing intellect of Swithin. Living in the heart of the country, she is nevertheless completely detached from rural society and indifferent to its occupations and pleasures – a Mrs Charmond, in fact, more sympathetically portrayed. As one of the rustic commentators observes: 'Ay, my lady is a walking weariness. I seed her yawn just at the very moment when the fox was halloaed away by Lornton Copse, and the hounds runned en all but past her carriage wheels. . . .' Swithin pursues his astronomical activities in an old tower on her land: there she meets him in the first chapter, there much of the action of the novel takes place, and there the story ends. The topography of *Two on a Tower* is extremely, almost allegorically, simple, but its few landmarks have suggestive overtones. Nearly all the events of the story occur at the tower or at the Great House, from which it is visible. The tower rises from a wood which itself stands on a hill, actually a prehistoric earthwork: surrounded by ploughed fields and unapproached by any road, it is as remote as a distant island or a tower of fairy-tale. Hardy's extraordinary archaeological imagination charges this setting with rich associations: sitting at the top of the column, Lady Constantine has 'a forest groaning under her feet, and palaeolithic dead men feeding its roots', and as Swithin prepares for his wedding we are reminded that 'embedded under his feet were possibly even now rude trinkets that had been worn at bridal ceremonies of the early inhabitants'.

The drama of these two socially unequal characters is played out against a background both of the course of human history, which links the life and emotions of prehistoric man with those of his late-Victorian descendants, and of the immensities of space revealed by the telescope. The spatial and temporal scope of the immediate action of the novel seems to be deliberately restricted in order to point the contrast most effectively, covering as it does only a few acres and, except towards the end, a few months. Yet Lady Constantine cannot escape being haunted by time, for she is some ten years older than Swithin, and this barrier is ultimately more potent than their social inequality in destroying the possibility of happiness. A period of a few years, totally insignificant in relation to the total span of history of which the Victorians had become aware, is shown by Hardy to be of crucial importance in the lives of human beings; just as, later in the novel, Swithin's absence on the other side of the globe, at a distance which is in astronomical terms infinitesimal, provides an insurmountable barrier to communication and has humanly disastrous consequences.

To summarize the main elements of the story: the vacuum in Lady Constantine's life is soon filled, first by an interest in Swithin and then by love for him (he is an 'intervention between herself and despair'). He is less prompt to reciprocate her feelings, for his passion is at first exclusively intellectual: 'That the magnificent comet of 1811 would not return again for thirty centuries had been quite a permanent regret with him.' The death of her husband, reported from Africa, leaves her comparatively poor and levels the distinction between them; again a commentary is provided by the rustic chorus: ' "I'd up and marry en, if I were she; since her downfall has brought 'em quite near together, and him as good as she in rank, as he was afore in bone and breeding." ' They marry in secret, somewhat implausibly continuing to live apart until Swithin has made his name and his fortune. At this point Hardy's plot-machinery creaks loudly several times: it is as if the potential of his initial situation, sufficient for a short story or a novelette but not for a three-volume novel, were becoming exhausted, and he falls back, not without desperation, on complications of an all too familiar kind. As he had produced

Paula Power's uncle (previously unheard of) to intensify the intrigue in *A Laodicean*, so in this novel he produces (from Brazil) Lady Constantine's scapegrace brother Louis; and furthermore, on the very day of his wedding, Swithin learns that he has been left a considerable annuity by (inevitably) an uncle he has never seen, the money to be forfeited if he marries young. Hardy also introduces a new character, the Bishop of Melchester, who – not realizing, of course, that she is already married – becomes a suitor for Lady Constantine's hand. Hardy defended himself from the charge of satire in the presentation of the bishop by insisting, in his preface, that 'the Bishop is every inch a gentleman'; but he must have forgotten what he had written, or have pretended to do so, for the arrogance and worldliness in the bishop's character are unmistakable, and his letter of proposal recalls, in its self-importance and tendency to self-parody, that of Mr Collins in *Pride and Prejudice*.

News then reaches Lady Constantine that her first husband is indeed dead but that, owing to a misunderstanding, his death was originally reported as having taken place earlier than was in fact the case: she is, therefore, not legally married to Swithin, concerning whose legacy, and the condition attached to it, she has meanwhile learned. After a struggle, she resolves not to marry him at once, but to encourage him to travel in pursuit of his astronomical researches until their marriage can take place without loss of the annuity. He has hardly left the country, leaving no address behind him, when she finds she is pregnant; and she is forced to marry the bishop to save her name and that of her unborn child. After a few years the bishop dies, and Swithin returns, intending to marry her, only to find that she has aged while he is in his prime. He leaves her, but rushes back to announce that he will marry her after all. She dies of shock in his arms; and the novel concludes, somewhat oddly, 'The Bishop was avenged'.

As this bald, but not altogether unfair, summary indicates, the action of the second half of the novel is a huddle of surprises, reverses and improbabilities. There is some attempt to show, by direct comment rather than dramatically, the inner tensions and perplexities of Lady Constantine, on whom attention is concentrated; but the development of the story proceeds too exclusively through external events, which fall out with an implausible obligingness. Important letters arrive at the most convenient moment from the narrator's point of view; crucial conversations are overheard by chance; the characters play a kind of hide-and-seek, and so forth. As in

A Laodicean, a genuinely original and fruitful theme falls victim to the routine demands of the romantic novel; though the problem was no doubt also quantitative, commercial and financial considerations forcing Hardy (as on other occasions) to stretch the material of an excellent short story or novelette into an unsatisfactory three-decker.

On the credit side, there are some admirable passages of humorous rustic dialogue, and, as often, Hardy's peasants talk much more convincingly, and certainly more delightfully, than his gentry and his intellectuals. The astronomical imagery, without being intrusive, is introduced at moments with considerable felicity, especially in pointing the contrast between the cosmic and the sublunary: '[Swithin's] were eyes which habitually gazed, not into the depths of other eyes, but into other worlds'; 'the masses of hair that were once darkness visible had become touched here and there by a faint grey haze, like the Via Lactea in a midnight sky'. Although the novel as a whole lacks solidity and substantiality in its presentation of the external world, there are some vivid weather-descriptions:

> Ten days passed without a sight of him; ten blurred and dreary days, during which the whole landscape dripped like a mop: the park trees swabbed the gravel from the drive, while the sky was a zinc-coloured archivault of immovable cloud.

In such a sentence the Hardyan touch is as evident in the unexpectedly homely comparison 'dripped like a mop' as in the somewhat self-consciously architectural 'archivault'. Finally, Hardy touches here on a theme that was to become increasingly dominant in later novels: the nature of a true marriage, and its relationship to the religious ceremony and the legal contract which ensure its social acceptance. The 'marriage' between Swithin and Lady Constantine, though legally invalid, is faithfully undertaken and, by any standards other than the legalistic, a truer marriage than either of the legal marriages she enters into. But the final assurance of the bishop's posthumous revenge undermines this argument and negates the moral courage of its advocacy, so that it is difficult to defend Hardy against the charge, brought by Michael Millgate, of 'artificiality and moral irresolution' in this novel.

The Well-Beloved

The Well-Beloved is the shortest of the novels and, as Hardy points out in his 1912 preface, 'differ[s] from all or most others of the series in that the interest aimed at is of an ideal or subjective nature, and frankly imaginative . . .', with the result that 'verisimilitude in the sequence of events has been subordinated to the said aim'. The 'ideal or subjective' theme is the pursuit by an artist, from boyhood to old age, of a 'migratory, elusive idealization he called his Love who . . . had flitted from human shell to human shell an indefinite number of times . . .'. Yet again, Pierston's background is socially ambiguous: his father is 'an inartistic man of trade and commerce', the prosperous owner of stone-quarries on the Isle of Slingers (Portland); but the latter's commercial success in providing the materials for many of London's finest buildings has enabled his son to train, and already to achieve a growing reputation, as a sculptor, creating delicate works of art out of the stone which his father dealt in only in the rough-hewn state. (We may note the suggestive autobiographical parallel: Thomas Hardy senior built houses, his better-educated son designed them, before he turned to designing novels.) The quest for human beauty, and the attempt to render it permanent and publicly accessible in his sculptures, is Pierston's profession; but the same quest is also a private obsession. His romantic existence has been paradoxically compounded of a single-minded idealistic devotion and what on the surface would appear to the unsympathetic reader to be a fairly commonplace roving disposition:

> to his Well-Beloved he had always been faithful; but she had had many embodiments. . . . Essentially she was perhaps of no tangible substance; a spirit, a dream, a frenzy, a conception, an aroma, an epitomized sex, a light of the eye, a parting of the lips.

In the early chapters, Hardy's dramatization of this theme carries little conviction, and the migrations of the 'spirit' from one individual to another are difficult to distinguish from mere sexual impressionability and irresponsibility on the young man's part. Having decided to marry a childhood sweetheart, for example, he permits himself to be attracted by a woman he accidentally encounters, travels to London with her, and implausibly proposes on the spur of the moment: ' "My queenly darling?" he burst out; "instead of going to your aunt's, will you come and marry me?" ' The explanation that the 'spirit' had now revealed itself in 'every fibre and curve of this woman's form' seems, at this stage in the novel, distinctly lame. (We may perhaps detect Hardy self-indulgently romanticizing a propensity of his own nature: his habit of falling in love with a pretty face, however briefly glimpsed, is amply documented and seems to have been one that age did not wither or custom stale.)

When the story gets into its stride, however, it is less open to such criticisms. Pierston's abandoned love, in the incident just described, later becomes the mother of the second heroine of the novel, and she in turn becomes the mother of the third; it is only after he has irrevocably lost Avice the First that Pierston comes to recognize her as the ideal love, and the successive generations seem to him to be reincarnations of this ideal – a fancy reinforced by strong physical resemblance (explained, with a deference to canons of realism which belies the prefatory rejection of 'verisimilitude', by the custom of intermarriage on the Isle). Yet with none of the three does he achieve a satisfactory or enduring relationship: as he had callously rejected the first, the second rejects him, and the third (young enough, of course, to be his grandchild) promises to marry him only to elope with a lover of her own age. For all his acceptance into fashionable society on the strength of his artistic celebrity (and again the parallel with Hardy suggests itself), Pierston's inner life is therefore a record of failure.

The Well-Beloved is not only, however, as this summary might suggest, a romantic fantasy or modern fairy-tale: it is also a fable of the artist's nature and condition. As Pierston reflects during one of his periods of misery:

> he would not have stood where he did stand in the ranks of an
> imaginative profession if he had not been at the mercy of every
> haunting of the fancy that can beset man. It was in his
> weaknesses as a citizen and a national-unit that his strength lay as
> an artist.

This is a romantic view of the artist, and the influence of Shelley, who is quoted on the title-page, is potent throughout the novel; but it also owes some of its force to personal convictions and even to self-analysis. The most memorable elements in this book are those related to the central and compulsive Hardyan preoccupations with the passing of time and the relationship of the past to the present. Pierston grows older in body, but his emotions remain as intense as ever: his attraction to Avice the Second leads him to reflect that 'In his heart he was not a day older than when he had wooed the mother at the daughter's present age. His record moved on with the years, his sentiments stood still.' When he is near her, 'he felt as he had felt when standing beside her predecessor; but, alas! he was

twenty years further on towards the shade'. This persistence of youthful emotions in undiminished vigour is the source of his creativity
as an artist; but, for the man, it is a penalty and a burden – even a
'curse' (the word is used more than once in the novel) – which make
him envy the easier if duller lot of his contemporaries, who 'had
got past the distracting currents of passionateness, and were in the
calm waters of middle-aged philosophy'. The cruel irony of a still-
intense emotional life compelled to inhabit a decaying body is expressed
elsewhere in Hardy's work, and seems to have been keenly and
personally felt. At one point Pierston asks himself: 'When was it to
end – this curse of his heart not ageing while his frame moved
naturally onward?', and this sentence is virtually a paraphrase of
one of the finest of Hardy's short poems, written at about the same
time as this novel:

> I look into my glass,
> And view my wasting skin,
> And say, 'Would God it came to pass
> My heart had shrunk as thin!'

The poem serves to confirm, in case there should be any doubt, our
suspicion that the impulse behind the presentation of Pierston's sense
of life's irony was largely personal.

In spite of the title, then, the real subject of this book (particularly
in its later stages) is not love, platonically and fancifully conceived,
but time and age. An epigram near the end observes of Pierston
that 'Time was against him and love, and time would probably
win'. Another of the epigraphs in the book is from Shakespeare's
Sonnet 73 ('That time of year thou may'st in me behold'); and
Shakespeare's sonnets represent, of course, a classic treatment of
the same themes of love and time. The second of that sequence
('When forty winters shall besiege thy brow') is strongly recalled
by Hardy's memorable description of a woman seen again after the
lapse of forty years: she is now

> the image and superscription of Age – an old woman, pale and
> shrivelled, her forehead ploughed, her cheek hollow, her hair
> white as snow. To this the face he once kissed had been brought
> by the raspings, chisellings, scourgings, bakings, freezings of
> forty invidious years – by the thinkings of more than half a
> lifetime.

(In the same way, the poem of Hardy's cited above echoes a favourite device in the sonnets: see, for example, Sonnet 3 ('Look in thy glass . . .') and Sonnet 77 ('Thy glass will show thee how thy beauties wear').) Pierston's ambition is to defy time: he meets Avice the Third at the very spot at which, two generations earlier, he had arranged to meet her grandmother; but even though 'a secondly renewed copy of his sweetheart had arisen to fill her place', the inescapable truth is that 'he, alas, was not renewed'. At the end of the novel, Pierston is compelled to renounce his wish to marry Avice the Third: instead, he marries the shrivelled Marcia, who can offer him friendship but not love. With his acceptance of the situation, and of the inevitability of his own physical decay, there comes to him a placidity he has never known before – but the price of it is a complete loss of his creative powers, and even of his capacity for aesthetic appreciation. As he accepts the role of an old man for the first time, his emotional life comes to an end: he abandons his studio, and finds no more pleasure in the paintings in the National Gallery than in the crude work of the pavement-artist outside. But his response to this discovery is one of relief: what he has lost is 'a faculty which has, after all, brought me my greatest sorrows, if a few little pleasures', and he thanks Heaven that he is 'old at last': ' "The curse is removed." ' In retirement he becomes a pillar of the community, and almost the last glimpse we have of him is on his way to a public meeting to advocate

> a scheme for the closing of the old natural fountains in the Street of Wells, because of their possible contamination, and supplying the townlet with water from pipes. . . . He was also engaged in acquiring some old moss-grown, mullioned Elizabethan cottages, for the purpose of pulling them down because they were damp; which he afterwards did, and built new ones with hollow walls, and full of ventilators.

I cannot accept George Wing's reading of this strange and haunting passage as a 'benevolently muted finale', or Michael Millgate's view of the novel's conclusion as expressing a Prospero-like 'resignation'. Pierston does not merely drown his book: he accepts, with reprehensible (though understandable) blandness, the death of his heart. If we recall that Hardy had not only read some of the novels of Hawthorne but had also seen some of Ibsen's dramas, we can hardly ignore the powerful symbolism of these final images – symbolism which both summarizes and judges, quite uncompromisingly, this epilogue to Pierston's curious career. The 'old natural fountains' are the sources of creativity which are stopped; the ancient cottages are his own past, his childhood and his only true love, now destroyed and replaced by something more comfortable and efficient but 'hollow'. The fable of the artist's condition is concluded only in these closing lines of the book; and to Hardy, who was now in his fifties and for whom the revision of *The Well-Beloved* several years after its original publication was virtually his farewell to fiction, there must have been considerable elements of self-identification and self-questioning in his account of Pierston's fate.

Few, if any, passages preceding this conclusion, however, have such a resonant quality: as a whole the book suffers from an emotional poverty and a thinness of local texture. Its lack of inner compulsion, for all the personal elements which I believe it contains, is most clearly manifested at the level of style, which makes it a matter for astonishment that its composition should have come between that of two such masterpieces as *Tess* and *Jude*, and especially that it should have immediately followed a novel as linguistically varied and accomplished as *Tess*. It is almost as if Shakespeare had taken time off, between *King Lear* and *Macbeth*, to write *The Two Gentlemen of Verona*. Perhaps a kind of lowering of creative pressure was necessary for Hardy between two phases of intense imaginative productivity. But for all its weaknesses, general and local, *The Well-Beloved* seems to be a variation, even if only a minor one, on some of Hardy's central themes.

It is only fair to add that this slight and, psychologically speaking, not very interesting tale (I refer, of course, to the psychology of the characters, not of the author) is given a measure of solidity and a badly needed dimension of vividness by the use of a precisely rendered environment. The peninsula – not quite an island, though very nearly so – is where Pierston begins and ends, and where his most intense experiences take place. It is itself a work of natural sculpture, carved out of 'a single block of limestone four miles long', and its landscape and landmarks dominate the sculptor's memory and experience. Because of its geographical isolation and the custom of intermarriage among its inhabitants, who regard those from the mainland as 'kimberlins' or foreigners, it has changed little even in the nineteenth century: 'the manners of the isle were primitive and straightforward, even among the well-to-do'. Tradition holds that it was settled by Roman colonists, and that 'a temple of Venus once stood at the top of the Roman road leading up into the isle'. An effective symbol is that of the church which, thanks to a landslide, has slipped into a ravine and lies in ruins: the image reinforces the notion that paganism still retains its hold, after two thousand years, on the inhabitants. The carefully evoked atmosphere of the 'island' gives it a substantiality that is lacked by most of the characters in this book.

4
Short Stories

Hardy wrote nearly fifty short stories – a substantial body of work, equivalent in length to four or five of the novels; but it has not received a proportionate amount of attention from his critics. It is true that the wide variation in quality characteristic of Hardy's writings is at least as prominent in the short stories as in the novels and poems; but the judgment of a recent critic that 'Most of them . . . are not worth salvaging' seems to overstate the case, and the comment in another study of Hardy that 'The short stories *are* pot boilers' seems to miss the point. All Hardy's fiction, like Shakespeare's plays, was prompted by motives that were, in part at least, opportunist and commercial; but this is, *per se*, hardly a damaging consideration in estimating their literary worth. The best of the stories are no more and no less pot-boilers than *The Return of the Native* – or, for that matter, *King Lear*.

Their author at least appears to have deemed most of them 'worth salvaging', since he collected thirty-seven stories in four volumes over a period of a quarter of a century. *Wessex Tales* (1888) contains six stories written between 1879 and 1888; *A Group of Noble Dames* (1891), ten stories mainly dating from 1889–90, though two had appeared considerably earlier; *Life's Little Ironies* (1894), nine stories written between 1882 and 1893, the majority of them belonging to the years 1890 and 1891; and *A Changed Man* (1913), twelve stories written during the period 1881–1900. (Firm evidence of the date of composition is often lacking, but it seems reasonable to assume that it did not normally precede that of magazine publication by more than a short interval.) All these stories had appeared before the public in a variety of British and American periodicals before being collected. Some of the uncollected stories date from a little earlier in the 1870s than any of those collected, the earliest of all ('Destiny and a Blue Cloak') having been first published in 1874. Hardy's career as a writer of short stories therefore extends over more than twenty-five years, beginning soon after he made his début as a novelist with *Desperate Remedies*, and continuing for a few years after the publication of his last novels. (Indeed, the two parallel careers, as novelist and short-story writer, are of exactly equal length.)

As to how many or which of these fifty items, varying considerably in length, are of permanent interest there seems to be little agreement. Hardy told his American admirer Miss Rebekah Owen that he considered 'The Son's Veto' his finest short story; her vote went to 'The Three Strangers'; Florence Emily Hardy on another occasion nominated 'On the Western Circuit'. John Wain's recent selection is limited to seven stories and includes neither the first nor the third of these titles; among critics who have taken the stories into account in their assessment of Hardy's achievement, Douglas Brown mentions ten by title, George Wing about fifteen. Most, however, are passed over in a silence that, given Hardy's recognized status as a novelist, is somewhat puzzling.

Nor need we feel obliged to take at face value Hardy's own occasionally disparaging allusions to this branch of his art: he made similar and oft-quoted references to his novels, but the attitude of contempt towards both stories and novels is belied by the careful attention both received in the processes of composition and revision. When we have the kind of manuscript evidence assembled for Hardy that exists for Dickens (notably in the work of John Butt and Kathleen Tillotson), the famous remark that limited his ambition as a novelist to being 'a good hand at a serial' will be conclusively seen for what it is – excessive modesty or assumed indifference.

As far as the short stories are concerned, there are, apart from the issue already raised of their intrinsic literary quality, at least three ways in which they merit the attention of the serious Hardy student: they show very strikingly the range of his art and his exceptional capacity for mingling disparate types of fictional convention; they stand in a significant relationship to the major novels written during precisely the same period; and they exhibit in miniature some of the complex problems of composition and revision that make Hardy's text a territory full of interest and by no means yet exhaustively charted.

In answer to those who dismiss the stories as mainly negligible pot-boilers, one can point not only to the successive rewritings that Hardy patiently bestowed upon many of them, but also to the care he took in collecting them in volumes intended to possess a reasonable degree of internal unity. As late as 1912, for example, he took pains to reverse the positions of two stories – 'A Tradition of 1804' in *Life's Little Ironies* exchanging places with 'An Imaginative Woman' in *Wessex Tales* – for this reason. Such continuing concern hardly looks like indifference. But the homogeneity of these collections must not be exaggerated, for all except *A Group of Noble Dames* contain a considerable range of types. Of the first three stories in the earliest volume, *Wessex Tales*, for instance, one is a realistic story of middle-class urban life with a bitterly ironic conclusion, one a stylized and ballad-like romantic tale set in the 1820s, and the third a macabre excursion into the supernatural; what unites them, perhaps superficially, is the Wessex setting.

More generally, four types of stories may be distinguished: (1) those revealing a humorous and affectionate observation of rustic life (e.g., 'A Few Crusted Characters' (1891, *LLI*: the date given is that of first publication, the initials those of the volume in which the story was collected) and 'The Distracted Preacher' (1879, *WT*)); (2) tales on romantic or supernatural themes, often reminiscent of balladry and folk-tales (e.g., 'The Withered Arm' (1888, *WT*) and 'The Fiddler of the Reels' (1893, *LLI*)); (3) realistic and often ironic or tragic stories of modern life, usually later in date of composition than most of those in the previous two categories (e.g., 'On the Western Circuit' (1891, *LLI*) and 'An Imaginative Woman' (1894, *LLI*)); (4) historical tales, set in the Napoleonic period ('A Tradition of 1804' (1882, *WT*), 'The Melancholy Hussar of the German Legion' (1890, *LLI*)) or earlier (*A Group of Noble Dames*). Though there is inevitably some overlapping between these groups, each of them may be related to a distinctive element in Hardy's work as a whole. (1) has obvious affinities with the rustic portions of the Wessex novels, (2) with the many poems of ballad type in the *Collected Poems*, (3) with the late novels, especially *Tess of the D'Urbervilles* and *Jude the Obscure*, and (4) with *The Trumpet-Major* and *The Dynasts*. The last of these groups is probably the least interesting: stories like 'A Tradition of 1804' seem to resemble a discarded episode from one of the longer works cited, and with the exception of the powerful story 'Barbara of the House of Grebe', *A Group of Noble Dames* shows neither Hardy's characteristic preoccupations nor his imagination as fully engaged. As always, he conveys a sense of the past most successfully when he is not explicitly working with historical or pseudo-historical material.

The examples in the first of the four groups are not without interest, but add little to the knowledge of Hardy that is derived from the major fiction. Such stories as 'The Distracted Preacher', in which observation and recollection are shaped into rustic romance, with a stimulating touch of astringency, belong to the world of *Under the Greenwood Tree* and to comparable passages in some of the other novels. But the second and third groups contain stories that are not only successful in their own right but constitute an extension of Hardy's art, taking up (it is true) elements that exist elsewhere but developing them with the clarity and concentration demanded by the genre. It is here that we find the by no means negligible best of Hardy's work in the short-story medium, though it has so far been accorded little recognition.

Since demonstration must be specific to be useful, it will be necessary to concentrate on a handful of examples. It is true that the impression conveyed by any selection of material is inevitably misleading, and only a reading of the collected stories in their entirety can convey a full sense of the variety and inventiveness of Hardy's handling of the genre. (The uncollected stories are mostly of inferior quality, and Hardy's judgment on them was sound, though 'Our Exploits at West Poley' (1892, but rediscovered and republished only in 1952) is an interesting example of the way in which his persistent moral preoccupations emerge even in the context of a boys' adventure story; and 'Old Mrs. Chundle', probably written in the 1880s, but unpublished during Hardy's lifetime, shows an impressive modulation from grotesque comedy, through irony, to genuinely touching sentiment.) What can be more directly demonstrated, however, is the relationship of the minor to the major writings, as well as the textual vicissitudes of some items, which throw a revealing light on Hardy's working methods and on his attitude towards editors and reading public. I shall discuss more fully, therefore, two examples from each of the second and third categories enumerated above.

The earliest of the four, 'The Romantic Adventures of a Milkmaid', was published in England and America in 1883 but waited thirty years before being collected in *A Changed Man*. Its quality has been a source of disagreement even among Hardy's admirers: Douglas Brown praises it as 'ballad-like' and showing 'inventive energy and delight,' but C. J. Weber, with unaccustomed tartness, dismisses it as a 'worthless trifle'. Whatever its weaknesses, it has a flavour that is sufficiently individual to raise it above the mass of late-Victorian magazine fiction. It opens in a familiar vein of careful realism that recalls Hardy's debt to George Eliot: it is 'half-past four o'clock on a

May morning in the eighteen forties', and the symphony of rural noises as life begins to stir in the dairy farm – 'the bark of a dog', 'the slamming of a gate', 'women's voices', and soon 'the milk . . . buzzing into the pails' – is muted by 'a dense white fog'. The musical metaphors of the opening passage are of more than local interest, since the climax of the story is to involve music and dancing. When Hardy introduces the heroine, it is with a meticulous precision of visual detail (she wears 'a small woollen shawl of shepherd's plaid', a white handkerchief tied over her straw bonnet, and carries 'a withy basket, in which lay several butter-rolls in a nest of wet cabbage-leaves'); but her name, Margery Tucker, suggests not merely a rustic stereotype but the world of nursery-rhymes and folk-tales (Margery Daw, Tommy Tucker). The suggestion proves well-founded, for this realistic prologue precedes a story that strays to the frontiers of the supernatural and contains hints of Byronism and diabolism, as well as a recognizable debt to the Cinderella story. It exhibits, that is to say, the typically Hardyan mingling of disparate elements, realistic and fanciful or fantastic, implicit here in the title with its unfamiliar collocation of *romantic* and *milkmaid*. Such merging of apparently incompatible genres can also be found in the novels (*The Mayor of Casterbridge* is a case in point), and has proved a fertile source of puzzlement and disapproval among Hardy's critics.

The same story also incorporates some of the commonest ingredients of Hardy's fiction: the theme of class-distinctions (the milkmaid and the baron reversing the more familiar roles of the poor man and the lady); the conflict of old and new ways (Margery's 'Reels, and jigs, and country-dances' are scorned by the fashionable world in which she makes a brief appearance and which has 'gone crazy' over the newly arrived polka); the intrusion of the discontented and *déraciné* outsider into a happy and stable community (the Baron von Xanten is a spiritual brother to Fitzpiers in *The Woodlanders*); and the sometimes bizarre use of symbolism. Indeed, we have almost an anthology of his thematic and other preoccupations, full of echoes of what he had written and anticipations of what was still to come: Margery Tucker might, for instance, be seen as a very tentative first sketch for Tess Durbeyfield. There is, perhaps, *too* much, even for what is a short novel rather than a short story (its American serialization was in seven weekly instalments): although the tale is in essence a fairly simple one, it is padded out with description and dialogue and would have gained from a more disciplined structure and from more stylistic self-denial. It might have been even better as a ballad-poem; and it can fairly stand as an example of Hardy's failure to accommodate the kind of imaginative response prompted by his theme to the genre in which he was working. Yet it remains more readable and even memorable than Weber's curt dismissal allows for: as often, even Hardy's inferior work has, at moments at least, a curiously vivid and compelling quality. In one other respect it exemplifies a feature familiar in Hardy's fiction as a whole; the ending originally intended was abandoned in favour of one more likely 'to suit the requirements of the summer number of a periodical, *The Graphic*, in which the story was first printed' (the words are Hardy's, from a note written in his copy of *A Changed Man*, dated 1927 and now in the Dorset County Museum).

Ten years later, diabolism and dancing recur in a story that has often been regarded as Hardy's finest, 'The Fiddler of the Reels', and which serves to show how, working with somewhat similar materials to those in the earlier story, he was capable of a more controlled kind of art. Again, the story is set in a previous generation (it opens in the 1840s and moves on to the time of the Great Exhibition); and, like the Baron, 'Mop' Ollamoor, with his 'un-English' appearance, 'rich olive' complexion, and long dark hair, is an exotic, an orchid in the Wessex hedgerows. He represents paganism (he 'had never, in all likelihood, entered a church at all'), and effects conversion to his own creed of sensuality through his violin-playing ('All were devil's tunes in his repertory'). It is not too much to claim that, in 'Mop', described at the outset as 'a woman's man', Hardy achieved the near-impossible for a late-Victorian popular novelist in his account of the irresistible power of the sexual impulse stirred by a practised seducer. He does it by poetic rather than realistic means, and by metaphor rather than statement or analysis (compare the poem 'The Dance at the Phoenix', in which an elderly woman married to a steady husband leaves her bed to dance wildly under the spell produced by the music of the King's Own Cavalry). Mop's fiddling produces a semi-hypnotic effect, an involuntary impulse to abandon normal decorum and to dance until the point of exhaustion is reached: these 'compelled capers' (in Hardy's phrase) lead to the girl's seduction; and, years later, when she has made a respectable marriage, a second bout of dancing ends in the disappearance of 'Mop' with the child: a rape, that is, in another sense. The nearest parallel in the novels is probably Sergeant Troy of *Far from the Madding Crowd*, but there the handling of the theme of sexual power seems relatively crude. The simple patterning of 'The Fiddler of the Reels' is entirely satisfying, and the power of Mop's music-making is a perfect symbol for his personal magnetism; at the same time, fantasy is kept under control, and for all the hints as to the protagonist's true nature, the background is reassuringly realistic – both in the rural settings and in the London scenes, with the excursion-train and the visit to the Exhibition.

The two stories discussed so far are poetic and romantic, with obvious affiliations to the early and middle-period Wessex novels. The remaining two show a different aspect of Hardy's art, one that recalls Gissing and George Moore, and which is exemplified in the major novels only by *Jude the Obscure*. 'On the Western Circuit' appeared alongside 'The Fiddler of the Reels' in *Life's Little Ironies*, but offers a striking contrast in mode. Set 'in the city of Melchester', its milieu is urban and bourgeois: the two protagonists are a young barrister and the wife of a prosperous wine-merchant; and, rather than looking back to a past generation, its period is apparently that of its composition. The situation is developed, and the central irony made plain, with admirable economy, and the story seems a sufficient response to critics who believe Hardy to have been incapable of a plot that was not mechanical and over-elaborate. It has, too, another kind of interest that is worth expounding, in the development of its text from manuscript to the various printed versions. Four distinct stages in its textual history may be observed: (1) Hardy's holograph, given to the Manchester Central Library in 1911, and described by Purdy (p. 84) as 'the original, unbowdlerized version'; (2) its first appearance in print in England, in *The English Illustrated Magazine* for December 1891 (and in America in *Harper's Weekly* for 28 November of the same year); (3) the galley-proofs of *Life's Little Ironies*, showing, according to Purdy, 'a number of interesting alterations', dated December 1893, and now in the Dorset County Museum; (4) the version in that collection, as published on 22 February 1894 by Osgood, McIlvaine & Co.

Purdy's description of the manuscript as 'the original . . . version' implies that, as on other occasions, Hardy first wrote the story he wanted to write, subsequently modified it to satisfy his editor and Mrs Grundy, and finally restored the original text when the story appeared in volume form. An examination of the manuscript, however, suggests that this is not quite what happened. The original version was indeed bowdlerized, as I shall illustrate more fully in a moment; but the final version represents not simply a restoration of the original but to some extent a revision of it in which the frankness in the handling of the sexual situation is markedly increased. There were, that is to say, changes introduced both in the transition from manuscript to serial and, later, from serial to volume. Hardy's own dating of the final version of the story in *Life's Little Ironies* as 'Autumn 1891' is therefore misleading. After briefly considering the nature of the story, some specific examples of the changes introduced will make the trend of his revisions clearer.

The theme, like that of *Jude the Obscure*, relates to 'the marriage question': a young woman, sexually and emotionally unfulfilled by a marriage of convenience to an elderly and disagreeable husband, enters into a correspondence with a young barrister who has seduced one of her servants. Since the girl is illiterate, her mistress agrees to compose and write her love-letters, unknown to the recipient, and soon she finds herself pouring her deepest feelings into the letters and forming a close if one-sided attachment to the young man whom she has seen only once and briefly. It is not until he has married the girl, whom he has made pregnant, that the truth emerges, and he finds himself, like his true correspondent, 'chained' for the rest of his days to an incompatible spouse. Hardy, whose own marriage had by this time proved disastrous, had a more than detached interest in such a situation; but, in any case, from the point of view of a periodical intended for a family audience, the situation was hardly less explosive than that of *Tess*, which was actually in the process of serial publication when the story under discussion was written. Hardy's revisions ranged from the alteration of a single epithet to the omission of whole paragraphs, but it will be enough to note two major adjustments comparable to the mangling of *Tess* which he had found himself obliged to perform a little earlier. The wife of the original becomes a widow, her husband's role being taken over more or less intact by an uncle: at a stroke, that is, any hint of infidelity, even of the spiritual kind, is avoided. The numerous minor revisions consequent upon this change need not be noted, but two of them are of interest. When the servant-girl suggests, naively but with unconscious irony, that writing love-letters for her can have no effect on her mistress's feelings, Hardy wrote as her comment, ' "Because you are married already!" ' For the same reason, the wife's despairing cry towards the end of the story, ' "Ah – my husband! – I forgot I had a husband!" ' is sacrificed. Both reappear in the final version.

Second, all references to the fact that the marriage is necessitated by the girl's pregnancy are scrupulously excised. It is worth noting, however, that two of the most striking sentences in the story as we read it today did not appear in the manuscript: one is the comment that the wife's marriage 'had left her still a woman whose deeper nature had never been stirred', the other the even more unconventional remark 'That he had been able to seduce another woman in two days was his crowning though unrecognized fascination for her as the she-animal'. Editorial hands were never held up in horror at such a frank diagnosis of the power of sexual needs and impulse, since the sentences were afterthoughts inserted after the appearance of the story in magazine form.

In summary, Hardy revised his original version of this story twice, at different times and for different reasons. On the first occasion the pressures were external – those of the editor and readers of a popular magazine; and the example shows on a small scale what *Tess* and *Jude* display more extensively in their textual history: that he was prepared to undertake major alterations of content in order to produce an inoffensive, and therefore commercially viable, literary commodity. The second revision seems to have been undertaken, on the other hand, to please himself: it is partly concerned with sharpening some of the stylistic effects, but also stresses even more fully than the earliest version the sexual element, by way of belated compensation, as it were, for what had been omitted and distorted in the interim. Not only is 'On the Western Circuit' one of the most powerful of Hardy's short stories, but it provides additional evidence of his preoccupation with the theme of marital disharmony during the years that saw the publication of *Tess* and the writing of *Jude*.

My final example, 'An Imaginative Woman', which was eventually to stand first in *Wessex Tales*, having been included in the new edition of 1896, belongs to the same period – it was written (according to Hardy's note) in 1893 and first published in April 1894 – and shares a similar setting and tone. The scene is 'a well-known watering-place in Upper Wessex', the social background is middle class (the heroine's husband is 'a gunmaker in a thriving city northwards'), and again the theme is a woman's attempt to find relief from an unsatisfactory marriage in fantasy – this time in an idealized relationship with a poet who has previously occupied their lodgings. Hardy seems to have been engaged on the planning of *Jude the Obscure* at the same time that this story was written, and *The Well-Beloved* had been completed and published for the first time in the previous year. 'An Imaginative Woman' seems to derive its theme from both novels – the yoking together in matrimony of dissimilar temperaments from the former, and the pursuit of an ideal lover from the latter (with a female protagonist in place of the sculptor Pierston). The poignant conclusion of the story, with the widowed husband's unfounded rejection of his child (who resembles the dead poet) as a bastard, prompted a defence of the plausibility of this device in Hardy's Preface to *Wessex Tales* (dated April 1896): he wrote there that the story 'turns upon a physical possibility that may attach to women of imaginative temperament, and that is well supported by the experiences of medical men and other observers of such manifestations'. It is interesting that Hardy, who had elsewhere published stories far more fantastic without explanation, should have felt it necessary to speak in his own defence: nothing, perhaps, could better underline the essential difference of kind between stories such as this one and the unashamedly romantic type referred to earlier.

The manuscript of 'An Imaginative Woman', like that of 'On the Western Circuit', is heavily corrected, especially in the opening pages: the second leaf alone, for example, contains nearly forty alterations, insertions and deletions, made (it appears from the handwriting) at different times and including the addition of a substantial passage on the verso evidently inserted as an afterthought. This is not the place to discuss the nature of Hardy's revisions in detail, but their very existence gives the lie not only to the view of him as a careless stylist but to the notion that these unjustly neglected tales were dashed off in the intervals of more serious literary labours to satisfy a commercial need. Hardy took pains over these and other stories; and, apart from those mentioned, there are a dozen or more that deserve to be read by virtue of their intrinsic qualities as well as on account of the reflected interest which belongs to the minor work of a major writer. I have said nothing, for instance, of such tales as 'The Three Strangers' (*WT*), 'The Son's Veto' (*LLI*), 'A Tragedy of Two Ambitions' (*LLI*) or 'The Waiting Supper' (*CM*). Hardy's supposed indifference to his short stories is belied by the considerable care he took in writing, revising and collecting them; he was in any case the most modest of great novelists where his own fictional achievements were concerned, and we would be wise not to insist upon taking the stories at his own valuation.

5
Non-fictional Prose

The present chapter describes the nature and extent of Hardy's prose writings apart from his novels and stories: his prefaces; various articles and other short pieces which it will be convenient to refer to as essays; his letters; his autobiography; and his notebooks and diaries. With the exception of the autobiography, none of these is of major significance in its own right; but all serve to some degree to illuminate Hardy's mind and personality, and often provide specific insights into the characteristic preoccupations which find more formal expression in his fiction and poetry.

Prefaces

Hardy composed at various times nearly forty prefaces for his volumes of fiction and verse, varying in length from a short note to a full-dress essay. The earlier novels were originally issued without prefaces, but at the time of their reissue in the first uniform edition (as 'The Wessex Novels' in sixteen volumes, 1895–6), he took the opportunity of glancing at them retrospectively, assessing their virtues and defects in the light of experience, and recalling their reception and subsequent history. In many cases he added a further preface or a postscript for the 'Wessex Edition', published from 1912. A 'General Preface to the Novels and Poems' was written in 1911 for the same edition. *Tess* and *Jude* are exceptional among the novels in possessing important prefaces written for their first editions: by that stage in his career Hardy seems to have felt sufficiently independent to nail his colours to the mast, but also sufficiently disquieted about public reactions to his novels to wish to forestall criticism. The various volumes of verse and *The Dynasts* also have their own prefaces.

Hardy was no Henry James, and his prefaces neither offer nor claim to offer a substantial or coherent body of critical theory or reflection:

they deal in the main with specific and *ad hoc* matters arising from the work in question, though some important exceptions to this generalization will be noted below. The prefaces to the minor novels, mostly written long after their composition, are often apologetic or dismissive. Of *Desperate Remedies* he confesses that it was 'written . . . at a time when he was feeling his way to a method', and later describes it as a 'sensational and strictly conventional narrative'; looking again at *A Pair of Blue Eyes*, he concedes the 'immaturity in its views of life and in its workmanship'; *The Hand of Ethelberta* is a 'somewhat frivolous narrative'; and *Two on a Tower* a 'slightly-built romance'. The preface to *The Trumpet-Major* is more interesting than most: the novel is based not only on documentary sources but on the recollections of 'old persons well known to the author in childhood . . . who were eye-witnesses of those scenes', and on his memories of 'casual relics [which] brought to my imagination in early childhood the state of affairs at the date of the war more vividly than volumes of history could have done'. Topics touched on elsewhere include the revival of the term 'Wessex' in *Far from the Madding Crowd*, the use of dialect in *The Mayor of Casterbridge*, and the chronology and topography of *The Return of the Native* (we learn that the action is set in the 1840s, and that Egdon is a conflation of 'at least a dozen' actual heaths).

As already noted, the prefaces to the later novels often anticipate, and attempt to answer, hostile criticism and charges of pessimism. One of Hardy's favourite defensive gambits is to disclaim any consistent or systematic philosophy in his work: by insisting, as he does in the preface to *Tess*, that 'a novel is an impression, not an argument', he is in effect refusing to accept personal responsibility for the ideas which a novel appears to enunciate, for he claims that the views embodied in a work of fiction are no more a permanent and settled expression of its author's convictions than those embodied in a short poem. In the same preface, written in 1892, he adds that the book was intended to be 'neither didactic nor aggressive', but 'representative' in the scenic portions, and 'oftener charged with impressions than with convictions'. Three years later he is more explicitly disparaging of the novel, and goes even further in the rejection of responsibility: 'the pages are allowed to stand for what they are worth, as something once said; but probably they would not have been written now'. In the same year the preface to the first edition of *Jude* pursues similar tactics: it is not to be read as propaganda fiction or a novel with a purpose, but as 'a series of seemings, or personal impressions'.

A more direct defence of this allegedly impressionistic and non-didactic method appeared a few years later in the preface to *Poems of the Past and the Present*: referring to the apparent lack of 'cohesion of thought' in his poetry, Hardy writes there: 'Unadjusted impressions have their value, and the road to a true philosophy of life seems to lie in humbly recording diverse readings of its phenomena as they are forced upon us by chance and change.' One of the formal embodiments of these 'diverse readings' is the dramatic monologue, and at several points Hardy insists on the prominence of this type of poem in his own work, and the impersonal nature even of poems which may bear all the signs of making personal statements. Our reaction to this insistence may be to object that Hardy protests too much; but this does not exempt us from confronting the elementary but vital critical problem implicit in his claims, a problem relevant to both fiction and poetry, and one to which it will be necessary to return in a later chapter: how far can we feel justified in identifying the narrator of the novels and the stories, and the 'I' of the poems, with the historical Thomas Hardy? There are clearly instances where such identification is difficult or impossible; but it is also hard to resist the suspicion that Hardy is anxious, for reasons of his own, to persuade us of the impersonality of more of his work than can credibly lend itself to this kind of interpretation. It was deep personal reticence which prompted the manifestly untrue statement that there is 'not a line of autobiography' in *Jude the Obscure*, and it would be unwise to apply too literally and too comprehensively his description of his poems (in the preface to *Late Lyrics and Earlier*) as 'fugitive impressions'.

The 'General Preface to the Novels and Poems' repeats the same claims with respect to his work in prose and verse over more than forty years. No 'consistent philosophy', he maintains, has been attempted: he offers 'mere impressions of the moment, and not convictions or arguments'. In the same essay he comments on his system of classification of the Wessex Novels into three categories, defends the geographical limitations of their settings on the grounds that the characters are typical of humanity in general, and claims that his accounts of Wessex possess historical authenticity as 'a fairly true record of a vanishing life'. A revealing distinction is made between the 'freedom' of the writer of verse and the bondage of the purveyor of serial fiction, who is liable to 'accidents' which obstruct 'the channel between the writer and the public'.

Essays

Apart from his prefaces, Hardy wrote some thirty or more prose pieces which may be loosely described as essays. These have been conveniently collected by Harold Orel, who also provides an annotated list of nearly seventy other items too brief or too limited in interest to be worth reprinting. The 'essays' include non-fictional contributions to British and American magazines, prefaces to volumes by other authors, letters to the press and speeches delivered on various occasions. The range of topics may be suggested by identifying a few sample items: a letter to the *Athenaeum* on dialect in novels, and another to the *Spectator* on the same subject; a moving obituary on the Dorset poet William Barnes; a review (apparently the only one Hardy ever wrote) of a volume of Barnes's poems; brief reminiscences of Stevenson and Meredith; a note on 'The Ancient Cottages of England'; an interview on Stonehenge; and a list of what he considered the finest views in Dorset. Most of them add little that is new or substantial to our understanding of Hardy; but four of the longer pieces, two on literary and two on non-literary matters, are worth singling out for separate discussion.

'The Profitable Reading of Fiction' was published in 1888 in a New York magazine. It distinguishes four reasons, apart from simple time-killing, for the reading of novels. By way of clearing the ground, Hardy takes those of lesser importance first. The 'sudden shifting of the mental perspective into a fictitious world' may be healthful for the reader, and aid 'renovation' – by which Hardy seems to mean not merely relaxation, but a kind of emotional therapy (he refers rather quaintly to 'hygienic purposes' in novel-reading). Such purposes require a particular kind of novel, offering a complete change of setting and subject-matter from the reader's actual existence, and an 'absorbing' narrative. For his part, the reader of this kind of fiction is required to suspend such critical faculties as he may possess: 'However . . . profusely [the novelist] may pour out his coincidences, his marvellous juxtapositions, his catastrophes, his conversions of bad people into good people at a stroke, and *vice versa*, let him never be doubted for a moment.' (This description fits the 'sensation novel', which Hardy had flirted with in *Desperate Remedies* but quickly abandoned.) The 'intellectual stir' which arises from the reader's identification of characters, events and issues in the fiction with the circumstances and problems of his own life is to be avoided. Such a function, though not beneath contempt, is hardly an exalted one; and little more can be said of Hardy's second reason for novel-reading: the 'intellectual or moral profit' which may arise not so much from the characters or action of the story as from 'the accidents and appendages of narrative'. By the phrase Hardy means the custom of providing the novel with a stiffening of aphoristic moralizing and miscellaneous information: 'didactic reflection', 'trifles of useful knowledge', 'statistics', 'queer historic fact', 'specimens of the manners of good or bad society', 'quotations from ancient and other authors'. Hardy notes that such novels, which generally fail to give 'a picture of life in action', are less common than formerly.

From these relatively trivial kinds of 'profitable reading', Hardy turns to more important considerations. Rather than presenting 'views *about* life', the novel can offer 'representations of life', in which the moralizing is implicit; such books can provide 'a humanizing education'. Paradoxically, this kind of novel may actually carry more ethical weight than the novel avowedly written with a moral purpose; the didactic novel is generally so unconvincing in imaginative terms as to lack moral force. Hardy makes a plea for moral honesty in the novelist, and it is at this point that one perceives the close relevance of the arguments he is advancing to his own practice as a creative writer. The novelist must present life as he sees it as truthfully as he can; yet 'realism' is not enough, for his province is not the photographic rendering of the surface of life, but the depicting of the 'eternal' and the 'essential', the 'perennial procedure of humanity'. Any estimate of the effect of such a truthful portrayal of life (and this part of the essay seems prophetic of the troubles with *Tess* and *Jude* that were soon to come) must concern itself with the mature adult reader:

> A novel which does moral injury to a dozen imbeciles, and has
> bracing results upon a thousand intellects of normal vigour,
> can justify its existence; and probably a novel was never written
> by the purest-minded author for which there could not be found
> some moral invalid or other whom it was capable of harming.

Fourth, an artistically constructed story can provide 'aesthetic training': a novel may have 'a beauty of shape' as much as a picture or statue, though few readers are conscious of this aspect of fiction. Hardy's appreciation of form in the novel is worth remembering as a corrective to the widespread notion that his fiction is the antithesis of that of his contemporary Henry James: James's preoccupation with form was certainly more explicit, more sophisticated and more persistent, but

F

Hardy was far from being the naive teller of artless tales he has some-times been depicted.

The essay concludes with a reference to 'the mentally and morally warped ones of both sexes, who will, where practicable, so twist plain and obvious meanings as to see in an honest picture of human nature an attack on religion, morals, or institutions.' Nearly two years later, Hardy took up the question of the misinterpretation of honest intentions in 'Candour in English Fiction', published in the *New Review*. In the interim, the troubles over *Tess* had infused Hardy's attitude to this question with a good deal of bitterness, and the later essay reflects the pressure of personal experience. Why, he begins by asking, is so much contemporary fiction 'a literature of quackery', which shirks 'things which everybody is thinking but nobody is saying'? Since there is no reason to suppose that the well of potential literary talent and imaginative power is shallower than in other epochs, the feebleness of the general level of fiction must be blamed on external causes. Literature ought to reflect, reveal and criticize life; and 'Life being a physiological fact, its honest portrayal must be largely concerned with, for one thing, the relations of the sexes'; but to the frank and full treatment of sexual relationships 'English society opposes a well-nigh insuperable bar'. Thanks to the two external forces which operate upon contemporary fiction, the magazine and the circulating library, the novelist is driven to cowardice and compromise: he can only satisfy editors and librarians at the expense of his own artistic conscience, and 'if the true artist ever weeps it probably is then'. As a result the major themes of great literature are excluded: Hardy invites us to contemplate the fate of Shakespeare submitting *Othello*, *Hamlet* or *Antony and Cleopatra* as novels to 'the editor of a London magazine', and a footnote points out that Sophocles, Aeschylus, Goethe and Milton would find their work similarly unacceptable. The 'young person' standard is vigorously attacked: 'all fiction should not be shackled by conventions concerning budding womanhood, which may be altogether false'; and the article concludes with some practical suggestions for reform: it ought to be possible to produce books cheaply enough for them to be bought and not borrowed from circulating libraries which interpose their own code of censorship between author and reader; serial stories for adults should be published in newspapers, as distinct from those for family consumption published in magazines; and there might be magazines intended specifically for adult readers rather than for a general reader-ship. The essay reveals that Hardy not only felt strongly on this subject, but had given thought to the sources of the problem and to practical remedies.

'The Dorsetshire Labourer', published 1883, makes interesting reading in conjunction with the Wessex novels, showing as it does Hardy's intimate knowledge of the life and customs of the rural labourer, and his understanding of the forces that were making for change. He exposes the familiar stereotype of 'Hodge' as over-simplified and erroneous:

> This supposed real but highly conventional Hodge is a degraded being of uncouth manner and aspect, stolid understanding, and snail-like movement. His speech is such a chaotic corruption of regular language that few persons of progressive aims consider it worth while to enquire what views, if any, of life, of nature, or of society are conveyed in these utterances. Hodge hangs his head or looks sheepish when spoken to, and thinks Lunnon a place paved with gold. Misery and fever lurk in his cottage.

Hardy refutes this picture, insisting that country folk, like all other men, are individuals capable of endless variety. He demonstrates a strikingly well-informed acquaintance with the circumstances of their lives: how they are hired, what they wear, how much they earn, even precisely how they load the carts when they remove their household goods; and he notes the increasing mobility of labourers and the depopulation of the countryside. He is far from being sentimental about change:

> the artistic merit of their old condition is scarcely a reason why they should have continued in it when other communities were marching on so vigorously towards uniformity and mental equality. It is only the old story that progress and picturesqueness do not harmonize. They are losing their individuality, but they are widening the range of their ideas, and gaining in freedom. It is too much to expect them to remain stagnant and old-fashioned for the pleasure of romantic spectators.

Hardy weighs judiciously the inevitability of progress and change against the loss of values associated with the older and more stable way of life, the 'intimate and kindly relation with the land he tills' and the influence of 'domestic stability' as 'a factor in conduct': 'with uncertainty of residence often comes a laxer morality, and more cynical views of the duties of life'. Many of the themes touched on in this essay were to be returned to, as Professor Orel points out, in *Tess of the D'Urbervilles*.

Finally, 'Memories of Church Restoration', published in the *Cornhill* in 1906, recalls Hardy's architectural career a generation earlier. Its most revealing statement maintains that 'the human interest in an edifice ranks before its architectural interest, however great the latter may be'. In a later passage he again distinguishes between the 'aesthetic' and 'associative' responses aroused by an old building, and insists that the latter are 'more valuable'. Hardy was to reiterate the point yet again in his autobiography, where he asserts the superiority of 'beauty of association' to 'beauty of aspect'. Applied to his novels, these statements help to define his use of background, both architectural and scenic: the emotional power of a building or a landscape depends ultimately on its quality as a record of the human lives which have been associated with it, as a surviving memorial to what would otherwise have been completely lost, and as a poignant reminder of the durability of the inanimate in contrast to the tenuousness of human existence.

Letters

The edition of Hardy's correspondence now being prepared by Professors R. L. Purdy and Michael Millgate will contain some 5,000 letters which have survived from the epistolary activity of more than sixty years and are now widely scattered in public and private collections. Their publication is likely to add little or nothing to Hardy's stature as a writer. As a correspondent, he was far from being a Keats or a Byron, delighting in the spontaneous expression of the thoughts and emotions of the moment: he was too withdrawn and self-watchful to be a great letter-writer, his letters tend to be brief and matter-of-fact, and moments of self-revelation are rare. They will undoubtedly provide, however, a source of useful material for biographical and scholarly work in many directions, and will offer occasional flashes – the more vivid for being rare – of his elusive personality. Inevitably, there will be some major gaps in the record, and important chapters in his emotional life will remain undocumented; for example, none of his letters to his first wife before their marriage appear to be extant, and although a substantial number of his later letters to her survive, there are none from her. What remains is often unrevealing, though its very taciturnities may themselves be significant. The trivial, conventional and humourless letters to his first wife suggest not so much the personal limitations of Hardy as the failure of their marriage and the absence of any close communion between them: as C. J. Weber has suggested, the exchange of views on serious topics such as literature and religion became impossible for them, and 'what was left was the weather, wedding receptions, and cats'. Perhaps the most eloquent feature of this group of letters is the gradual change in the salutations and signatures, from 'My Dearest Emmie' to 'Dear E', and from 'Tom' to 'T.H.'.

There are a few other letters to members of his family, but most of Hardy's correspondence is either professional – to editors, publishers, illustrators, anthologists and the like – or to a wide circle of literary and other acquaintances. He exchanged letters with many of the most notable writers of his time, including some whose notions of literature were very different from his own; and 'his time', of course, extends from the mid-Victorian period to the Georgian, so that his list of correspondents includes not only Swinburne, Meredith, Morris, Gissing, Housman and Stevenson, but Yeats, Pound, Wells, Siegfried Sassoon and Virginia Woolf. Others include publishers and editors such as Alexander Macmillan, Leslie Stephen and W. E. Henley; theatrical figures such as Ellen Terry and Harley Granville-Barker; and a wide range of notabilities, including Asquith, who, as Prime Minister, offered Hardy a knighthood (which he refused) in 1908. There also survive more substantial collections of letters written to and from an inner circle of close friends. Sir George Douglas, Scottish baronet and man of letters, was a sympathetic correspondent whose friendship covered nearly forty years. Edward Clodd, banker and patron of the arts, was another long-standing friend, who entertained Hardy at Aldeburgh and corresponded with him frequently. Sir Sydney Cockerell, Director of the Fitzwilliam Museum, Cambridge, was entrusted by Hardy with the distribution of a number of his manuscripts to various institutions in 1911. The earliest important item in Hardy's correspondence is a group of letters from Horace Moule; Hardy's side of the correspondence seems to have vanished, but Moule's letters, written between 1860 and 1873, give a clear impression of the nature of their relationship. Moule served as literary mentor to Hardy when he was learning to write, and his letters contain advice on points of style and grammar, and some frank but friendly criticism of the early novels.

Most of the surviving letters, however, are from Hardy's later years, when he was an established literary figure with an international reputation. They include an extensive fan-mail, and show him to have been a voluminous, prompt and scrupulous letter-writer, often replying fully and kindly to unknown correspondents – except when they seemed disposed to enquire into his personal life and its relationship to his work.

The publication of the collected letters is unlikely to offer much help towards the resolution of the biographical problems confronting the student of Hardy: the two bonfires of 1919 and 1928 no doubt involved the destruction of the most intimate and revealing letters. But the considerable number which survive – an even larger number if we add the letters written *to* Hardy, from which interesting inferences can sometimes be drawn – furnish a mass of information on such topics as contemporary book- and magazine-publishing, as well as many insights into Hardy's attitude to his work and its reception. They present, moreover, a striking and in some ways unfamiliar portrait of Hardy as a man of many, diverse and enduring friendships – one very different from the gloomy recluse or awkward countryman that he is sometimes supposed to have been.

Hardy's Autobiography

The Life of Thomas Hardy, which in spite of appearances is almost entirely an autobiography proceeding from Hardy's own hand, is his last major work in prose, and is probably the strangest as well as the most directly revealing of all his books. According to Leon Edel, Henry James was convinced that the author who found himself the object of biographical curiosity should 'do his utmost to assure the silence of the tomb' and to win 'a victory for privacy'. In the autobiography, Hardy tries in a remarkable and perhaps even unique way to win such a victory – paradoxically, though, not by silence but through a process of apparent revelation. James seems to have had in mind the destruction of evidence; Hardy's different solution to the same problem (though the destruction of evidence was also involved) was to manufacture a version of the truth convincing enough to discourage further attempts. Its publication involved premeditated deception and sustained pretence; and even today the full nature of the literary fraud or confidence-trick that it represents has not been universally admitted.

Fully to appreciate its oddity, it is necessary to begin at the beginning. One of the privileges, or penalties, of longevity for a writer is to enjoy, or endure, the kind of retrospective surveys of his life and work which are normally reserved for the mighty dead – with all the inaccuracies, half-truths and wrong emphases to which such undertakings are prone. By way of compensation, he has the opportunity of setting the record straight, or of providing his own version of the truth, through autobiography; or of selecting his biographer and providing the materials for the latter's authorized labours. Hardy's solution to this was characteristically and curiously devious. He had always been morbidly sensitive to criticism of his work, and resentful of intrusions into his personal privacy. When the *Spectator* gave a fairly harsh review to his first published novel, 'he wished he were dead'; when the first two full-length studies of his novels appeared in 1894, he wrote to a friend that 'they are not in bad taste on the whole, if one concedes that they had to be written which I do not quite'. He consistently cold-shouldered aspiring biographers, did his best to discourage their efforts, and dissociated himself from them if they reached fruition. In correspondence with those who wished to investigate his personal life, he can be uncharacteristically curt and ungracious, making little secret of his wish that the task might never be pursued; and his letters contain many caustic references to the intrusions and inaccuracies of journalists and interviewers ('penny-a-liners' is his favourite term). In his preface to *Tess of the D'Urbervilles* he deplores the activities of critics who 'pervert plain meanings and grow personal under the name of practising the great historical method'; and he can be palpably untruthful in his endeavours to put investigators off the scent – in his insistence, for example, that there is not a word of autobiography in *Jude the Obscure*.

Not surprisingly, his reserve prevented him for a long time from taking a hand in the writing of his own life, though he was often urged to do so. In November 1915, for example, we find his friend Sir George Douglas asking in a letter, 'When are you going to write your Reminiscences?' – a question which must have been put by others on many occasions. Since Hardy was seventy-five at this time, such a proposal was scarcely premature. Coincidentally, a letter from another friend, Sir Sydney Cockerell, written only a few days after Douglas's, implies that the possibility had already been canvassed in conversation:

> I am again impelled to urge you to write down something about yourself – and especially about that youthful figure whose photograph I have got, and of whom you told me that you could think with almost complete detachment. Your sister's death will have revived many sleeping memories and set your thought travelling over those early days.

If some discussion can be assumed on the basis of this letter, it would appear to be the earliest surviving evidence that the possibility of an autobiography had been entertained. It is true that, more than two years later (in March 1918), we find Hardy responding in discouraging terms to the suggestion of the editor of the *Evening News* that he should write his reminiscences for publication, and stating his decision not to undertake an autobiography; but this must have been intended to mislead, since Hardy was almost certainly actively engaged on his reminiscences by this time. A letter written in 1919 by Mrs Hardy to Macmillan's strongly suggests, indeed, that the work had been begun early in 1916.

A few years earlier than the episodes I have referred to, the appearance of a book written in French and published in Paris may well have helped him to overcome his deep-rooted distaste of writing about himself. This was F. A. Hedgcock's *Thomas Hardy: penseur et artiste*, a full-length study containing much biographical material both factual and speculative. Hardy's own copy of the book, extensively annotated, has survived; and the annotations, particularly heavy in the portion dealing with his early years, very clearly indicate the indignation and contempt he felt on reading it. Reading between the lines of Hardy's tart and angry marginalia, one senses that two features of the book especially irritated him: the emphasis upon his humble origins, and the speculations on the relationship between his fiction and his own experience. There had also been other instances of published interviews, authentic and otherwise, which offended Hardy deeply. He would certainly have agreed with the well-known views of W. H. Auden on an author's right to privacy, and with A. E. Housman, who remarked on one occasion that 'the wish to include a glimpse of my personality in a literary article is low, unworthy, and American'. It seems reasonably clear that the cumulative effect of these intrusions, and the promulgation of what he believed (or at least claimed) to be misrepresentations of the facts, led him, against the grain of his own instincts, to undertake the writing of his life. By design, it was not published until after his death; it then appeared, and has continued to appear to this day, with the name of Florence Emily Hardy, his second wife, on the title page; and although the fact of Hardy's authorship of almost the entire work has been recognized for many years, the various editions of the book have contributed to the impression that it is a pious biographical memorial. Perhaps for this reason it is still surprisingly common to meet references to it as the 'biography' of Hardy 'by his widow'. The history of its composition has never been described in detail; but in spite of the wholesale and systematic destruction of private papers before and after Hardy's death, enough has survived to make possible a reconstruction – sometimes tentative, but in general outlines sufficiently clear – of the making of this remarkable book. Such an undertaking shows Hardy to have been frequently devious and occasionally dishonest, concealing even while apparently engaging in the task of revelation. The autobiography – heavily circumstantial, crammed with information – appears to be digressively full and frank; it presents, however, a carefully doctored version of the truth, and in some respects an incomplete one. The process of reconstruction also suggests that this book was an important preoccupation of the last ten or dozen years of his life – the same period, that is, which produced a large proportion of the poems in his last three volumes of verse, poems whose impulse must often have owed something to the recollection and reliving of emotion and experience produced by the composition of the *Life* and the perusal of old diaries and letters which it entailed.

The circumstances in which the *Life* originally appeared suggest at once that it is something other than a straightforward official biography. The first of the two volumes of original publication, *The Early Life*, was sent to the publisher within less than three weeks of Hardy's death, and was published before the end of the year; the second volume, *The Later Years*, appeared seventeen months later. If this remarkably prompt delivery of the manuscripts by Hardy's widow and supposed biographer provoked any questions as to their origins, they seem not to have been pursued; and the title page and prefatory note to the first volume provided little enlightenment. The title page declares the book to have been 'compiled largely from contemporary notes, letters, diaries, and biographical memoranda, as well as from oral information in conversations extending over many years by Florence Emily Hardy' – a formula which calls up a picture of the wife or widow working dutifully through her husband's papers, and searching her memories for the conversations of past years. Such a picture certainly bears no resemblance to what actually took place. With some inconsistency, the prefatory note speaks of Hardy himself setting down 'headings of chapters, etc., and, in especial, memories of his early days whenever they came into his mind' – a gross understatement of Hardy's share in the sifting of materials and the writing of the book, but nevertheless admitting a more deliberate participation by the subject. Knowing what we do, it is difficult not to catch a trace of irony in the penultimate paragraph of the same note:

It may be added that in the book generally Mr. Hardy's own
reminiscent phrases have been used or were written down at the
time of their expression *viva voce*. On this point great trouble
has been taken to secure exactness.

The 'phrases' are exact for the excellent reason that they were written
down by Hardy, as was, almost certainly, the note itself: the implied
situation, in which conversations were recalled or recorded Boswell-
fashion, simply never existed. There is, incidentally, an unconscious
irony which would have appealed to Hardy in the description of the
Early Life by a *Times Literary Supplement* reviewer as 'this last work of
Hardy's which Mrs. Hardy has so faithfully made in his image', and
in which his friends will seem to 'hear the stories that he told, echoed
. . . with his very accent'. Not only the language and tone of the book
but the surviving evidence of its composition reveal that Hardy
himself was the sole author of 34 chapters or about 90 per cent of the
complete work, as well as having a hand in the remaining 4 chapters –
a hand which even extended to a projected final sentence. In the
account of a visit to Thomas Hardy in Virginia Woolf's diary, she
notes that, while they were waiting for the great man to come down,
Mrs Hardy made conversation 'with great docility and readiness, as
if she had learnt her part'. It was a perceptive observation; and where
the pseudo-biography was concerned, Florence Hardy certainly
learned her part with great faithfulness, and kept the secret until her
death in 1937.

Of the problems of literary biography, Vladimir Nabokov has
said:

Sometimes the thing becomes a kind of double paper chase:
first, the biographer pursues his quarry through letters and
diaries, and across the bogs of conjecture, and then a rival
authority pursues the muddy biographer.

When the biographer is actually an autobiographer in disguise, the
paper chase takes on a dream-like quality; and certainly in this case
there is no shortage of paper: it would be out of place here to itemize
the materials for the kind of reconstruction of Hardy's autobiographical methods that may be undertaken, but they range from
extensively revised drafts of the complete book to fragments jotted
on scraps of paper, and also include notebooks, diaries and letters.

Initially Hardy may well have regarded his own contribution to the
Life as being confined to the provision of source-materials and the

laying down of general lines concerning what might be included; and preliminary work may have proceeded in 1916 or soon after on this basis. Sooner or later, however, he evidently resolved to write the book himself, without abandoning the fiction of his detachment from the task. The surviving material shows that the project was pursued with considerable patience and fastidiousness; it must have been enormously time-consuming, and the *Life* may well be one of the most deliberately and painstakingly composed of all Hardy's prose works. There is evidence, too, that he did not reach the point of putting it aside as complete (in so far as his own hand in it could be concluded), but was still giving thought to it towards the end of his life, and even within a few weeks of his death.

A major part of this preliminary work consisted in the careful reading and classification of old letters, diaries and other papers, the selection of material that might be utilized, and the destruction of much of the remainder. For a man with Hardy's sense of the past and its reality in the present, these tasks must have been not merely tedious chores of authorship but a considerable and sustained emotional experience. It seems, too, that the dimensions of the task grew as Hardy proceeded. Whereas the self-declared autobiographer must set himself a cut-off date, often some years earlier than the date of composition, the autobiographer masquerading as biographer, although he can hardly narrate his own death and burial, is likely to be unwilling to relinquish to another hand more of the final portion than is absolutely necessary. Hardy's time-defying decision was to have as large a share as possible in the production of material extending to the day of his death.

His working method seems to have been to read, thin out and classify the papers of a long lifetime; and, using them as an aid to memory and a source of plentiful quotation, to draft a manuscript version which was typed by Mrs Hardy and then destroyed. The typescripts were themselves submitted to extensive revision, and in some instances were retyped; a number of these typescripts, with manuscript additions and revisions and in various states of completeness, have survived. Of the two resulting volumes, the *Early Life* (slightly over half the complete biography) is entirely Hardy's work, as are the first fifteen chapters of *Later Years*, covering the period up to 1918. (This date may have been chosen as marking the end of the war, but possibly provides a clue as to the date of detailed planning and composition.) Two more chapters, covering 1918–20, were roughed out by Hardy and completed by his wife; the final two, covering 1921–8, were written by Mrs Hardy with the assistance of a memorandum book compiled by Hardy, eked out with her own diary and other sources. 1920 is a natural terminus for Hardy's own share in the work: he was eighty in that year, and may have felt his life was near its end; but he continued to accumulate material until within a few weeks of his last illness. There survives one rather touching fragment which, though undated, cannot have been written earlier than the end of November 1927, only six or seven weeks before his death. It must have been one of his last writings, and to have been destined for inclusion in the *Life* (though in the event it was ignored or overlooked). It is entitled 'Hardy's Altruism', and since it has never been published it is worth quoting in full:

> It must not be forgotten that Hardy's own life and experience had been smoother and happier than many – perhaps than the majority. It was his habit, or strange power, of putting himself in the place of those who endured sufferings from which he himself had been in the main free – or subject to but at brief times. This altruism was so constant with him as to cause a complaint among his readers that he did not say 'all's well with the world' because all was well with him. It should really have caused commendation.

So much, he seems to be saying, for all those books and articles on Hardy's pessimism; yet the claim that he had a happy life hardly fits with some of the evidence from earlier periods – with his confession to a friend in 1892, for instance, while he was working on *Jude the Obscure*, that 'I have passed through glooms such as I hope you will never see'. The fragment suggests, though, that at the age of eighty-seven and on the brink of his final illness, Hardy was still anxious to impose on posterity his own version of the truth.

It seems, then, that the autobiography is not only a work of reminiscence but the projection of a carefully calculated image of its subject; and to study the revisions in these typescripts is often to have a sense of a carefully considered effect being produced, of Hardy nicely calculating less and more. A few examples will show what I have in mind.

Hardy's habit of becoming infatuated with a pretty face – a habit which has already been referred to – was at first illustrated with a good deal of frankness; but second thoughts were more cautious, and his impressionability was played down in the process of revision. Mrs Julia Augusta Martin was the local lady of the manor and possible prototype of the long line of upper-class ladies in Hardy's fiction who are loved, usually unsuccessfully, by their social inferiors. 'She had been accustomed', the *Life* notes, 'to take [him] into her lap and kiss [him] until he was quite a big child', and 'he quite reciprocated her fondness'. He met her again at the time of his first marriage, and the typescript at this point indulges in a romantic fantasy which on reflection was carefully cancelled:

> Thus though their eyes never met again after his call on her in London, nor their lips from the time when she had held him in her arms, who can say that both occurrences might not have been in the order of things if he had developed their reacquaintance earlier, now that she was in her widowhood, with nothing to hinder her mind from rolling back upon her past.

Prolonged fantasy-making is also involved in his boyhood romance with Louisa Harding, daughter of a wealthy farmer and subject of three poems written in his old age. 'A nameless green mound in the corner of Mellstock Churchyard', he wrote, 'was visited more than once by one to whom a boyish dream had never lost its radiance'; and this passage too was struck out, as were a number of later references to women: one, for instance, to the 'voluptuous' lips of a minor poetess, 'that most impassioned and beautiful woman'; one to Mrs Henniker, who has been nominated as the model for Sue Bridehead ('some of his best short poems', he notes, 'were inspired by her'); and a slightly indecorous reference to a member of the Royal Family ('not a bad-looking girl, and a man might marry a worse'). Not all the cancellations concern women: there is a long attack on 'that infamous blackguard George Moore', which discretion later removed, and a caustic passage concerning Henry James and Robert Louis Stevenson – James's well-known comments on *Tess of the D'Urbervilles* had been published posthumously in his letters. This was prudently abridged, retaining the description of the two authors as 'the Polonius and Osric of novelists' but omitting a more devastating sentence: 'How indecent of those two virtuous females to expose their mental nakedness in such a manner.' Apropos of James, it may be mentioned that Hardy is guilty of a curious untruth in saying elsewhere that James was rejected for membership of the Rabelais Club on account of his lack of literary 'virility': as he must have known quite well, James *was* a member, and his name appears on several membership lists preserved among Hardy's papers. These are all details; but the cumulative effect of the kind of revisions and suppressions which I have illustrated is of course to soften the hard outlines of an astringent personality, and to present Hardy as a much blander, less impulsively emotional, man than in fact he was.

Another striking feature of the book is the way in which, among so much factual detail and so many minutiae of reflection and comment, certain matters of substance are either treated in a curiously cursory manner or passed over in complete silence. The autobiography is a mass of information, much of it trivial and incidental; and it is not easy for the reader picking his way through the undergrowth to spot certain lacunae on points of special sensitivity. There is, for instance, only the briefest possible reference, in the middle of a sentence concerned with other matters, to his 1874 honeymoon: his first marriage was probably the most important milestone in his emotional life and the culmination of a long courtship, the wedding trip was his first journey abroad and served as the occasion to collect material for a new novel; and it was fully documented in both Hardy's diaries and his wife's. The entire episode, which might have received extended treatment, is merely glanced at rather ambiguously as 'a short visit to the Continent'. Hardy's reasons for not wishing to revive the unbearably poignant associations of that period of his life, evoked in the finest of all his poems, are not hard to surmise; but at such points the autobiography is far from being as complete a record of his experience as it may appear to be. He is also guilty of falsification in claiming that his first wife's family were in favour of the match, when in fact there was strong opposition which must have been deeply wounding to his pride. In another area, Hardy's difficulties with editors, publishers and critics receive less than completely frank treatment: for example, some long and bitter passages on Mrs Oliphant's attack on *Jude the Obscure* are cancelled; and there are other instances of an unwillingness to revive and place on record a painful experience.

The book is dense with quotations from letters, diaries and other contemporary documents; and where the originals have survived, Hardy can sometimes be detected in the act of treating them somewhat cavalierly, revising and omitting for reasons that were certainly not always stylistic. A letter from Leslie Stephen, for example, is quoted to the effect that Sainte-Beuve and Matthew Arnold 'are the only modern critics who seem to me worth reading': Stephen's letter happens to have survived, and includes also the name of Lowell, but Hardy seems to have had no love for Americans, and his name is absent in the printed text. Again, individual instances are trivial, but they have the effect of undermining one's confidence in material of which the accuracy cannot be verified.

These examples might be multiplied many times, but enough has perhaps been said to suggest that, for the student of Hardy, the *Life* is a work of unique interest and serious unreliability. It claims the status of an authoritative biography, and still, nearly fifty years after Hardy's death, is generally accepted as the standard and unrivalled account of his life – and, to that extent, he must be considered as having achieved his aim; but it partakes of the inevitable limitations and distortions of an autobiography. It is the fullest manifestation of a tendency which became marked in Hardy's last decade, and can also be seen in his correspondence of the period, when he wrote in his own hand drafts of letters which were then typed and signed as if they had been written by another – a retreat into the third person, a strategy of indirectness which in the *Life* is elevated into a formal narrative technique. Hardy may even have derived a certain ironic relish from the ambiguity of such phrases as 'the present writer' and 'the writer of these pages'. The Hardy we come to know through the autobiography is the Hardy that Hardy wanted us to know: his life has thus become a work of fiction of the kind which English novelists have practised so successfully, using the material of life but taking liberties with it.

Seen for what it is, and not for what it pretends to be, this last major prose work is in harmony with the rest of Hardy's achievements of a lifetime. Of the narrative art of his fiction, J. Hillis Miller has written:

> His goal seems to have been to escape from the dangers of direct involvement in life, and to imagine himself in a position where he could safely see life as it is without being seen and could report on that seeing. To protect himself and to play the role of someone who would have unique access to the truth – these motives lie behind Hardy's creation of the narrative voice and point of view which are characteristic of his fiction.

It is also, one may add, a very close description of the *Life*. For the 'invisible coat' which cloaked his watching and eavesdropping activities was a garment shared by Hardy the novelist, his narrators and some of his characters, by Hardy the poet, and by Hardy the autobiographer. Graham Greene has said, in *his* autobiography, 'I suppose every novelist has something in common with a spy'; and a recurrent type in Hardy's novels is the watcher in the shadows, the

self-effacing but sympathetically presented figure who sees and over-
hears rather than participating in the action: Diggory Venn the
reddleman is constantly spying and eavesdropping, Mr Percomb the
barber, at the beginning of *The Woodlanders*, peers into a lighted
room, Gabriel Oak puts his eye to a crevice in Bathsheba's hut. In
the poems, too, Hardy assumes a variety of disguises, often teasing
the reader and baffling his attempts to discover the identity of the
poetic voice.

Just occasionally, the disguise slips and there is a flash of self-
revelation. If the *Life* strikes us, for the work of a great novelist, as a
rather dull piece of narrative, this may be partly because novelists on
the whole do not write first-class autobiographies (Trollope's, for
example, is less interesting than most of his novels); but it is also
because it is a *deliberately* conventional and pedestrian book, just as
Hardy – like E. M. Forster, and possibly for somewhat similar reasons –
seems to have cultivated a dowdy, old-fashioned physical appearance.
Published at the end of the 1920s, in the age of Huxley and Waugh,
it is essentially a late example of the Victorian life-and-letters tradition;
and it does the same kind of whitewashing for its subject that, for
example, John Forster did for Dickens and Mrs Gaskell for Charlotte
Brontë. Nevertheless, the flashes *are* there: the vignette of the young
Hardy coming to the conclusion (echoed by the young Jude) 'that
he did not wish to grow up'; the confession of his 'faculty . . . for
burying an emotion in my heart or brain for forty years, and exhuming
it at the end of that time as fresh as when interred'; his admission that
he cared nothing for public office or sitting on committees, but pre-
ferred to be (like his voyeur-heroes) 'the man with the watching eye'.
At such moments we come a little closer to knowing this writer whose
work is so intensely personal, deriving its nerve and muscle from the
minute detail of intimate daily experience, but who took such pains
to remain, if not unknown, at least remote and tantalizingly enigmatic.

I mentioned earlier a tiny but astonishing piece of evidence of
Hardy's anxiety to exert control from beyond the grave over the
erecting of his own biographical monument – the fact that he left
among his papers a couple of sentences apparently intended to form
the closing words of the book. They run as follows:

Hardy often said that a poet's writings could not be judged till
the last line had been written, which was the death of the author.
The opinion was particularly true of his own poetry, and indeed
of all his productions.

These sentences were not used to conclude the *Life*, though the first of them appears, in a different form, as a diary entry from 1899.

Notebooks and Diaries

The Dorset County Museum possesses a number of Hardy's manuscript notebooks, together with various annotated scrapbooks. Some of these notebooks contain selections made by Hardy from old diaries which were subsequently destroyed; the task was undertaken as part of the preparation for writing the autobiography, and other important portions of the lost diaries survive embedded in that book. Other notebooks are in effect commonplace books, containing records of Hardy's wide and varied reading over several decades. There is also a 'Schools of Painting' notebook dating from 1863, which contains notes on art history, and a 'Trumpet-Major Notebook' with a record of Hardy's researches into historical sources during the writing of that novel. The same collection also possesses diaries and other writings by the first Mrs Hardy, and fragments of a diary kept by the second lady of that name. As with the letters, the record is far from complete: much was systematically consigned to the flames (there are accounts of a bonfire before, and another shortly after, Hardy's death), and some of what has survived was clearly intended for destruction (a diary covering the years 1921–7, for instance, is headed: 'To be destroyed'). But enough remains to be of considerable interest to the serious student of Hardy, and although most of it as yet remains unpublished, arrangements are in hand for some of the major items to appear. As the more significant material becomes available, it is likely to stimulate fresh lines of thought and enquiry, especially in relation to the influence of Hardy's reading upon his creative work.

The commonplace books give a fascinating if incomplete picture of his reading for pleasure and profit, and of the intellectual discoveries he deemed worthy of preservation. The earliest of them is incomplete, has the date 1867 on the flyleaf, and consists mainly of short quotations from a wide variety of authors in prose and verse, with a preponderance of the latter. At this time, which coincides with his first attempt at writing fiction, Hardy was evidently studying not only the English classics (including Shakespeare, Bunyan, Johnson, Gray and Keats) but various contemporaries (George Eliot, Trollope, Swinburne, Herbert Spencer), as well as French writers (Corneille, Musset, Hugo). There is a good deal of underlining of striking phrases (for example, Keats's 'sun-burnt mirth', and Shelley's 'pestilence-stricken multitudes'):

the youthful reader who had already written verse of his own was obviously anxious to play the sedulous ape and to learn what he could from the language of the masters. Another volume, apparently belonging to the 1870s and 1880s, contains extracts from a highly eclectic choice of sources: newspapers and journals from the *Daily News* to the *Cornhill*, textbooks on astronomy and natural history, biographies and novels, Spinoza and Schlegel, Shakespeare and Henry James. A third notebook, started in the 1880s and continued well after the turn of the century, shows Hardy keeping up with recent literature: he read works by Wilde, Dowson, Kipling, H. G. Wells and Emily Dickinson, and took the trouble to copy out a long passage from T. S. Eliot's *Prufrock*. One has the impression in these commonplace books of a wide-ranging, if somewhat unselective and desultory, curiosity, and an insatiable appetite for facts, the odder the better. Some of the topics covered by his notes are: Schopenhauer on pessimism; a French literary journal on realism and naturalism; Lombroso on the insanity of genius; the population of Dorset as recorded in Domesday, and that of Whitechapel in 1876; the career of Verdi; famous varieties of coffee; prosody, parasites, homing pigeons, prize cows, and the history of roller-skates. Conceivably they were made partly with the practical objective of providing a stock of information for the busy novelist to turn to – the note on types of coffee, for instance, might have enabled a writer of society novels (as Hardy seems at one time to have aspired to be) to indulge in some impressive name-dropping. Occasionally a parallel may be spotted, as when an observation on the behaviour of ants taken from a popular work of natural history by J. G. Wood turns up in *The Return of the Native* (when Mrs Yeobright, nearing exhaustion, watches a colony of ants at work, she remembers that 'this bustle of ants had been in progress for years at the same spot – doubtless those of the old times were the ancestors of these which walked there now').

Yet another notebook is titled 'Facts', contains dated and undated material covering the years 1882 to 1913 or thereabouts, and concentrates on local information from newspapers, memoirs and similar sources. Picturesque and macabre incidents are very prominent, including some accounts of wife-selling which were utilized in *The Mayor of Casterbridge*, and the prototype of the episode in *Tess* wherein the horse is killed by a shaft of a passing vehicle. There is also a brief reference to a christening in a bedroom (apparently taken from Walpole's letters) which may have prompted another scene in *Tess*. Again, this highly miscellaneous gathering of evidence bears the signs of having been accumulated as source-material for the busy novelist and story-writer to resort to when invention flagged. If truth is stranger than fiction, as Hardy certainly believed, there was no reason why fiction should not sometimes borrow from truth. The real-life tragedies recorded include seductions, crimes of passion, suicides (and crossroads burials), deceived husbands and abandoned babies, as well as robberies, frauds and horse-stealing. Some of the situations verge on tragi-comedy, and even at moments recall Harry Graham's 'ruthless rhymes': a man climbing over a wall to keep a tryst with his sweetheart falls into a water-butt; an alcoholic who has killed himself is found to be a successful temperance lecturer; an American visiting a Civil War graveyard finds a tombstone bearing his own name. This patient documentation of the sadness and oddity of human experience, blending the pathetic, the grotesque and the absurd, parallels some of the most memorable incidents in the fiction and poetry, where a similar fascination with the 'satires of circumstance' and the 'little ironies' of life is in evidence.

6

Verse

In an oft-quoted diary entry made in 1875, and reproduced in the autobiography, Hardy set down some reflections on 'the whole secret of a living style', which (he wrote) lay for him in 'not having too much style – being, in fact, a little careless, or rather seeming to be, here and there'. Elsewhere he drew a parallel between this cultivated carelessness and the spirit of Gothic architecture: 'He knew that in architecture cunning irregularity is of enormous worth, and it is obvious that he carried on into his verse . . . the Gothic art-principle in which he had been trained – the principle of spontaneity.' It is tempting to comment that Hardy's conception of 'style' is excessively restricted: he seems to equate it in the first of these quotations with polish or correctness, and to fail to perceive that the kind of deliberate lack of finish he is advocating, so far from being an offence against 'style', is itself a legitimate stylistic quality. Fortunately, however, Hardy is much more successful as a practitioner than as a theorist of literature; and the remarks quoted (although the first of them in its context refers to prose) seem to offer a useful starting-point for a consideration of the distinctive features of his verse. He practised a variety of poetic genres – lyrics, narrative poems, dramatic monologues, epigrams, pastiches – and employed an extraordinary range of metrical and stanzaic forms; but almost throughout there is a remarkable uniformity of tone and a wholly individual use of language: without displaying the immediately apparent innovative boldness of a Hopkins or a Pound (both of whom were his poetic contemporaries), he forged an idiom that is unmistakably personal.

What are the characteristics of the peculiar Hardy note? When, in a sense, every poem is typical, there is a temptation to select for purposes of illustration passages in which Hardy seems to carry his stylistic doctrines to extremes, and almost to lapse into self-parody. F. R. Leavis, in an admirable essay on the poetry, and perhaps unconsciously echoing the diary entry quoted above, suggests that he 'made a style out of stylelessness', and reinforces his claim with a handful of samples of Hardy's more bizarre linguistic contortions. For example:

> Her death-rumour smartly uplifted
> To full apogee.

What is striking in such lines is the almost perverse defiance of contemporary poetic orthodoxy: Hardy is fearless in disappointing the conventional expectations of the era in which he wrote (the age, initially, of Tennyson and Swinburne, and later, of the Georgian poets). Part of his achievement was to compel readers and critics to revise their notions of what constitutes an appropriate language for verse. 'Death-rumour' and 'uplifted' are, it is true, somewhat unlovely coinages; their meaning, however, is perfectly clear. 'Apogee' belongs primarily to the language of science, and recalls the recurrent complaint of the early critics of Hardy's fiction that he indulged a taste for 'pedantic phraseology' (the phrase comes from the *Spectator* review of *Tess*). Rather than stigmatizing such language as clumsy or pedantic, however, we ought to give Hardy the credit due for breaking through the narrow restraints of late-Romantic poetic diction. If the revolution he quietly led involved occasional acts of verbal violence, that was part of the necessary price. Another of Leavis's examples is the following:

> Your form has never darked its doors,
> Nor have your faultless feet once thrown
> A pensive pit-pat on its floors.

Here, 'pensive pit-pat' is startling in its sudden descent into homely informality. It is worth pointing out that Hardy's manuscript shows that he originally wrote 'The faintest pit-pat', and subsequently transferred the epithet 'pensive' from the previous line ('pensive feet'); in other words, his revising hand steered these lines firmly in the direction of the unexpected – the oddity, if it exists, is the result not of unconscious awkwardness or lack of polish, but of an act of calculation. A similar instance occurs in the 'Lines to a Movement in Mozart's E-flat Symphony': 'We looked together upon the pestered sea!', where the manuscript shows that the more conventional *burnished* and *capricious* were successively rejected in favour of the striking *pestered*. 'Pensive pit-pat' is also typical of Hardy's second thoughts in its movement towards alliteration; in the final stanza of that haunting (and biographically puzzling) poem 'The Division', the printed version runs:

> But that thwart thing betwixt us twain,
>   Which nothing cleaves or clears,
> Is more than distance, Dear, or rain,
>   And longer than the years!

But the manuscript shows that the first line originally read: '. . . that dark cloud . . .': the archaisms of the revised version both avoid the cliché of 'dark cloud' and increase the sinewy strength of the line when it is read aloud.

In such an instance, the use of archaism, which at first glance seems to expose Hardy to a charge of overripe Romantic poeticizing, turns out to be justified; and indeed, in his best poems, his apparently extravagant or irresponsible diction generally proves on closer inspection to be defensible. There might at first glance appear to be little to be said for such a coinage as *unhope*; but its placing as the final word of the poem in 'In Tenebris', and as a rhyme-word, enables it to convey a sense of bleak stoicism that is exactly right in the context:

> Black is night's cope;
> But death will not appal
> One who, past doubtings all,
>   Waits in unhope.

Hardy's notions of the subject-matter as well as the language and metre of poetry showed almost from the beginning a defiance of orthodoxy; so that his failure to persuade magazine editors of the 1860s to publish his work is hardly a matter for astonishment. It is true that the poems that have survived from his twenties include some rather conventional sonnets, in which the influence of Shakespeare can be detected; but already in 'Hap', dated 1866, and still more in 'Neutral Tones' in the same year, the forging of a personal style can be seen to be in process: theme, mood and language alike make no concessions to popular tastes or assumptions. In notable contrast to Hardy the novelist, indeed, Hardy the poet seems to have been very little concerned to please the public. A striking aspect of much of his verse is its private nature: rather than writing for an audience, he seems to be writing to please himself; and one result of this is that he can disregard normal assumptions about the subject-matter of verse. No experience or reflection is too large, or too small, to form the basis of a poem: in reading his verse in bulk, we find ourselves constantly required to readjust our perspective as we turn from, for example, the cosmic vision of 'At a Lunar Eclipse' to the soft-spoken intimacy of 'Nobody Comes'; and if there is a boldness in tackling the theme of the one in a short poem, there is also a kind of unostentatious audacity in venturing to make, and to print, verse of such unassuming pretensions as the other. Hardy's audacity extends also to technique and language. His boldness often takes the form of selecting a metrical and rhyming pattern for a poem that seems to be at odds with its theme and mood – of, for instance, casting a serious and contemplative poem into a mould reminiscent of lilting song or vigorous hymn – and then, at any rate in the most successful instances, of bringing off the gamble triumphantly. Linguistically, his originality consists partly in a simultaneous openness to many areas and levels of language: whereas most Victorian verse-writers seem to operate within a more or less narrowly defined poetic 'register', and with certain well-defined assumptions concerning the language of poetry, one feels that with Hardy almost any word could turn up at any moment, and words which rarely share the same context are liable to be encountered in collocation. It is possible to disparage this characteristic as unevenness or uncertainty of tone; more justly, however, it can be viewed as a remarkable flexibility – the result not of carelessness, nor of affectation, but of freedom from restrictions and inhibitions.

In, for instance, 'He Never Expected Much', the stanza-form with its refrain-like repetitions, its lines of varying lengths, and its intricate rhyme-scheme, might seem fussy and restless, damagingly at odds with the meditative, retrospective mood; yet Hardy has the capacity to give us a double surprise, first in using such an improbable medium and then in leaving us with a sense of its rightness. And from the bold opening ('Well, World . . .'), reminiscent in its controlled casualness of Donne's *Songs and Sonnets*, to the Wordsworthian second stanza ('that mysterious voice you shed/From clouds and hills around'), and the wholly individual blend of precision, archaism, and conversational awkwardness in the final stanza ('Just neutral-tinted haps and such'), this short poem embodies an impressive range of verbal effects.

Hardy's achievement in his best poems is to exercise such masterly (yet usually unobtrusive) control over the demands of metre and rhyme that his utterances seem natural and effortless even while they gain strength from the formal qualities of the verse. He can begin a poem with the offhand, tentative movement of informal speech:

Whenever I plunge my arm, like this,
In a basin of water, I never miss
The sweet sharp sense of a fugitive day . . .

('Under the Waterfall')

yet, within three lines, the combined forces of metre, rhyme and alliteration intensify the reader's response, the verse moving from relaxation to tension as if miming the pressure of emotionally charged memories breaking through the tranquil surface of a commonplace action in the present. Sometimes the most powerful feelings are expressed in verse of considerable technical complexity, as in the second stanza of 'The Going'. Simple language there gains strength from the emphasis appropriately effected by metre ('Or utter a wish for a word . . .'); a normally neutral and colourless word acquires weight and power from its position as a rhyme-word ('your great *going*'); the occasional word (*lip, harden*), not unfamiliar in itself but in its usage in this context, lends an invigorating sense of unpredictability to the diction; and the complex stanzaic form and rhyme-scheme are justified by their function in imposing a necessary discipline upon the expression of what might easily have been an unmanageable over-indulged emotion. Moreover, examination of the whole poem of which this is the second stanza ('The Going' stands first in the series of 'Poems of 1912–13') reveals a firm overall structure: of the six stanzas, the first, third and fifth begin with the word 'Why', so that the pattern is of question and response, of a baffled self-searching and the attempt to reach, if not a solution, at any rate an acceptance of the inevitable.

Hardy's poetic syntax, too, can seem wilfully to run against Tenny-sonian or Swinburnian notions of fluidity and undisturbing musicality. The last stanza of 'Midnight on the Great Western' eschews smooth-ness and the dying fall as dishonest to the emotion conveyed:

Knows your soul a sphere, O journeying boy,
    Our rude realms far above,
Whence with spacious vision you mark and mete
This region of sin that you find you in,
    But are not of?

The poem expresses a puzzlement and a sense of painfully groping enquiry which the tortuous syntax seems to mime: dying falls, Hardy seems to imply, are all right for poets for whom all's right with the world. Often the departures from conventional word-order stem from an attempt to catch the naturalness of spontaneous speech: as P. N. Furbank has noted, 'who else would begin a poem "Her laugh was not in the middle of her face quite"? Or construct a whole poem . . . from the germ of this utterly natural fragment of spoken rhythm?'

Metrical inventiveness and ingenuity are evident throughout the *Collected Poems*. At worst, Hardy's constant experimentation with intricate stanzaic forms and rhyme schemes can seem like a preoccupation with technique for its own sake – the self-indulgence of a skilled craftsman taking pleasure in setting himself new problems; and there is some disconcerting evidence that, on occasion at least, he devised a metrical pattern before finding words to fit it. But in his best poems the form serves a more positive purpose: his characteristic emotional range, with its emphasis on nostalgia and yearning and its preoccupation with the minute and momentary dramas of the heart, is one that could very readily topple a poem over into sentimentality or whimsicality without the check of a rigorous formal element. 'Poetry', as Hardy himself once said, 'is emotion put into measure.' It is relevant, too, to recall Hardy's inherited and lifelong love of music and song: the lilting quality of much of his verse seems to cry aloud for music – or even to make its own music:

– The yachts ride mute at anchor and the fulling moon is fair,
And the giddy folk are strutting up and down the smooth parade

and again:

A little cloud then cloaked us, and there flew an irised rain,
And the Atlantic dyed its levels with a dull misfeatured stain,
And then the sun burst out again, and purples prinked the main.

One of his finest and most representative poems. 'During Wind and Rain', is cast in a stanza-form which points a contrast between the joy and vitality of the distant past surviving in memory and the desolation of the present, conveyed through imagery of disease and death:

They are blithely breakfasting all –
Men and maidens – yea,
Under the summer tree,
    With a glimpse of the bay,
While pet fowl come to the knee. . . .
    Ah, no; the years O!
And the rotten rose is ript from the wall.

In each of the four stanzas, the piercing recollection of time past is communicated through a sharp visual image of social activity (singing together, making a garden, an outdoor breakfast, moving house), poignant as an old photograph; each image is dissolved, or rather shattered, however, by the inescapable knowledge of the destructive work done by time ('the years O!'), and each stanza ends with a highly charged line in which another, very different visual image – so powerful in its compression of statement as to be almost an Imagist poem in itself – overlays the earlier one: 'How the sick leaves reel down in throngs!', 'See, the white storm-birds wing across!', 'And the rotten rose is ript from the wall', and, in the final stanza, the intensely powerful line, 'Down their carved names the rain-drop ploughs'. Feeling and form, emotion and 'measure', are perfectly married.

Not the least characteristic quality of 'During Wind and Rain' is the teasing sense that we are being offered fragments of deeply significant memories, as if one were reading Hardy's account of his emotional life by flashes of lightning. (Evelyn Hardy has pointed out that several details of the poem are paralleled in a short memoir written by Emma Lavinia.) Hardy is one of the most obsessively personal of poets, at once self-absorbed and self-concealing; and so many of his poems seem to offer themselves to the reader as auto-biographical riddles. It will already have become apparent, however, that the biographical problem is not the only problem posed by this large corpus of verse, the sheer bulk of which poses a practical problem for the reader and the student. It may be as well, therefore, to attempt a systematic charting of some of the features which tend to make Hardy's verse as a whole, and the typical Hardy poem, difficult of access.

The most immediately obvious of these problems relate to the quantity and quality of his poetic output. Leaving aside the verse plays, including the 500-page 'epic drama' *The Dynasts*, there are nearly 1,000 short poems written over a period of more than sixty years. It is a remarkable body of material; but one need not read very far into the *Collected Poems* to perceive that Hardy was almost totally unselective in publishing and reissuing his poetry. The volume contains some of the finest of modern lyrics, but also much that is trivial or embarrassingly feeble: to adapt one of Hardy's most famous lines, the reader's search for the Better exacts a full look at the Worst. Just *how* much is of value is a matter for argument, and a question to which very different answers have been given. For F. R. Leavis, 'any real claim [Hardy] may have to major status rests upon half-a-dozen poems'; Philip Larkin, on the other hand, trumpeted the assurance a few years ago that 'one reader at least would not wish [the] *Collected Poems* a single page shorter' – a view not necessarily opposed to the letter of Leavis's judgment, but very different in its tone of defiant championing from Leavis's ruthless thinning out of inferior specimens. The unevenness of Hardy's verse, the mingling of the superb with the indifferent, has led critics to adopt somewhat contorted positions in assessing his poetic status: John Crowe Ransom, for example, who clearly admired Hardy's poetry, reached the curious conclusion that he was 'a major minor poet', and for Leavis, although he wrote some major poems, Hardy is not a great poet.

Another problem is chronological. Hardy wrote poetry for longer than almost any other English poet, but one of the clichés of Hardy criticism is that in all this time he showed scarcely any development and that the mid-Victorian Hardy is not significantly different from the late-Victorian, the Edwardian or the Georgian Hardy. The truth is, however, that we are not in a very strong position to make authoritative judgments concerning Hardy's development or lack of it: the *Collected Poems* follows the order of publication, which is a very different matter in Hardy's case from the order of composition, and we have no way of dating the majority of the poems except very tentatively. The curious pattern of his literary career has already been described: he inherited the Romantic conviction that poetry is a higher form of expression than prose, and wrote poetry in his youth; by his mid-twenties he was sending it to magazines, totally without success, and with consequent discouragement. An examination of the poems which have survived from the 1860s makes those editorial decisions understandable: often gloomy in mood and sometimes perverse or obscure in expression, they were scarcely qualified to brighten a corner of a popular magazine. For a quarter of a century he wrote mainly prose, though a few poems also date from this period; in his usual economical way, he occasionally slipped a prose paraphrase of one of his unpublished poems into a novel. Then, after *Jude the Obscure*, he abandoned fiction – a decision which has produced its own mythology – and wrote verse almost exclusively for the last thirty years of his life. None of his poetry was published until he was nearly sixty, and the apparently inexplicable change of direction by a novelist with an international popularity was slow in winning acceptance from critics and readers. Some of the reviews of *Wessex Poems*, his first collection of verse, express puzzlement at what they saw as the curious and ill-advised whim of an accomplished novelist venturing into literary territory which he was ill-equipped by talent or experience to explore; the irony of their criticism can scarcely have been lost upon Hardy. As late as 1909, we find him writing bitterly to a friend:

'Here I am again, settling down to the revision of copy that I have promised to send . . . to be printed for a public which does not desire a line of it.' And when the poet laureate, Alfred Austin, died in 1913, Hardy, the most eminent man of letters of the day, was passed over – perhaps, because, as a historian of the laureateship has observed, Hardy's poetry was 'not consonant with the laureate mood'.

When he put together a volume of verse, his habit was to include poems recently composed mixed in with others dating from earlier decades: he evidently had a reservoir of old poems into which he went on dipping right to the end of his life. As late as 1924, for instance, he was asked by a literary agent to compose a Christmas poem; after confessing his inability to write poems 'to order', he goes on to say in his letter of reply: 'after a search I find I have a fairly good one which I had quite forgotten. . . . It was only roughly scribbled down in pencil a long time ago, and was abandoned for some reason or other' – and he promises to tidy it up and send it along. The notion of Hardy, in his eighty-fifth year, poking among the papers of a lifetime on the chance of unearthing a forgotten poem is indeed a strange one.

Just how far these old poems were revised it is impossible to say, since he tended to destroy earlier drafts as each fresh one was completed (not so much, I think, from a conscious motive of covering his tracks as from a genuinely modest conviction that no one was likely to regard them as having any interest or value). He refers in his autobiography to changing 'a few words' and 'rewriting . . . a line or two', but in speaking of his revisions Hardy tended to understate the truth, and some of the surviving manuscripts show very extensive rewriting. To give only one tiny example: the opening line of one of his most familiar poems, 'When the present has latched its postern behind my tremulous stay', originally ran: 'When night has closed its shutters on my dismantled day' – and there are hundreds, and perhaps thousands, of other revisions. Professor Purdy, normally the most reliable of bibliographers, is for once seriously misleading in describing the poetical manuscripts as 'fair copies', when a large portion of them are nothing of the sort. When a variorum edition of Hardy's poems becomes available, there is likely to be abundant material for a. fascinating study of his craftsmanship.

Hardy's volumes of verse, then, contain a mixture of old and new, with nothing in their arrangement to indicate the order of composition – the title of one of them, *Poems of the Past and the Present*, would serve for all. The first collection, *Wessex Poems*, published in 1898, contains fifty-one titles, of which exactly one-third date from the 1860s, a few from the 1870s, and others from the 1890s. He evidently drew only selectively on his store of old poems, however, for nearly a quarter of a century later he notes in the preface to *Late Lyrics and Earlier* that 'about half the verses were written quite lately', and it seems that the poems in that volume in fact range over fifty-five years, from 1866 to 1921. Finally, and most strikingly, in the posthumously published *Winter Words*, he brought together poems written over a period of more than sixty years, in which every decade of his career except the 1870s seems to be represented. Hardy did not quite fulfil his ambition to be the first English poet to publish a book on his eighty-eighth birthday, but it is hard to match the chronological inclusiveness of that final volume.

In summary, then, one can suggest, rather tentatively, that Hardy wrote a good deal of verse in the 1860s, and preserved some of it for publication decades later; that he wrote comparatively little during the 1870s, 1880s and 1890s, when he was busy writing fourteen novels and nearly fifty short stories; but that his output increased in the last years of the century and continued through the Edwardian period; that his most productive years were in the decade which followed the completion of *The Dynasts* in 1909 and saw the most momentous events, private and public, of his lifetime – the death of his first wife, and the Great War; and that he went on composing, arranging and publishing until very near the end of his life – one of his best poems, for example, was written about his eighty-sixth birthday. Hardy could scarcely have made a better job of discouraging efforts to trace his poetic development if he had set out to do so; and though he clearly shows nothing approaching the phases or periods of a poet such as his near-contemporary Yeats, the handy generalization that he was a Victorian novelist and a twentieth-century poet is not the whole truth. If he was the contemporary of Eliot and Pound (and, incidentally, he corresponded with the latter, and his notebooks show that he read *Prufrock* with professional interest), he also belonged to the age of Browning and Swinburne.

The mention of Pound's name recalls a further problem – the relationship of Hardy's verse to his fiction. 'Now *there* is a clarity', wrote Pound of Hardy's poetry; 'there is the harvest of having written twenty novels first'. Pound's facts are shaky; and the sense in which the poems were the 'harvest' of the years of prose-writing is perhaps not a very obvious one; moreover, it is very doubtful whether Hardy himself would have taken the observation as a compliment – he habitually played down his own achievement as a novelist, and regarded (or affected to regard) the fiction as a prolonged and tedious interruption of his true vocation. There is, it is true, a fairly obvious continuity of theme and tone between fiction and verse; but Pound's word *clarity* suggests qualities of vision and style. Let us dispose first of all, though, of Hardy's own public estimate of the relative value of his fiction and his verse. His notorious declaration, early in his career, to Leslie Stephen that his ambition was limited to being considered 'a good hand at a serial' has – like similar off-the-cuff utterances by other authors – been made to carry rather more weight than it will properly support; but it is true that, after he renounced fiction and all its works around the turn of the century, Hardy showed frequent signs of irritation at the general and surely pardonable tendency to regard him as a leading novelist who happened to have written a few poems. In his own mind, of course, he had always been a poet who had been driven into a shotgun marriage with the art of fiction, and who had had the courage (after twenty-five years) to return to his first love; but it was a long time before this estimate began to win acceptance, and it is certainly not universally held even today. In 1915 we find him advising a critic to 'treat my verse . . . as my *essential* writings, and my prose as my *accidental*, rather than the reverse'; and a few years later, writing to an anthologist who asks for advice on what should be included, he tells him 'I don't care an atom what prose you select', but goes on to make very precise suggestions of poems that might be used. But, as so often with Hardy, his declared attitudes don't quite square with the facts. If he really cared so little for the art of fiction, why did he take such pains with it, beyond the call of duty, so that the manuscripts of even his pot-boiling short stories show him shaping and polishing with scrupulous care? And if, having abandoned the novel, he really felt so little interest in his past achievements, why did he go on revising his novels minutely for new editions (over 200 changes in the 1912 text of *Jude the Obscure*, for example)? There is a kind of folklore of Hardyan attitudes and methods which is largely unsupported by the evidence; and that he was a slapdash writer of prose, cynically manufacturing serials for the market, is an example of such a popular belief which, it is only fair to say, was given currency partly by Hardy himself, but to which study of his manuscripts effectively gives the lie. When further accounts of the development of Hardy's text on the lines of J. T. Laird's recent study of *Tess of the D'Urbervilles* become available, we shall be closer to a true understanding of Hardy's artistry as a prose writer.

As for the relative merits of his verse and his fiction, Hardy's shade can now begin to say, nearly fifty years after his death, 'I told you so'; for both the quality of his best poetry and the extent of his influence have in the last few years been increasingly recognized. The major novels seem likely to retain their own place as classics; if Hardy is not quite in the first rank as a novelist, he stands very high in the second rank. But the reputation of his poetry has steadily grown, and larger claims have lately been made for it than have ever been made for the novels. Recently, for example, Donald Davie declared that 'in British poetry of the last fifty years . . . the most farreaching influence, for good and ill, has been not Yeats, still less Eliot or Pound, not Lawrence, but *Hardy*'; and the *Times Literary Supplement* in a front-page review referred to 'the present-day reappraisal of Hardy as the father of modern British poetry, and one of the supreme poets of the past two hundred years'.

But we have not yet finished enumerating the problems raised by Hardy's verse. There is also the narrowness of his range of poetic themes and moods: as E. K. Chambers perceptively noted in a review of *Wessex Poems*, 'He is entirely dependent for his inspiration upon this curiously intense and somewhat dismal vision of life, which is upon him almost as an obsession.' Reading his verse in bulk, one almost has the illusion of reading the same few poems over and over again, and the preoccupation with time and change, regret and remorse, the death of emotion and the indifference of nature (already familiar, of course, from the fiction) seems to recur almost endlessly. And, as suggested earlier, there are also, pervasively and insistently, the questions of style and metrics: why does Hardy adopt such wilful eccentricities of diction and syntax, and such restless and random variations of metre? No one, I think, has described these stylistic stumbling-blocks better than F. R. Leavis, who, in the essay already cited, recognizes them as extremely, even 'aggressively', characteristic of Hardy in their curious blending of strength and weakness:

> There is something extremely personal about the gauche unshrinking mismarriages . . . of his diction, in which, with naif aplomb, he takes as they come the romantic-poetical, the prosaic banal, the stilted literary, the colloquial, the archaistic, the erudite, the technical, the dialect word, the brand-new Hardy coinage.

Leavis is enunciating a version of one of the central and familiar truths of Hardy criticism: that a writer who ought frequently by all the rules and precedents to be downright bad somehow contrives to bring off a highly individual success. Whatever may be said against Hardy's poetic style (and Max Beerbohm's parody says some of it quite neatly), he contrived to speak with an unmistakably personal voice. His earliest surviving poem shows the influence of Wordsworth; his favourite poet was Shelley; and he admired Swinburne; but nearly all his poetry rejects the fluidity of nineteenth-century verse in favour of an idiom – gnarled, dislocated, unpredictable, often wilfully un-melodious – which owes a little to Browning and Barnes (notably to their experiments with speech-rhythms and colloquial diction), but is almost wholly original. His debts to other poets are slight; his real debt in his best poems was to the living language, the idioms and rhythms of spontaneous and casual speech, and when he fails it is more likely to be through excessive boldness than through timidity; it is only fair to recognize that his unorthodoxy derives not from ignorance but from policy.

Nor does it seem to be easy to decide what *kind* of poetry Hardy wrote, and what his best poems offer. Early critics tended to view them primarily as vehicles for ideas; and Hardy bibliographies bristle with titles like 'Pessimism in the poems of Hardy' (1899) and *Hardy and his Philosophy* (1928). But, formally and informally, Hardy repeatedly deprecated attempts to set him up as a thinker, and insisted that his poems recorded subjective and fleeting impressions, and were never intended to form part of a coherent and consistent system of ideas. In a letter to Edmund Gosse he writes that 'so few of the critical trade recognize what you know well – a poem expresses a mood that some-times ends with the very writing of it, and not a scientific conviction'; and in the last sentence to the preface of his final collection, *Winter Words*, he repeats what he had so often said before: 'that no harmonious philosophy is attempted in these pages – or in any bygone pages of mine, for that matter.'

One other type of problem calls for mention, and I have saved to the end of the list the most teasing kind of difficulty encountered in reading Hardy's poetry: the enigmatic quality of the personal allusions. If we are tempted to believe that with this key Hardy unlocked his heart, we soon find that the key does not fit the lock. Poem after poem, including some of the best, appears to present personal experience minutely and circumstantially; yet it is as if, in the process of making public art out of private experience, Hardy had shirked the full and final revelation, and we are left with a series of riddles. What, for instance, are we to make of the ghosts that haunt him in one of his most memorable poems, 'Wessex Heights'?

There's a ghost in Yell'ham Bottom chiding loud at the fall of the
     night,
There's a ghost in Froom-side Vale, thin-lipped and vague, in a
     shroud of white,
There is one in the railway train whenever I do not want it
     near,
I see its profile against the pane, saying what I would not hear.

This seems to me very characteristic of Hardy in its combination of
geographical precision and autobiographical vagueness: we sense the
nature of his emotion, but we can only guess at the human circumstances which gave rise to it. There has been a tendency among Hardy
scholars to treat the poems as reliable biographical material, and to
quarry them, as one might quarry letters or diaries, for insights into
the real Thomas Hardy. This seems to me to take too much for
granted, and to forget both that evasiveness was second nature
to Hardy, and that he had had long experience as a maker of
fictions.

When we look at what Hardy says explicitly about the interpretation of his poems, we find that the question is obscured rather
than clarified, and that Hardy in effect tries to warn us off the forbidden
territory of biographical criticism as he might have warned a trespasser
off his property at Max Gate – that property which, symbolically
enough, he surrounded with young trees which, as they grew, made
the house dark inside and virtually invisible from the road. As I have
indicated already, he insisted that the poems attempted no more than
to capture passing moods and thoughts: that they were, in his own
phrases, 'unadjusted [and] fugitive impressions', which aimed at no
'cohesion of thought' or 'harmonious philosophy'. Such disarming
admissions, quietly knocking the ground from beneath the interpreter's feet, echo what he had earlier said of the novels – the description of *Jude the Obscure*, for instance, as 'a series of seemings, or
personal impressions', and the famous dictum in the preface to *Tess of
the D'Urbervilles* that 'a novel is an impression, not an argument'.
These disclaimers may have been partly prompted by the rash of books
and articles on 'Hardy's philosophy' which began to appear very
early: this gentle but firm sabotaging of efforts to scrutinize his ideas
and beliefs, and to trace a system of secular pieties in his work, would
be very much in character. But he also goes beyond this and denies
that his poems are personal documents. In the preface to his first
collection, he writes that 'the pieces are in a large degree dramatic or

personative in conception; and this even where they are not obviously so'. The very rare word *personative* is defined by *OED* as meaning 'involving dramatic representation', and this passage is one of only two examples cited. Perhaps the word was misunderstood as meaning 'personal', for when Hardy repeated the point in the preface to his second collection, he used a less puzzling word: 'much is dramatic or impersonative even where not explicitly so'. Hardy may well have had Browning's dramatic monologues in mind here; but the purpose of his warning is clear enough – he is doing what he can to discourage the reading of the poems as personal documents. But since he was capable of going to almost any lengths in order to safeguard his privacy, we need not feel obliged to take these statements at face value, and the question remains an open one.

If we look at his first published verses – in the 1898 volume, *Wessex Poems,* the very title of which suggests a continuity with the world of his fiction – we find the problem of the speaker's identity very prominently raised; for of just over fifty poems in this volume, almost exactly four-fifths are presented as monologues. There is a small number in which the speaker is unmistakably Thomas Hardy – for example, the title of 'Thoughts of Phena at news of her death', in conjunction with the date, March 1890, makes it quite clear that he is speaking from personal experience; and if further confirmation is needed, it is provided by an account in the autobiography of the writing of this poem. (The poem refers to the death of his cousin Tryphena Sparks, who has been claimed as a prototype of Sue Bridehead and – much less plausibly – has been cast by some recent students of Hardy's life in the role of lost love, ex-mistress and mother of his illegitimate son and sole offspring.) Such a poem stands, in very restricted company, at one extreme of a line of identification of monologuist with poet. At the other extreme is a much larger group of poems in which the speaker is quite certainly *not* the poet but an invented character. Such examples as 'The Peasant's Confession', a melodrama set in the Napoleonic period, and 'She at his funeral', in which the speaker is a woman, are dramatic monologues in Browning's sense. Between these two extremes lies a doubtful territory of poems in which the speaker may or may not be the poet; this is a large group, and different degrees of likelihood are involved, but there seems to be no means of settling the question conclusively. It is likely enough that the last poem in the volume, the finely characteristic 'I look into my glass', is autobiographical, and that the self-observing 'I' is Hardy:

I look into my glass,
And view my wasting skin,
And say, 'Would God it came to pass
My heart had shrunk as thin!'

One is on much less certain ground, though, if one seeks to attach
names to the 'hearts grown cold to me' of the second stanza. Is Hardy,
as so often, combining a degree of self-revelation with a shrinking
from full disclosure? or is the instinct of the story-teller at work,
turning a *cri de cœur* into a fictional situation? In any case, the solemn
lining-up of cold-hearted candidates seems likely to tell us little of
value about Hardy or his poem. Even less confidence can be felt in
classifying the first poem in the volume, 'The Temporary the All', as
a direct expression of personal experience; Professor Bailey's suggestion (among others) that the 'visioned hermitage' of that poem can
be identified with the vicarage which Hardy, as a clergyman *manqué*,
aspired to occupy, seems to me ludicrously misconceived. Post-
romantic poetry is surely crowded with whole suburbs of visioned
hermitages, and to let biographical interpretation act as a substitute
for attention to style and genre is to do no service to poetry or common
sense.

Wessex Poems, then, consists largely of poems which, at first glance,
seem to be personal; yet on closer examination only a small minority
can be regarded as indisputable fragments of autobiography, and
many are quite certainly nothing of the kind. In his typically trail-
confusing manner, indeed, Hardy uses the first person in his poetry to
represent a variety of stances, both personal and objective; whereas in
his autobiography and his letters he does the opposite, and tends to
conceal personal statements behind the mask of the third person. The
problem, of course, is not that he uses the first person but that he does
so ambiguously, shifting its function not merely from poem to poem
but within a single poem. A poem titled 'On the Departure Plat-
form', for instance, begins with what appears to be an instant of
remembered experience; but before the end the old man who is
writing the poem refers to the protagonist and speaker as 'young man'
– a deliberate inconsistency which must have been designed to baffle
interpreters, and has succeeded only too well. 'Under the Waterfall',
one of his longest poems, reads remarkably like a personal recollection
(as indeed it is), and it is only in the penultimate line that we learn that
the speaker is a woman. At such moments we seem to catch Hardy
in the act of fictionalizing his own experience, blending confession

with invention – an act which can, perhaps, be justified by saying that its effect is to generalize a particular and secret emotion. The lesson of all this for the explicator must surely be that, for all but a minority of Hardy's poems, the search for biographical solutions to the riddles they pose is likely to be an irrelevance – an excursion into what Nabokov, speaking of the perils of literary biography, calls the 'bogs of conjecture'; and that emphasis should shift to enquiring how successfully the dramatic persona has been created.

Similar conclusions emerge if we take a later group of poems, the twenty-six 'love lyrics' in the 1909 volume *Time's Laughingstocks*. This group ranges widely in date: nearly half of the poems belong to Hardy's youth forty years earlier; others cannot be dated with certainty, but probably belong much closer to the date of publication. When we align what we know of Hardy's personal life at this time with the dominant themes of these poems – separation, disillusionment, marriage as destructive of romantic love, illicit passion and betrayal, the consciousness of time and of physical decay – it is of course tempting to seek equations between poetry and experience; but again the temptation ought, I believe, to be resisted. In the 'love lyrics' Professor Bailey finds allusions to various Victorian and Edwardian ladies, sometimes offering us a choice of candidates; but many of the poems read to me more like exercises in poetic forms and modes than personal confessions – not so much chapters of autobiography as fictional variations on the theme of love. A very early poem, written in 1867 and titled '1967', is both a fairly conventional Victorian piece and at the same time typical of Hardy in its wry acceptance of human impermanence: a century hence, youth and emotion will survive, but not for these individuals:

> With nothing left of me and you
> In that live century's vivid view
> Beyond a pinch of dust or two. . . .

If we start enquiring, however, to whom the poem is addressed, we may be asking a question that is not only unanswerable but need never be asked. The poem *may* speak to a genuine love; but it is at least as likely that it is a fiction, like the sonnet by the sleepless lover that follows it, or the bitter little anecdote of a loveless marriage recounted in 'Four Footsteps', which might indeed have served as the germ of one of Hardy's own short stories.

I have been trying, then, to enter a perhaps somewhat long-winded caveat to the effect that, though Hardy's poems may be more frequently personal than he was prepared to admit, they may also be much less consistently and reliably so than many of his commentators have chosen to assume. By way of testing this suggestion at its weakest link, I want next to consider a group of poems that appear to offer themselves as insistently and unambiguously personal, their origins in Hardy's private experience being known to us in considerable detail. These are the twenty-one 'Poems of 1912–13', first published in 1914 and by general consent including much of the best of all Hardy's verse. Their occasion was the death of his wife, and they are the record both of his immediate reactions to bereavement and of the vicissitudes of a marriage that had lasted for forty years. These are the poems of a survivor, in whom the sense of loss is given an extra dimension by the contrast between the golden memories of mid-Victorian courtship and early marriage, and the bitterness of the later estrangement. Hardy is, therefore – like an autobiographical novelist, such as the Dickens of *Great Expectations* – looking backward with a double perspective: seeing the distant past not only as it was but in the ironic and painful light shed by later experience. They are mid-winter poems, using the familiar seasonal symbolism of desolation and sterility:

Where we made the fire
In the summer time
Of branch and briar
On the hill to the sea,
I slowly climb
Through winter mire,
And scan and trace
The forsaken place
Quite readily.

Now a cold wind blows,
And the grass is gray,
But the spot still shows. . . .

For once, however, the symbolism is justified by historical facts: Emma Lavinia Hardy died on 27 November 1912, and the poems followed in the next three or four months. In March 1913 Hardy made a penitential pilgrimage to Cornwall, where he had first met her: with his unfailing instinct for the significance of an anniversary, he timed it exactly forty-three years from the original momentous journey. He confessed later that the visit was 'a very painful one', and the sense of laceration is strong in the poems which record it. The 1912–13 poems reflect, however, not a single mood but a variety of stages or faces of grief: incredulous shock, remorse, tender acceptance of the inevitable, a sense both of irremediable absence and of a haunting presence, wry reflections on the ironies which life conspires to provide, such as the catalogue of fashions which the postman brings for her who is now 'costumed in a shroud'. 'The verses came', Hardy told A. C. Benson (who recorded the remarks in his diary), 'it was quite natural; one looked back through the years and saw some pictures. . . .' And yet naturalness is not quite the quality one thinks of first in reading these poems: not only in viewpoint and tone but in metre, diction and syntax they range from the direct and spontaneous to the contrived and eccentric. The lilt and tempo of the very first poem in the group, for instance, almost succeed in distracting attention from its highly patterned structure and the artifice of its elaborate stanza-form:

> Never to bid good-bye,
> Or lip me the softest call,
> Or utter a wish for a word, while I
> Saw morning harden upon the wall,
> Unmoved, unknowing
> That your great going
> Had place that moment, and altered all.

The accents of regret are here conveyed through a style that oddly blends formality with a bold indifference to conventional language – a linguistic correlate of Hardy's shunning of conventional consolations. For him there can be no prospect of reunion or renewed communication: she is 'past love, praise, indifference, blame'. Momentarily the pathetic fallacy may intrude, as when he recalls an experience which lasted a minute and has been preserved for a lifetime: they have climbed a hill in Cornwall together, their lives shrunk to nothing by a Victorian consciousness of geological time, as Tess is dwarfed by Stonehenge – and yet they possess their own irreducible uniqueness:

> Primeval rocks form the road's steep border
> And much have they faced there, first and last,
> Of the transitory in Earth's long order;
> But what they record in colour and cast
> Is – that we two passed.

Within a few lines, though, the recollection imposes itself that such moments survive only conditionally, in the memory of one who must, reasonably enough, have regarded himself as close to death.

The poems of 1912–13 constitute a kind of acid test of Hardy's poetic style. How well does his poetic idiom serve him when he writes (as he does not always write) from the pressure of intense feelings which bring together past and present? The answer is, as usual, unevenly – but very much less so than usual. There is a hit-and-miss quality about the bulk of Hardy's verse of which he was well aware: of the 1914 volume, for example, he says (in an unpublished letter) that not all the poems are exactly what he would now write – he is presumably thinking of the older material refurbished for publication – but, he goes on: 'There is . . . in me, a little of Pilate's feeling: "What I have written I have written".' (It is curious that Hardy should have been so meticulous about the *text* of his poems, endlessly fussing over it, and so indifferent to the overall level of its quality.) With the 'Poems of 1912–13', however, the proportion of hits to misses is notably higher than usual. He is still capable of beginning a poem on his wife's grave with archaic fustian:

Clouds spout upon her
Their waters amain
In ruthless disdain . . .

in which the crudity of language and rhythm seem utterly at odds with the tenderness of the feeling: this particular 'contraption', one feels, ought to have been more tactfully constructed. But much more characteristic of this group of poems is a quietly colloquial tone which creates the illusion in the reader of overhearing a private self-communing – as, for example, in 'The Walk':

You did not walk with me
Of late to the hill-top tree
By the gated ways,
As in earlier days;
You were weak and lame.
So you never came,
And I went alone, and I did not mind
Not thinking of you as left behind.

I walked up there to-day
Just in the former way;
Surveyed around
The familiar ground
By myself again:
What difference, then?
Only that underlying sense
Of the look of a room on returning thence.

Or again, 'Without Ceremony', in which he recalls Emma's impulsive
ways (not always a source of gratification in her lifetime, one might
surmise), and reflects that her sudden death has been a final example of
her habit of abrupt departures without the formality of a goodbye:

> And when you'd a mind to career
> Off anywhere – say to town –
> You were all on a sudden gone
> Before I had thought thereon
> Or noticed your trunks were down.

It may be that, after reading Lionel Trilling's recent book, we can
never again speak quite so readily and unselfconsciously of sincerity
and authenticity – but here they surely are, the language and tone
exquisitely conveying the sense of a mind in the process of coming to
terms with an overwhelming experience. If we pause for a moment,
however, to consider this latter poem as a personal record, we are
pulled up short by the fact that Emma's death was not as sudden as it
suits the poems to pretend: she had suffered from heart trouble for
some time, and however much Hardy was shocked by his own reactions to her death, the event itself cannot have come as such an utter
surprise. He seems to be busy, indeed, once again fictionalizing his
experience, shaping the truth with the practised story-teller's instinct
for a telling situation; and similar reflections are prompted by an
examination of these poems collectively – they display a care in
arrangement unusual for Hardy, a calculated contrasting of moods and
viewpoints (one poem in which the dead woman speaks to him is
followed, for example, by the well-known 'The Voice', in which he
listens to her imagined words). We need perhaps to treat Hardy's
claims for their artlessness and spontaneity with a degree of scepticism:
knowingly or otherwise, he is a less than reliable guide to his own
work. And before we leave this group of poems, one feature of their
public appearance is worth noting. Hardy seems to have hesitated – as
well he might – before giving to the world these intimate confessions
of remorse and regret, for at the end of June 1914 we find him writing
to a friend: 'I am . . . exercised on what to do with some poems.
When I am dead and gone I shall be glad – if I can be anything – for
them to have been printed, and yet I don't quite like to print them.'
But within a few months they were in print; and it is a matter for
speculation why Hardy should have been in such a hurry to publish
these intensely private documents – and to publish them with some
very strange bedfellows in a volume titled *Satires of Circumstance*.

Perhaps the public declaration of his grief and remorse was, like his journey to Cornwall, part of an 'expiation' – the word he himself used to describe the poems I have been discussing.

There are some exceptions to the claim frequently and not unjustly advanced that Hardy's poetry is characterized by an unusual degree of uniformity, and that his range of themes and moods is considerably narrower than that of most major poets. The *Collected Poems* includes, for instance, a number of ballads and narrative poems falling into two classes: those dealing with legendary and historical themes and settings, and those dealing with modern (or at least nineteenth-century) life. The versifying in these poems can sometimes be routine and pedestrian, but the best of them combine deft and economical story-telling with a remarkable metrical skill and rhyming ingenuity. The first group range from 'The Lost Pyx', an exercise in William Morrisy medievalism characteristically localized (according to Hardy's note) 'between High-Stoy and Bubb-Down', to a group of poems (e.g., 'The Peasant's Confession') set in the Napoleonic period. Several of the poems of modern life are worth singling out for special mention: 'A Sunday Morning Tragedy' employs archaic diction and the traditional ballad stanza to deal dramatically with a social problem which was, Hardy noted, 'of growing prevalence', that of abortion; 'A Trampwoman's Tragedy', written in 1902 and rejected by the *Cornhill*, is arguably the best of Hardy's longer poems (although the action is set in the 1820s, one of its long-dead characters, the celebrated horse-thief Blue Jimmy, is linked with the experience of the living in a manner very typical of Hardy, since he is said to have stolen a horse 'belonging to a neighbour of the writer's grandfather'); 'Satires of Circumstance' is a series of fifteen grim anecdotes based on ironic or macabre situations which might well have found their way into the accommodating plots of Hardy's fiction; in similar vein, 'Ah, Are You Digging On My Grave' is an amusingly anti-sentimental poem. Aside from these ballads or narrative vignettes, many of which furnish additional evidence of Hardy's interest in local history, there is a handful of epigrams and translations, including the 'Epitaph on a Pessimist' ('From the French and Greek'):

I'm Smith of Stoke, aged sixty-odd,
  I've lived without a dame
From youth-time on; and would to God
  My dad had done the same.

and the bitter 'Christmas: 1924':

'Peace upon earth!' was said. We sing it,
And pay a million priests to bring it.
After two thousand years of mass
We've got as far as poison-gas.

In different mood, there are a few humorous poems, such as the delightful 'Liddell and Scott'. But all these occupy only a fraction of Hardy's poetic output: the bulk of his poems, and nearly all the best of them, are personal, speaking of private emotions in a tone so restrained as to make the words seem less heard than overheard. If the emotions are intensely personal, however, this is not to say that they are not often prompted by the external world: by landscape and weather, for instance, or by houses and furniture and what Hardy calls, in a passage in *The Woodlanders* quoted earlier, 'the world of little things'. The preoccupation with time, and with human experience in the perspective of history, which has already been noted as character- istic of Hardy's fiction is equally evident in his verse. Even so slight a lyric as 'A Wet Night' contrives to shift its focus within a few lines from the trivial and transient to the universal and timeless, placing individual sensations in the context of generations of fellow-sufferers: even when he feels most alone in an indifferent universe, man enjoys the bleak consolation of taking his place in the age-old pattern of suffering humanity. In a fine and very characteristic poem, 'The Clasped Skeletons', the time-perspective is abruptly lengthened at the end: the prehistoric lovers, 'surmised date 1800 B.C.', who have been unearthed in 'an Ancient British barrow near the writer's house', are first compared with the great lovers of legend and history, remote from us but more recent than the skeleton-lovers:

So long, beyond chronology,
  Lovers in death as 'twere,
So long in placid dignity.
  Have you lain here!

then, in a stanza which recalls the scene on the cliff in *A Pair of Blue Eyes*, the lovers of prehistoric Dorset are shown as belonging only to yesterday in relation to the history of the earth and of a groaning creation:

Yet what is length of time? But dream!
  Once breathed this atmosphere
Those fossils near you, met the gleam
  Of day as you did here.

Again, in the two stanzas of 'Evening Shadows', Hardy's thought moves from an awareness of the insignificance of his own life-span to an impersonal consciousness of the Christian era as merely a phase in the endless course of history; in each case, the sense of impermanence (of the individual life which must end, and of a world-changing movement which must also decline and disappear) is conveyed through a visual image (the shadows of the house he has built, the shadows of 'the neighbouring pagan mound'). To move from the quiet perception of a momentary and commonplace experience to a statement of his deepest convictions concerning life, faith and history – and all within a dozen lines – is a remarkable achievement, and one that Hardy pulls off in poem after poem.

Among the poems which seem to come closest to expressing Hardy's feelings about life (feelings to which it is more convenient than helpful to give the label of pessimism) are 'Childhood Among the Ferns' and 'A Wish for Unconsciousness'. Both express a sense of the burden of being alive, the ache of human responsibility. The former, seeing childhood as the only time of contentment, expresses a wish not to grow up – the same wish that Hardy expressed in his autobiography ('he came to the conclusion that he did not wish to grow up') and ascribed to Jude Fawley ('If he could only prevent himself growing up!'). The latter goes even further in wishing for extinction or non-being:

> If I could but abide
> As a tablet on a wall,
> Or a hillock daisy-pied,
> Or a picture in a hall,
> And as nothing else at all . . .

But not all of Hardy's poems are as sombre, or as self-absorbed, as these: he can write of other people with affectionate recollection, sometimes of identifiable individuals such as his mother, his grandmother, William Barnes, Florence Dugdale (later the second Mrs Hardy) and his early loves ('To Lizbie Browne', 'To Louisa in the Lane'). Others bear the signs of treating of actual personalities and experiences (e.g., 'A Broken Appointment'), but resist more or less stubbornly attempts to fit them neatly into the poet's biography. Perhaps the gravest dangers in pursuing the biographical trail too zealously lie in the risk that the genuine sources of Hardy's distinction as a poet – his delicately individual handling of metre, language and tone – will be obscured.

No account of Hardy's verse can omit a reference to *The Dynasts*, the 500-page 'epic drama of the war with Napoleon' to the researching and composition of which Hardy devoted so much time and energy during his seventh decade. His interest in the Napoleonic period was, of course, of long standing, and he had been steadily accumulating material and mentally shaping his conception of the work for many years before composition began. His enthusiasm for the Napoleonic Wars dated from boyhood, and had been nurtured by precisely the kind of personal and family links with the period that were necessary to activate the Hardyan historical imagination. His grandfather had served as a volunteer and had subscribed to an illustrated periodical titled *A History of the Wars* which the young Hardy found in a closet and pored over, fascinated by the 'melodramatic prints of serried ranks, crossed bayonets, huge knapsacks, and dead bodies'. As a boy he also encountered soldiers from the nearby barracks who had been invited by the local squire as dancing-partners for the farm-girls at a harvest-supper: thus began (as he notes in his autobiography) his 'extensive acquaintance with soldiers of the old uniforms and long service, which was to serve him in good stead when he came to write *The Trumpet-Major* and *The Dynasts*'. His putative connection with his namesake Admiral Sir Thomas Hardy, captain of the *Victory* and a Dorset man, also fed his Napoleonic interests. The amassing of material for *The Dynasts* involved systematic research in the British Museum Library and the forming of a respectable collection of historical works in French and English in Hardy's own library at Max Gate. But his feeling for the past was not of a kind that could find stimulus or sustenance in words alone; and he made two visits to the site of the Battle of Waterloo, and on several occasions talked with Chelsea Pensioners who remembered that battle and the Peninsular Campaign. As late as 1878, for instance, he was able to interview a 'palsied pensioner' who had served under Sir John Moore and later fought at Waterloo: 'it was extraordinary', he wrote in his diary, 'to talk and shake hands with a man who had shared in that terrible winter march to Coruña, and had seen Moore face to face.' The same diary entry indicates his fascination with the barbarism of contemporary army life. To seek and to find living links with what had already passed into history is highly characteristic of Hardy's approach to the task of recreating the past.

Characteristic, too, is the steady and (apart from a few private references) silent growth of the project in Hardy's mind over many years, during which its scope developed from narrative poem to

dramatic trilogy. The circumstances of its publication have already
been described in Chapter 1. Although reviewers of the early portions
expressed some reservations about the enterprise, the complete work
received high praise: Sir Henry Newbolt, for example, remarked in
the *Quarterly*, 'I do not care to imagine a time when Englishmen will
not read this poem with delight.' It cannot be said, however, that
The Dynasts has worn as well as Hardy's fiction or his shorter poems,
and few present-day readers are likely to live up to Newbolt's expectations or to reach the end of the nineteen acts without occasional sighs
and yawns. As an exercise in the long poem – that genre which so
many Victorian poets attempted, and in which so few succeeded –
The Dynasts can hardly be judged a complete success. Hardy's distinctive lyric gift shows itself in occasional flashes: in the third line of

> Friends, foemen, mingle; heap and heap –
> Hide their hacked bones, Earth! – deep, deep, deep,
> Where harmless worms caress and creep.

and in the tenderly controlled movement and Swinburnian alitera-
tion of

> What will be seen in the morning light?
> What will be learnt when the spring breaks bright,
> And the frost unlocks to the sun's soft sight?

and occasionally he forgets that he is engaged in a grandiose historical
undertaking, and reverts to his more familiar unpretentious manner:
the song 'Budmouth Dears', like the local beauties it celebrates, is
'fresh as peaches'. But long stretches of the verse are stiffly prosaic,
showing all too clearly the signs of being rendered into metre from
their sources in weighty historical accounts. Meredith's comment
that the work would have been 'more effective in prose' is damaging
but not unfair.

And yet the whole has an impressiveness that it is difficult to localize
in its parts: not only the grandeur of the conception but also the
technical interest of Hardy's manipulation of point of view justify the
time spent reading it. John Wain's suggestion that the reader who feels
inclined to skip should omit the dialogue and not – as might seem more
reasonable – the lengthy stage-directions and 'Dumb Shows' may seem
paradoxical, but serves to underline the importance of the novelistic
element in this 'epic-drama'; and Hardy, who had some years earlier
retired from storytelling, displays considerable skill and power in his
narrative. His narrator's vantage-point, however, is no longer behind

a convenient tree or on the other side of a half-open door, but up in the firmament:

> Europe is disclosed as a prone and emaciated figure, the Alps shaping like a backbone, and the branching mountain-chains like ribs, the peninsular plateau of Spain forming a head. . . . The point of view then sinks downwards through space, and draws near to the surface of the perturbed countries, where the people, distressed by events which they did not cause, are seen writhing, crawling, heaving, and vibrating in their various cities and nationalities.

Comparisons of humanity to insects (ants, caterpillars, cheesemites, etc.), for which precedents can be found in the fiction, abound. This work, 'intended', as Hardy insists, 'for mental performance', is able to employ a 'migratory Proskenion' and enjoys a flexibility and a free-dom from spatial constraints that even the Elizabethan dramatist might have envied. The picture-making powers of the reader's imagination, so often called into play in the Wessex Novels, also have heavy demands made upon them here; and Hardy repeatedly shows his concern with what he calls at different times 'point of observation', 'point of sight', and 'point of view': we even find, at moments, a trace of the jargon of the studio:

> Behind all, the heights of Salinas close the prospect, the small river Alberche flowing at their foot from left to right into the Tagus, which advances in foreshortened perspective to the town at the right front corner of the scene.

Hardy's descriptive writing produces some vividly characteristic phrases: the light of the bonfire on the heath, recalling scenes in *The Return of the Native* and *The Trumpet-Major*, reveals 'the purple rotundities of the heath show[ing] like bronze, and the pits like the eye-sockets of a skull'; and, in verse,

> . . . the shining eyeball,
> (Called a trice from gloom by the fleeting pan-flash) . . .

– both reminiscent of the chiaroscuro effects often obtained in the novels.

In writing *The Dynasts*, Hardy probably owed something to his early study of Greek tragedy, as well as to Goethe's *Faust* and Shelley's *Prometheus Unbound*. For most of its early readers, however, its appeal seems to have been less literary and dramatic than philosophical: the notion of humanity as 'one great network or tissue' (an echo of the idea and image of 'the great web of human doings' already expressed in *The Woodlanders*); the concept of the 'Immanent Will'; the choruses and commentaries of the Spirit of the Years and the Spirit of the Pities – these, accompanying and counterpointing the human drama of war and death, victory and defeat, depicted at many levels, were taken very seriously by readers whose generation felt the overwhelming impact of the Great War. (Hardy wrote to his publisher on 15 July 1914, urging that his verse should be included in a limited edition of his works, and adding – almost apologetically, or perhaps ironically – that many readers evidently considered *The Dynasts* his most important work.) In so far as it still wins readers, however, the appeal of *The Dynasts* is likely to rest less on the elaborate supernatural machinery and the pervasive philosophical ideas than on the historical narrative and the technical interest of its presentation: 'the presiding eye', John Wain has said, 'is that of the film camera, called into being by the imagination of a major writer before it existed in the physical world.' Something of the specialist's passion, too, comes across to the reader: when he was correcting the proofs of the last part, Hardy wrote to a friend that he had studied Wellington's campaigns so intensively that he could almost believe he had taken part in the Battle of Waterloo himself; and he succeeds in communicating to us his enthusiasm for and deep absorption in the period.

It is fitting, perhaps, to take farewell of Hardy by glancing at two poems which stand on the last pages of his final volume; neither of them was published during his lifetime. 'A Private Man on Public Men' sets up an antithesis which reflects one of the paradoxes of Hardy's own nature: the conflict between his resolute quest for success and fame, and his longing to be unobserved and even untouched by others (he seems to have had a physical disinclination to even such conventional forms of contact as shaking hands). The poem belongs to a long tradition of verse in praise of the cloistered and obscure life, and the wisdom of seeking contentment by renouncing ambition:

I lived in quiet, screened, unknown,
Pondering upon some stick or stone,
Or news of some rare book or bird
Latterly bought, or seen, or heard

and it looks at first sight like an act of self-justification by one who had not feared to shun the world and its ways. But the now familiar problem insists on reappearing: once again, insidious though the temptation is, there are difficulties in the way of reading the poem simply as a personal declaration. Its contempt, for instance, for those whose energies are devoted to 'raking riches into heaps' comes oddly from one who had long since made a considerable fortune by catering for the tastes of a large public; and though Hardy's existence was 'screened', it was certainly not 'unknown'. We are driven, in fact, to accept the poem as yet another fiction, even if it is one that reveals personal yearnings.

Finally, the last poem of the whole collection, 'He Resolves to Say No More'. Coming on page 887 of the *Collected Poems*, and near the end of more than sixty years of continuous authorship, the decision to 'say no more' was hardly precipitate. Its repeated assertions – 'What I discern I will not say', 'What I have learnt no man shall know' – imply a stoical self-sufficiency, a refusal to indulge in the luxury of self-expression: yet the poem surely dramatizes a momentary impulse rather than presenting a considered resolution, and there is no reason to suppose that, had he lived another ten years, Hardy would not have gone on writing poetry and arranging for its publication precisely as he did in the last year of his life.

Hardy is, of course, far from unique in the kinds of poetic deception that I have tried to illustrate: the pseudo-autobiographical fragment, the mendacious 'I', are common enough, especially in Romantic verse. We may search the museums in vain for Keats's own particular Grecian urn, and recall that when Wordsworth tells us he listened to the singing of the solitary Highland lass he lies in his teeth. What is striking in Hardy's case is the persistence of this vein of fiction in his verse, and the continuity it provides with his other, earlier, career, combined with the disconcerting readiness of some of his commentators to take virtually all his work as composing a sustained autobiographical document. Even when he is obviously writing what amounts to pastiche of the sentimental or melodramatic folksong or ballad, his preoccupation with the traditional themes of adultery, infidelity and the like has been seized on as evidence of hidden guilt. Hardy's topographical precision has led scholars who should know better to expect comparable precision in referring to personalities and events. He wrote the kind of poetry, as he wrote the kind of novels, which habitually places imaginary figures in real landscapes; and his habit of shaping reality with the tools of the maker of fictions provides one of the links between his two careers, as novelist and poet. In reading the poetry we ought always to bear in mind that the impulse of self-expression and self-revelation is constantly overlaid by the urge to make a formally satisfying 'contraption'.

The Works of Thomas Hardy: A Select List

(Dates of publication refer to the first appearance in volume form, unless otherwise stated.)

Novels

Desperate Remedies (1871).

Under the Greenwood Tree (1872).

A Pair of Blue Eyes (1873; previously serialized monthly in *Tinsley's Magazine*, September 1872–July 1873).

Far from the Madding Crowd (1874; previously serialized monthly in *Cornhill Magazine*, January–December 1874).

The Hand of Ethelberta (1876; previously serialized monthly in *Cornhill Magazine*, July 1875–May 1876).

The Return of the Native (1878; previously serialized monthly in *Belgravia*, January–December 1878).

The Trumpet-Major (1880; previously serialized monthly in *Good Words*, January–December 1880).

A Laodicean (1881; previously serialized monthly in *Harper's New Monthly Magazine*, December 1880–December 1881).

Two on a Tower (1882; previously serialized monthly in *Atlantic Monthly*, May–December 1882).

The Mayor of Casterbridge (1886; previously serialized weekly in the *Graphic*, 2 January–15 May 1886).

The Woodlanders (1887; previously serialized monthly in *Macmillan's Magazine*, May 1886–April 1887).

Tess of the D'Urbervilles (1891; previously serialized weekly in the *Graphic*, 4 July–26 December 1891).

Jude the Obscure (1895; previously serialized monthly in *Harper's New Monthly Magazine*, December 1894–November 1895).

The Well-Beloved (1897; previously serialized weekly in the *Illustrated London News*, 1 October–17 December 1892).

Short Stories

Wessex Tales (1888; all five stories had been previously published in magazines; a sixth story – 'An Imaginative Woman' – was added when the book was reissued in 1896).

A Group of Noble Dames (1891; all ten stories had been previously published in magazines).

Life's Little Ironies (1894; all nine stories had been previously published in magazines).

A Changed Man (1913; all twelve stories had been previously published in magazines).

(There are about a dozen other uncollected stories, but the above four volumes contain most of Hardy's significant work in this genre.)

Poems

Wessex Poems (1898; contains 51 poems).
Poems of the Past and the Present (1901; contains 99 poems).
Time's Laughingstocks (1909; contains 94 poems).
Satires of Circumstance (1914; contains 107 poems).
Moments of Vision (1917; contains 159 poems).
Late Lyrics and Earlier (1922; contains 151 poems, and an important prose 'Apology').
Human Shows (1925; contains 152 poems).
Winter Words (1928; contains 105 poems; posthumously issued, this collection was not finally revised by Hardy).

Plays

The Dynasts, Part I (1904); Part II (1906); Part III (1908).
The Famous Tragedy of the Queen of Cornwall (1923).

Autobiography

The Early Life of Thomas Hardy, by F. E. Hardy (1928).
The Later Years of Thomas Hardy, by F. E. Hardy (1930).
(Since 1962 the autobiography has been available in a single-volume edition titled *The Life of Thomas Hardy, 1840–1928*.)

Miscellaneous Prose

All the prefaces and essays, and some other material of interest, are contained in Harold Orel's edition of *Hardy's Personal Writings* (1966).

Information concerning past and forthcoming editions of Hardy's letters and notebooks will be found in the Bibliographical Notes to Chapter 5.

Collected Editions

The Wessex Novels, 16 volumes (1895–6).

The Wessex Edition, 24 volumes (1912–31; the first twenty volumes appeared in 1912–13 and provide the definitive text of the novels).

Collected Poems (1919; subsequently expanded to include the collections of verse published after this date).

The Short Stories of Thomas Hardy (1928).

A Note on Hardy's Manuscripts

The Dorset County Museum possesses the MSS. of *Under the Greenwood Tree*, *The Mayor of Casterbridge*, and *The Woodlanders*; *Tess of the D'Urbervilles* is in the British Museum; *Jude the Obscure* in the Fitzwilliam Museum, Cambridge; *The Trumpet-Major* in the Royal Library, Windsor Castle; and *The Return of the Native* at University College, Dublin. Two others are in America: *Two on a Tower* at Harvard, and an incomplete MS. of *A Pair of Blue Eyes* in the Berg Collection at the New York Public Library. Of the collections of verse, *Human Shows* is at Yale; *Late Lyrics and Earlier* at Dorchester; *Moments of Vision* at Magdalene College, Cambridge; *Poems of the Past and the Present* at the Bodleian; *Time's Laughingstocks* at the Fitzwilliam; *Satires of Circumstance* at Dorchester; *Wessex Poems* at the City Museum, Birmingham; and *Winter Words* at Queen's College, Oxford. *The Dynasts* is in the British Museum. MSS. of the short stories are widely scattered. Some other material is in private hands, but the MSS. of several early novels have not survived. Most of the MSS. repay careful study; microfilms of most of those in the Dorset County Museum are now available commercially.

Bibliographical Notes

Bibliographies

Hardy has been well served by bibliographers. R. L. Purdy's *Thomas Hardy: A Bibliographical Study* (1954) is a model of its kind, and goes beyond the promise of its title in providing a great deal of biographical information. Also useful are: C. J. Weber's *The First Hundred Years of Thomas Hardy, 1840–1940* (1942, 1965) and G. S. Fayen's guide to Hardy scholarship and criticism in *Victorian Fiction: A Guide to Research*, ed. L. Stevenson (1964), to which a supplementary volume covering the years 1963–74, with a section on Hardy by Michael Millgate, is in course of preparation under the editorship of George Ford (publication expected about 1977). G. S. Fayen has also compiled a short but helpful bibliography, with select criticism up to 1967, in the *New Cambridge Bibliography of English Literature*, vol. III (1800–1900), ed. G. Watson (1969). The fullest guide to Hardy criticism, including that of his contemporaries, is *Thomas Hardy: An Annotated Bibliography of Writings About Him*, by H. E. Gerber and W. E. Davis (1973).

Chapter 1   Life and Career

There is at present no entirely satisfactory biography of Hardy. The *Life* which purports to be by his widow remains indispensable, but presents problems which are examined in Chapter 5. C. J. Weber's *Hardy of Wessex* (1940, revised edition 1965) and Evelyn Hardy's *Hardy: a Critical Biography* (1954) are both useful, but are likely to be superseded by the biography on which Professor Michael Millgate is currently at work. Robert Gittings's *Young Thomas Hardy* (1975) and *The Older Hardy* (1978) are executed with scrupulous historical accuracy and set the record straight on some important biographical questions, including the notorious 'Tryphena' problem. M. Williams's *Thomas Hardy and Rural England* (1972) contains some useful material on the historical and socio-economic background.

Material relevant to Hardy's professional career will be found in the *Life* and in Purdy's bibliography. The following also contain material of interest:

W. Tinsley, *Random Recollections of an Old Publisher* (1900); C. L. Graves, *Life and Letters of Alexander Macmillan* (1910); C. Morgan, *The House of Macmillan, 1843–1943* (1943); S. Nowell-Smith (ed.), *Letters to Macmillan* (1967). Hardy contributed a substantial account of Leslie Stephen as an editor to F. W. Maitland's *Life and Letters of Leslie Stephen* (1906); see also Hardy's sonnet 'The Schreckhorn'. There is much unpublished material in the Dorset County Museum, including correspondence between Hardy and his publishers, editors and illustrators, and in the Macmillan Archive (Add. 54923) in the British Museum. Horace Moule's letters to Hardy are in the Dorset County Museum. For Virginia Woolf's account of her visit to Hardy in 1926, see *A Writer's Diary* (1953), pp. 89–94. The contemporary reception of Hardy has been conveniently documented by R. G. Cox in *Thomas Hardy: the Critical Heritage* (1970). F. B. Pinion's *A Hardy Companion* (1968) is a useful work of reference.

Chapters 2, 3, 4   Major Novels; Minor Novels; Short Stories

Two of the best book-length studies of Hardy's fiction are A. J. Guerard's *Hardy: the Novels and Stories* (1949), and Michael Millgate's *Thomas Hardy: his Career as a Novelist* (1971). Other notable accounts include Douglas Brown's *Thomas Hardy* (1954); Irving Howe's *Thomas Hardy* (1967); J. Hillis Miller's *Thomas Hardy: Distance and Desire* (1970); and George Wing's *Thomas Hardy* (1963).

There is as yet no complete critical edition of Hardy's novels. The 'New Wessex Edition' (Macmillan) has some useful annotation, but the introductions are uneven. Critical editions of *Tess of the D'Urbervilles* and *The Return of the Native* have been published by Norton & Co. (New York), who also have other novels in preparation. Nor is there yet in print an adequate study of Hardy's manuscripts or of the complex question of the serialization of his novels. M. E. Chase's *Thomas Hardy from Serial to Novel* (1927) performed an important pioneering task, but is seriously incomplete. It is to be hoped that J. T. Laird's recent book *The Shaping of 'Tess of the D'Urbervilles'* (1975) will be followed by studies of the evolution of the other novels from manuscript to final printed form.

Among countless articles on individual novels and special aspects, a few of particular interest may be mentioned: J. F. Danby argues the case for a higher estimate of *Under the Greenwood Tree* in *Critical Quarterly* (1960), and Barbara Hardy deals similarly with *The Trumpet-Major* in her preface to the New Wessex Edition of that novel (1974); David Lodge has a good chapter on *Tess of the D'Urbervilles* in his *Language of Fiction* (1966), and there is a brilliant essay by Tony Tanner on the same novel in *Critical Quarterly* (1968); Douglas Brown has a monograph on *The Mayor of Casterbridge* in Arnold's 'Studies in

English Literature' series (1962), and John Paterson one on *The Making of 'The Return of the Native'* (1960); an important article in French on *Jude the Obscure* is that by F. Lagarde in *Caliban*, published by the University of Toulouse (1966), and A. Alvarez's introduction to the same novel in the New American Library edition (1961) is worth looking up. On Hardy's pictorialism, see articles by A. Smart in *Review of English Studies* (1961) and L. Fernando in *A Review of English Literature* (1965). R. W. King has an interesting article on verse and prose parallels in Hardy in *Review of English Studies* (1962).

Chapter 5   Non-fictional Prose

Hardy's prefaces, essays and miscellaneous non-fictional prose writings are conveniently collected in H. Orel's *Hardy's Personal Writings* (1966).

A number of Hardy's letters have been published at various times. His surviving letters to his first wife appeared as *'Dearest Emmie'*, ed. C. J. Weber (1963), and a group of letters to Mrs Florence Henniker, covering the period 1893–1922, were published as *One Rare Fair Woman*, ed. E. Hardy and F. B. Pinion (1972). On Hardy's letters to Sir George Douglas (now in the National Library of Scotland), see an article by W. M. Parker in *English* (1963). C. J. Weber's *Hardy and the Lady from Madison Square* (1952) discusses his correspondence with Rebekah Owen. The same scholar's *The Letters of Thomas Hardy* (1954) gives the text of over 100 letters. The *Colby Library Quarterly* has frequently included material on Hardy letters contained in the important Hardy collection at Colby College, Maine. The Thomas Hardy Memorial Collection in the Dorset County Museum, Dorchester, contains over 5,000 letters, of which about 850 are by Hardy; a descriptive checklist, *Thomas Hardy's Correspondence at Max Gate*, has been compiled by C. J. and C. C. Weber (1968). The first volume of a projected seven-volume edition of the *Collected Letters* (ed. Purdy & Millgate) appeared in 1978.

For editions of Hardy's autobiography, see the list of his works above. R. Taylor's edition of Hardy's notebooks now in preparation will also include all the passages omitted from the original typescripts of the *Life*; for examples of deletions from the typescripts, see my article 'Hardy, Mrs. Oliphant, and *Jude the Obscure*' in *Victorian Newsletter* (1974). Brief comments on the authorship of the *Life* will be found in the *Times Literary Supplement* for 18 November and 30 December 1960, and 6 April 1962.

As noted above, Dr Richard Taylor has in hand an edition of Hardy's notebooks, due for publication shortly. Lennart A. Björk has recently published the first volume of a two-volume edition of Hardy's 'Literary Notes' (*Gothenburg Studies in English* 29, 1974). Hardy's architectural notebook has been edited by C. Beatty (1966). The title of *Thomas Hardy's Notebooks*, ed. E. Hardy (1955) is misleading – only two notebooks are reproduced, with extracts from a third – and the text is unsatisfactory in places. Emma Hardy's *Some Recollections* has been edited by E. Hardy and R. Gittings (1961).

Chapter 6   Verse

James Gibson has recently edited *The Complete Poems of Thomas Hardy* for the New Wessex Edition (1975); this volume includes notes as well as a few poems not previously included in the *Collected Poems*. Mr Gibson also has in preparation a variorum edition of Hardy's poems. Among the many selections which have been made, a few may be mentioned. Hardy's own *Selected Poems* (1916), in the Golden Treasury series, includes 129 poems; his *Chosen Poems* (1929), the arrangement of which was one of his last literary labours, dropped a few and added others, enlarging the selection to 161. Useful recent selections include those by P. N. Furbank (1966) and James Gibson (1975). C. J. Weber has edited *Hardy's Love Poems* (1963).

    J. O. Bailey's *The Poetry of Thomas Hardy: A Handbook and Commentary* (1970) is sometimes helpful, but much of the detail and many of the speculations are distracting rather than illuminating. Among critical studies, those by Samuel Hynes (*The Pattern of Hardy's Poetry* (1961)) and Kenneth Marsden (*The Poems of Thomas Hardy* (1969)) may be recommended. The American journal *Southern Review*'s centenary issue in 1940 contains important essays by W. H. Auden, F. R. Leavis, John Crowe Ransom, and others. But the definitive study of Hardy's poetic technique, based on his manuscripts as well as his entire output of verse, remains to be written.

    There are book-length studies of *The Dynasts* by J. O. Bailey (1956), H. Orel (1963), and W. F. Wright (1967). A new edition of *The Dynasts*, by Professor Orel, is due for publication shortly.

Index

Index

Forster, John, 150
Fortnightly Review, the, 16, 28
Frith, W. P., 13, 73
Furbank, P. N., 158

Gaskell, Elizabeth, 10, 12, 26, 98, 150
Gibson, James, 190
Gissing, George, 127, 139
Gittings, Robert, 6, 62, 99, 187
Goethe, J. W. von, 180
Good Words, 105, 184
Gosse, Sir Edmund, 17, 51, 161
Granville-Barker, Harley, 21, 139
Graphic, the, 15, 27, 79, 126, 184
Gray, Thomas, 2, 59, 151
Greene, Graham, 149
Gregor, Ian, ix, 42
Guerard, A. J., 188

Haight, Gordon, 31
Harding, Louisa, 147, 177
Hardy, Admiral Sir Thomas, 178
Hardy, Barbara, 188
Hardy, Emma Lavinia, 9, 11, 94, 148, 151, 160, 163, 171–5, 189
Hardy, Evelyn, 160, 187
Hardy, Florence Emily, 22, 122, 142–6, 151, 177
Hardy, Frederick, D., 67
Hardy, Thomas (senior), 5, 115
Hardy, Thomas: Autobiography (*The Life of Thomas Hardy*), 8, 22, 26, 64–6, 71, 72, 109, 140–51, 154, 177, 185, 187; 'Candour in English Fiction', 15, 136–7; *Changed Man, A*, 37, 121, 124, 126, 185; *Desperate Remedies*, 9, 10, 14, 24–5, 33, 35, 37, 91–4, 95, 96, 122, 132, 134, 184; 'Dorsetshire Labourer, The', 50, 62, 137–8; *Dynasts, The*, 7, 12, 21, 32, 123, 131, 160, 163, 178–81, 185, 186; Essays, 134–8, 185; *Far from the Madding Crowd*, 10–11, 26–7, 28, 32, 35, 37, 39–40, 43, 45, 46, 50, 51, 68, 74, 81, 82, 98, 126, 132, 184; *Group of Noble Dames, A*, 28, 37, 121, 123, 185;

Hand of Ethelberta, The, 11, 28, 35, 37, 41, 45, 97–101, 132, 184; 'How I Built Myself a House', 7; *Human Shows*, 21, 185, 186; *Jude the Obscure*, 16–17, 18, 19, 20, 27, 29, 30, 31, 36, 37, 43–4, 48, 50–1, 56–7, 58, 60, 62–3, 64, 67, 74, 82–8, 95, 107, 110, 123, 127, 128, 129, 131, 132, 133, 135, 141, 146, 148, 150, 161, 164, 167, 168, 177, 184, 186, 189; *Laodicean, A*, 12, 36, 37, 45, 106–10, 113, 184; *Late Lyrics and Earlier*, 19, 133, 163, 185, 186; Letters, 138–40; *Life's Little Ironies*, 37, 121, 123, 127, 128, 185; *Mayor of Casterbridge, The*, 13–14, 26, 33, 36, 37, 45, 46, 47, 51–2, 59, 61, 64, 73, 74, 77–82, 124, 132, 152, 184, 186, 188; 'Memories of Church Restoration', 138; *Moments of Vision*, 21, 185, 186; Notebooks and Diaries, 151–3; *Pair of Blue Eyes, A*, 10, 25, 35, 37, 45, 57, 94–7, 132, 184, 186;
POEMS:
'Afternoon Service at Mellstock (About 1850)', 56; 'Afterwards', 88; 'Ah, Are You Digging On My Grave', 175; 'At a Lunar Eclipse', 57, 156–7; 'Broken Appointment, A', 177; 'Childhood Among the Ferns', 177; 'Christmas: 1924', 175–6; 'Clasped Skeletons, The', 176; 'Dance at the Phoenix, The', 126; 'Division, The', 155–6; 'During Wind and Rain', 159–60; 'Epitaph on a Pessimist', 175; 'Evening Shadows', 177; 'Four Footsteps', 170; 'Going, The', 158; 'Hap', 156; 'Heiress and Architect', 110; 'He Never Expected Much', 157; 'He Resolves to Say No More', 182; 'I Look into my Glass', 117, 168–9; 'In Tenebris', 156; 'Liddell and Scott', 176; 'Lines to a Movement in Mozart's E-flat Symphony', 155; 'Lost Pyx, The', 175;

Index

Joyce, James, 23

Keats, John, 55, 151, 182
King, R. W., 188
Kipling, Rudyard, 152

Lagarde, F., 188
Laird, J. T., 164, 188
Larkin, Philip, 160–1
Lawrence, D. H., 3, 23, 42, 43, 165
Leavis, F. R., 154–5, 160–1, 165, 190
Lodge, David, 188
Lowell, J. R., 13, 148

MacMillan, Alexander, 8, 13, 24,
    25, 34, 35, 139, 188
MacMillan's Magazine, 14, 15, 27,
    184
Marsden, Kenneth, 190
Martin, Julia, 5, 146–7
Meredith, George, 9, 134, 139, 179
Mill, J. S., 62, 65
Millais, J. E., 72, 74
Miller, J. Hillis, 149, 188
Millgate, Michael, ix, 19, 94, 114,
    118, 138, 187, 188, 189
Moore, George, 127, 147
Morley, John, 9
Morris, Mowbray, 15, 27
Morris, William, 139, 175
Moule, Henry, 4
Moule, Horace, 6, 7, 42, 52, 95,
    139, 188
Murray's Magazine, 15, 28
Musset, Alfred de, 151

Nabokov, Vladimir, 144
National Vigilance Association, 30
Newbolt, Sir Henry, 179
Newman, J. H., 8
New Review, the, 136

Obscene Publications Act, 30
Oliphant, Margaret, 148
Orel, Harold, 134, 138, 185, 188,
    190
Owen, Rebekah, 122, 189

Pall Mall Gazette, the, 16

Palmerston, Lord, 8
Parnell, Charles, 44
Paterson, Helen, 98
Paterson, John, 44, 188
Pinion, F. B., 188
Pound, Ezra, 139, 154, 163–4, 165
Pre-Raphaelite Brotherhood, 69–70
Procter, Anne, 2
Punch, 98
Purdy, R. L., 17, 127, 138, 162,
    187, 189

Quarterly Review, the, 15, 179

Ransom, J. C., 161, 190
Richardson, Samuel, 56
Ricks, Christopher, 60
Rossetti, D. G., 69
Royal Academy, 72
Ruskin, John, 31
Rutland, W. R., 57

Sainte-Beuve, C. A., 148
Sassoon, Siegfried, 139
Saturday Review, the, 15, 16, 49
Schlegel, F. von, 152
Schopenhauer, Arthur, 152
Scott, Sir Walter, 5, 68, 71
Shakespeare, William, 5, 117–18,
    136, 151, 152, 156
Shaw, G. B., 16, 101
Shelley, P. B., 151, 166, 180
Smart, Alistair, 188
Smith, George, 13
Society for the Suppression of Vice,
    30
Sparks, Tryphena, 63, 168
Spectator, the, 9, 10, 14, 70, 93, 134,
    141, 155
Spencer, Herbert, 151
Spinoza, B. de, 152
Stephen, Sir Leslie, 10–11, 13, 26–7,
    28, 139, 148, 164, 188
Stevenson, R. L., 134, 139, 147
Swinburne, A. C., 3, 31, 139, 151,
    166, 179

Tanner, Tony, 53, 188
Taylor, Richard, 189